MORE CYBERPRAISE FOR *CYBORG CITIZEN*

"In *Cyborg Citizen*, Gray manages to bridge the understanding gap between technology and politics. He uses a wealth of historical perspective to look into the future of a cyber-augmented culture, and shows us with depth and clarity what the changes will mean to our lives as individuals and as a society. The book is readable by people with all different levels of technological sophistication, and has much new to offer no matter how much you have already thought about the issues."

—**Terry Winograd**, Professor of Computer Science, Stanford University

"Chris Gray is emerging as one of the most important thinkers about the effects of new technologies on society. Gray's intelligent, humane and hyperactive mind ranges across an astonishing array of phenomena from the effects of the internet and genetic engineering to the history of the vibrator and the Pentagon's plans for a new generation of cyborg warriors. Gray's encyclopedic mind, his refreshingly energetic prose, and his progressive politics make him an engaging guide to the promises and perils of 21st-century technology. An avowed 'Jeffersonian anarchist,' his perspective is always original, informed, and intelligent."

—**Hugh Gusterson**, author of *Nuclear Rites: A Weapons Laboratory at the End of the Cold War*

cyborg citizen

POLITICS IN THE POSTHUMAN AGE

Chris Hables Gray

ROUTLEDGE
New York and London

Published in 2002 by
Routledge
29 West 35th Street
New York, NY 10001

Published in Great Britain by
Routledge
11 New Fetter Lane
London EC4P 4EE

Routledge is an imprint of the Taylor & Francis Group.

First Routledge paperback edition, 2002.
Printed in the United States of America on acid-free paper.

10 9 8 7 6 5 4 3 2

Library of Congress Cataloging-in-Publication Data

Gray, Chris Hables.
    Cyborg citizen : politics in the posthuman age / by Chris Hables Gray.
        p. cm.
    Includes bibliographical references and index.
    ISBN 0-415-91978-9 — 0-415-91979-7 (pbk.)
    1. Politics. 2. Cyborgs. 3. Human Machine Systems. I. Title.

TA167 .G75 2000
303.48'3—dc21   00-030731

To the grandparents of my sons:
George Gray, Benita Hables Gray, Ted Wilson,
and Mary Lovett Wilson.
From the present it is so easy to see how much
of our hope for the future is based on what you have
accomplished in the past.

contents

postmodern politics

CYBORG WARRIORS   55

promulgating cyborgs

 INFOMEDICINE AND THE NEW BODY   69

 CYBERNETIC HUMAN REPRODUCTION   87

 ENABLED CYBORGS, LIVING AND DEAD   99

THE HOPEFUL MONSTERS OF GENETIC ENGINEERING   113

cyborg society

cyborgology

POSTHUMAN POSSIBILITIES   187

acknowledgments

This book depends on a growing community of researchers who look at cyborgs, cyberculture, and related issues. In particular, my friends from the History of Consciousness Board of Studies at the University of California at Santa Cruz, where I earned my Ph.D., have remained important influences: Donna Haraway, Ron Eglash, Sara Williams, Joe Dumit, Paul Edwards, Nöel Sturgeon, T. V. Reed, Sandy Stone, Jennifer González, and Che Sandoval. Steve Mentor, Heidi Figueroa-Sarriera, Diane Nelson, Mark Driscoll, and Joseba Gabilondo have also been wonderful colleagues.

I also want to thank my friends and colleagues from the University of Great Falls: Joe Schopfer, Lyndon Marshall (my "attack Dean" because he is so fierce in supporting his faculty and students), the Circus Numicus research group (Dennis Weeks, the "cattle prod" of the group in particular), our President Fred Gilliard, and finally my students in my classes on cyborgs and related phenomena. They have inspired me with their interest and their skepticism, as have the students and faculty I work with through Goddard College's off-campus B.A./M.A. program.

Funding from the Oregon State University Center for the Humanities, the NASA History Office, and the Eisenhower Foundation (which sent me to the home of the golem, the Czech Republic, on a teaching fellowship) was welcome and invaluable.

It has been my great good fortune to have strong support (even money in advance!) from Routledge. In particular, Bill Germano and Adrian Driscoll have been sympathetic and interested commissioning editors. Amy Reading was an extraordinary close editor of the text. My readers, Steve Mentor and Ron Eglash were wonderful, supportive, and critical. I only wish I could have fixed everything they thought was flawed.

Finally, there is my family: my parents and brothers who have always believed in me, my in-laws (especially Ted Wilson, who buys and reads all my books), my nieces and nephews, my two wonderful sons, Corey and Zackary, and, most important of all, my partner, Jane Lovett Wilson.

All errors are not my own—the construction of meaning is so complicated—but as the authorial money is mine, I'll take the responsibility as well.

a note on texts

This is actually a multilayered text, not all of which is here in this book, although the main narrative line is. The layers in this book are the main text, the notes on each chapter at the end of the book, the illustrations, the bibliography, and the index. There is an extensive academic and personal commentary with notes and links, organized as a hypertext, and illustrations on the Internet at http://www.Routledge-ny.com/CyborgCitizen. The notes in this text are quite limited, giving only the source of quotations. Books and articles mentioned in the text are listed in the bibliography. All other academic source information is on the Web site. If some of the arguments in the main narrative strike you as unsubtle or even specious, please explore the thinking behind them in the hypertext before you send me a dismissive letter. Correspondence is very welcome, electronically from the website or through the mail, courtesy of Routledge.

slouching toward the posthuman—does participatory evolution require participatory government?

THE CRIPPLING OF SUPERMAN

In 1995, Christopher Reeve, the actor famous for portraying Superman in the movies, fell from his horse Buck and became a quadriplegic. A sad story? Yes, certainly, but also a heroic cyborg tale. Instead of wallowing in his fate as a barely mobile creature, dependent on and intertwined with machines, a cybernetic organism trapped in power beds and wheelchairs, Christopher Reeve has chosen to become a militant advocate for more intimate cyborgizations. Within a year of his accident he appeared on the cover of *Time* magazine and as a featured speaker at the 1996 Democratic National Convention.

Using his special status as the crippled Superman and his considerable charisma, Reeve has catalyzed the unification of most of the patient groups in the United States who focus on paraplegia and other spinal cord injuries. This unified front of invalid cyborgs and their families now confidently predicts that science will master the reconstruction of the spinal cord within 30 years. Their goal is to accelerate this medical breakthrough by decades. Despite the obvious difficulties in predicting scientific discoveries, their basic claim is quite reasonable. There is an excellent chance that doctors will master nerve restoration soon, *if* enough resources are mobilized. Indeed, in August of 1996 researchers announced that they had successfully repaired totally severed spines in experimental mice.

Cyborgs such as Reeve certainly have their own political priorities, but on closer examination we see that they are not that different from the priorities of the rest of us. Almost all of us are cyborged in some way, as this

1

book will show in detail, though most of us are not as clear on our status as Christopher Reeve has to be.

A cyborg is a self-regulating organism that combines the natural and artificial together in one system. Cyborgs do not have to be part human, for any organism/system that mixes the evolved and the made, the living and the inanimate, is technically a cyborg. This would include biocomputers based on organic processes, along with roaches with implants and bioengineered microbes. This book focuses on human cyborgs and uses a particularly broad definition. If you have been technologically modified in any significant way, from an implanted pacemaker to a vaccination that reprogrammed your immune system, then you are definitely a cyborg. Even if you are one of those rare people who is in no way a cyborg in the technical sense, cyborg issues still impact you. We live in a cyborg society, no matter how unmodified we are as individuals. So as we humans continue to technologically transform ourselves, this process will play an increasingly important, eventually fundamental role in politics—and not always for the better.

There are as many frightening cyborg futures as there are idyllic ones. Most of our possible futures are difficult to conceive of at all. Yet helping to conceive them, in both senses of the word, is the goal of this book. This is particularly important in times like these, when so many fear the future, what it might be, and what we might be in it. From our beginnings, it seems, we humans have feared the possibility of some intelligent *other*; a superrace of genii or titans or gods. Some of these imagined creatures have been humanoid, many not. Some were friendly, but most seemed unsympathetic. Such fantasies have never really waned. The overt fear of vampires may be relegated to novels, movies, and Halloween, yet it represents real anxiety. Fear of aliens also represents our obsessive terror of the superior creature that dethrones us, enslaves us, maybe even eats us. Götterdämmerung. Armageddon. Rapture. Extinction. It is an old, dread song.

The irony is that we will almost certainly bring about our end ourselves, either directly through chemical, biological, or nuclear war or ecocide, or through the creation of our successor species: cyborgs. Deep down we know it is our hubris that will seal our doom—our hubris and our great talent for making and remaking even ourselves.

Signs of our cyborg society are all around. The few of us who are not in some way already 'borged through immunizations, interfaces, or prosthetics are embedded nonetheless in countless machinic/organic cybernetic systems. From the moment your clock radio wakes you in the morning, your life is intimately shaped by machines. Some of them we merge with almost unconsciously, such as the car we drive, the computer we work with, or the television we zone out in front of. Others involve more conscious interfacing. Overall the effect is an extraordinary symbiosis of humans and machines. This is a fundamentally new development in the history of the human. Now, with the advent of genetic engineering, we not only can consciously evolve and invent our machine companions, we can do the same for our bodies. This is clearly a major step beyond natural selection and the careful breeding Darwin called artificial selection. It is, in a phrase coined by Manfred Clynes in the same "Cyborgs and Space" article in which he devised the term cyborg, participatory evolution. This immediately raises the question: Does participatory evolution require participatory government? The goal of this book is to show why the answer is "yes."

Evolution is an open-ended system with a tight link between information and action. We have an opportunity, if we take participatory evolution seriously, to be free of both the rule of blind chance–necessity (the Darwinian perspective) and its opposite, distant absolute authority (creationism). Participatory evolution means we should shape our future through multiple human choices, incomplete and contradictory as they often are. Participatory government is the same. The spectacular failures of the Marxist command economies in the twentieth century should be a warning to those who believe in command politics and economics as well as to those who would support hierarchically controlled government and/or corporate evolution from above. Decisions about evolution should be made at the grass roots, just as political and economic decisions should be, especially now that we have begun to recognize the political evolution of cyborgs.

THE PROLIFERATION OF CYBORGS

Let us start with an origin story. Whether you call it myth, tradition, scholarship, or family gossip, the origin story exerts a powerful fascination, and those stories about humans, tools, machines, magic, and science are among the most beguiling. We go back to the very beginning of the human, which some 'ologists say began with *Homo faber*, man the maker, the tool user. Some versions of this story have very materialist plot lines: eye-to-hand-to-tool makes the brain grow, and repeat; others are more nuanced. All share a particularly grounded approach to the question: "What are the origins of humans?" The evidence points to tools and the body, that very first human tool.

Tools define ages (pastoral, agricultural, urban), especially war tools (bronze, iron, steel). Countless tools were invented while humans assembled increasingly complicated social machines to produce community (tribes, familes, villages), war (armies), and economic development (irrigation systems, cities, ports), and to scratch our insatiable itch for knowledge (religion, art, magic). In the thousands of years of cities, the borders between human and tool and the very idea of machine-as-complex-system have been carefully explored, usually in religion, art, and magic. Cyborgs were a dream long before there were even machines. Some of our tales today will probably come true, just as old stories of seamless artificial limbs or creating talking machines have now been instantiated in flesh and metal.

Humans have always designed our own sentient creatures in myths, beginning with ancient Greek and Hindi tales that describe strange, half-flesh/half-metal creatures, and many other stories that frame humans as automatons, artifacts animated by gods and goddesses. Automatons have a long history, from Hero's mechanical tableaus (300 B.C.E.), through the cock of Strasbourg (1574) and Jacques de Vaucanson's famous shitting mechanical duck (1741), to the profitable creations of Disney's imagineers today. They are all complex feats of religious engineering.

The tradition of automatons thrived around the world, peaking in China, Japan, and Europe approximately 500 years ago. Then in Europe it exploded into the general cultural transition, which birthed modern science, modern war, and the modern nation-state that quickly bought about the contemporary world. Automatons led to automatic looms when Vaucanson was ordered to turn his hand to practical machines, and eventually the modern world witnessed the creation of automatic weapons and other machinery as well as a whole range of control systems, from puppets to prosthetics.

This was the time of the golem, of talking heads and homunculi, of prosthetics that really worked, such as the interchangeable artificial arms wielded by Count Goetz von Berlichingen—one for court, one for fighting. It was the age when the conceit that the body was a machine was translated through the theater of anatomy and autopsy medicine into a working hypothesis. The body was intellectually autodeconstructed and its organs physically displayed for the scientific gaze.

And it was the age when science began to inform not just ballistics but logistics, armies became efficient machines, and Machiavelli brought to war and politics the calculus of rationality. It has been a mad rush since then. In the last few hundred years, industrial and scientific revolutions have more than kept pace with political changes. Mary Shelley crafted Frankenstein's monster for a storytelling contest with her husband Percy Shelley and their friend Lord Byron, from her state-of-the-art scientific and technological knowledge and her insights into the hidden aspirations of modernity. Byron's daughter, Ada Lovelace, became the first computer programmer and worked on the first modern military research and development contract, Charles Babbage's deal with the Royal Navy to produce ballistic and navigational calculations. This link between the future imaginary (art or science fiction or war plans) and the reality of technoscience is real and dynamic and it breeds monsters, hopeful and otherwise—daily.

The incredible speed of our cyborgization and the economics of publishing have inspired Routledge and me to create a sort of cyborg text, a hybrid of a traditional book and electronic publishing. The book contains the heart of my argument about the importance of cyborg citizenship, written for the intelligent reader without footnotes and with a minimum of digressions into complex French philosophy. On the accompanying Web site hosted by Routledge (http://www.Routledge-ny.com/CyborgCitizen) there is an extensive commentary on the main text, including enough academic language and references to choke a horse. There will also be continually updated links to the latest technological information on cyborg breakthroughs and to the many Web sites that discuss the political and ethical implications of our cyborg society. And there will be forums where readers can correct, argue with, or even praise the book itself.

While a first glance at the Table of Contents may depict a book that seeks to cover the whole range of cyborg society, that is far from the case. My focus is the politics of the cyborg phenomena. Cyborg literature and mass culture, the impact of cyborgization on religion, and consciously cyborg art, for example, are only discussed in relation to their political implications. The incredible range of cyborg engineering, science, medicine, and other practices, in all their technical glory, are only briefly touched on as they pertain to politics. Even the legal implications of cyborgization are only sketched.

I slight areas such as art because in this book there is barely enough room to take the politics of cyborgization seriously, let alone the aesthetics. However, beauty can help us understand cyborg politics. Take Diego Rivera's great mural *Pan American Unity*, painted in 1927 on a wall in San Francisco's City College, as an example. This mural is not what first comes to mind when one thinks of cyborg art. It is not Robert Longo's *All You Zombies* or Robocop or even Eva from the movie *Metropolis*. It is a huge picture dominated by a giantess, half Indian goddess, half robot machine. For Rivera it represented the unification of the anima of South America with North America: ancient wisdom/magic with technological power/magic. Remember, Rivera was a leftist in an age when work was honored as it should be. Rivera's mural seems to say that workers of both hemispheres, with their tenacity and innovative genius, can build a beautiful future.

Diego Rivera described *Pan American Unity* as a "fusion of the genius of the South...religious ardor and plastic expression and the genius of the North...creative mechanical explosion...a colossal cauldron of life." Perhaps this can be our future. Along with his affirmation of both the organic and the machinic, Rivera also rejects a whole range of other dichotomies: north versus south, cyborg or goddess, nature contra city. That is a good start for this book, which at the very least should disrupt all simple dichotomies no matter how fundamental—from living and dead to ally and enemy.

While shopping this book around to publishers, I received a response that startled me. One senior editor who read the proposal responded with a stark declaration: "I got your proposal and I took a look. I think I'm your enemy." Because I write at length about cyborgs, she seems to have assumed I am a wholehearted proponent of the complete cyborgization of humanity. But it is not so simple. It is not a matter of being procyborg or anti. The Luddites, for example, were not against all machines. In fact, their struggle against the weaving machines that made factory cloth production possible were in defense of an earlier generation of machines that had allowed the growth of a thriving cottage industry that produced the same goods. Tools are here to stay, machines are here to stay, cyborgs are here to stay. The real issue is which tools, which machines, which cyborgs we will have in our society and which will be excluded or never created.

This is how truth is constructed. Choices lead to possibilities that lead to other possible choices. We cannot have all the truth there is; we are not equipped to process it. Perhaps we will get the truth we need. To do so we have to remember what those harried TV FBI agents, Muldar and Scully, have discovered: "The truth is out there."

Which means, at the least, that: 1. There is truth. 2. It may be surprising. 3. We have to go get it; it will not come to us.

postmodern politics

the cyborg
body politic

THE POSSIBILITIES OF POSTHUMANISM

We're going to be as Gods, we might as well get good at it.
—Stewart Brand

In another thousand years we'll be machines, or gods.
—Afriel, a Shapist, from the science-fiction story "Swarm"

In the summer of 1995 I visited MIT's Media Lab and met a couple of grad students working on wearable computers and sophisticated human-machine interfaces who happily labeled themselves cyborgs. Steve Mann was connected to his computer through satellite signals; next to his head antenna he wore a camera that constantly broadcasted images onto two tiny TV screens he wore as glasses. He could set his camera to show everything upside down or sideways, which he had done to see how long it would take his brain to adapt. Or he could set his camera to infrared and "see" electrical cords in the walls and even trace power lines to hidden cameras in Harvard Square shops. Since he broadcast his camera output onto his Web page, he had been banned from several of these stores. Steve called his existence "mediated reality," because everything he saw was mediated through his camera—quite different from virtual reality where primary sense data is fabricated by a computer, or mutual reality, where two or more people experience the same artificial world.

Steve's colleague, Thad Starner, was working on augmented reality. He wore a small laser that painted a computer screen onto one of his retinas. His other eye observed the physical world. He controlled his computer through a one-handed keypad. He also had wireless access to the Internet. Most of the time he existed in cyberspace and Massachusetts at the same time, his senses simultaneously accessing both worlds.

Within a few years these two cyborgs had multiplied into a small band of students with various types of constantly improving wearable computers. Research into improved interfaces and power technologies, such as athletic shoes that generate electricity when you walk in them, is ongoing. For many young people, being 'borged is empowering.

These cyborgs are also clearly cyborgologists, working consciously at expanding the possibilities for human-machine integration. But many other scientists and engineers are also cyborgologists, whether they use that term or not: computer designers working on interfaces, surgeons on transplant teams, bioengineers improving tools and machines such as prosthetic limbs and timed drug release systems. There is another group of cyborgologists who seek to understand the social and philosophical implications of our cyborgization. Some claim the label cyborgologist proudly, such as the historians of technology whose special interest group on computers called itself "The Cyborgs" for a while, or the anthropologists who issued a manifesto for a cyborg anthropology.

Other academics are trying to put these changes into perspective without using the image of the cyborg. The historian David Channell sees our current culture as a merging of the long-standing Western ideals of organic order ("The Great Chain of Being") and mechanistic rationality ("The Clockwork Universe"). He argues that today these two trends come together in the idea of the vital machine. Bruce Mazlish, of MIT's History Department, tells a slightly different story, an epic about the human quest gradually to transcend our illusions. It starts with the rejection of the pretense that we are at the center of the cosmos (the Copernican Revolution), then the illusion that we are fundamentally distinct from animals died (overthrown by evolutionary theory), followed by our realization that we are not even completely rational (thanks to Freud and the unconscious). Finally, the "Fourth Discontinuity," as he calls it in a book of the same name, will have to go. This is the artificial divide we have drawn between the organic and the machinic, life and machines.

Inevitably people have begun to see the earth itself as a cyborg system. As Donna Haraway put it, referring to the Gaia theory that the biosphere is a self-regulating system, Gaia is a "cyborg world." Considering the domination of humans and our technologies in the biosphere, this seems inarguable. Gregory Stock, a physicist and science writer, has given this insight a masculinist twist in his book *Metaman*. He postulates that the earth is one cyborg creature with its own needs and desires, including the procreation of other metamen throughout the galaxy. As cartoonish as it sounds, when you combine the dynamics of the Gaia theory with Stock's impressive documentation, it almost becomes a convincing story.

Something is happening. Whatever you call it, the living system we are part of is clearly both organic and machinic—and it is evolving.

In 1960 Manfred Clynes and Nathan Kline created the term "cyborg" and discussed its implications, the foremost being participatory evolution. Clearly, if humans are modifying themselves to live in space and other strange places, the dynamics of natural evolution have been supplanted, at least temporarily, by artificial evolution. Now we can consciously shape our own evolution, but it is a limited participation so far because of technical constraints and our different, often conflicting goals. Artificial evolution is not just the conscious breeding of farm animals that Darwin discussed; it now includes the direct modification of human bodies and genes. Our interventions are presently crude, but new technosciences promise that soon we will be creating creatures from ourselves that cannot even be classified as humans. Whatever the motivations, whether profit or power or the maximization of the glories of human potential, this process is fundamentally political. Politics will determine what values we build into posthumanity.

The probability of posthuman cyborgs horrifies some people and thrills others. We see the beginning of these divisions in the debates on cloning. The Catholic Church and many governments call for a ban on human cloning experiments, while scientists sign petitions calling for more research. There are even groups like the Extropians, who label themselves "transhumanists" and hail the approaching proliferation of human-based "post" creatures as inevitable and wonderful.

But these simple dichotomies are not adequate. First, there are many different types of cyborgs and many different ways to categorize them. For example, cyborgs can be restorative, normalizing, reconfiguring, and enhancing. People are used to thinking of cyborgs as people for whom lost functions have been restored, maybe even to the extent that they seem "normal" again, but we have largely ignored the ethical implications of reconfigured and enhanced posthumans. Only in 1997 did the Human Genome Project fund research on the social implications of using genetic engineering to enhance and reconfigure humans. Other researchers have proposed schemes for analyzing cyborgs that focus on the systems level of the cyborg (postulating meta- and semicyborgs, for example) and that look at the relative balance between biological and machinic elements.

The second problem with these dichotomies is that they may not be the most important ones. Steven Mentor, Heidi Figueroa-Sarriera, and I make this point in our essay "Cyborgology" in *The Cyborg Handbook*, where we discuss Maureen McHugh's novel, *China Mountain Zhang*. The protagonist, a Chinese-American engineer, comes to terms with his own cyborgization when he realizes that: "Soon, perhaps, it will be impossible to tell where human ends and machines begin." We go on to argue that such confusion is fine, because, there are:

> more important distinctions to make, between just and unjust, between sustaining and destroying, between stable and erratic, between pleasure and pain, between knowledge and ignorance, between effective and ineffectual, between beauty and ugliness.... Once, most people thought that artificial-natural, human-machine, organic and constructed, were dualities just as central to living, but the figure of the cyborg has revealed that it isn't so.

The essay ends with a call to go beyond dualistic epistemologies altogether and consider the epistemology of cyborgs:

THESIS, ANTITHESIS, SYNTHESIS, PROSTHESIS, and again.

Reality is not a simple swinging to and fro, nor is it a straightforward march to completion. We are not determined just by our technology. We do not only construct the world socially. Our technologies, our cultures, our will, and nature are weaving a future from the present. Reality is dynamic and lumpy. Some things follow from others, some persevere, some disappear, others seem to just appear. But that is because we cannot comprehend all of reality. We can understand a great deal *but not everything*, and any epistemology that pretends we can know it all is seriously flawed. For good or ill (probably for both) the era of posthuman possibilities is beginning. To deny it is dangerous. To recognize it is to begin to understand, perhaps even control, our postmodern present and the political future of our cyborg society.

POSTMODERN: THE TIMES WE LIVE IN

Postmodernism is the intellectual equivalent of nervous laughter.
—Jeff Reid

The postmodern condition is a technoscientific one.
—John Rajchman

[W]hat appears on one level as the latest fad, advertising pitch, and hollow spectacle is part of a slowly emerging cultural transformation in Western societies, a change of sensibility for which the term "postmodernism" is actually, at least for now, wholly adequate.

—Andreas Huyssen

What is this? Postmodern? Cyborg? The worst of academic jargon married to a science-fiction monster? Why not talk about something real? Why not something important? Well, cyborgs are real, from grandmothers with pacemakers to astronauts in space, and whether you like the label postmodern or not, it is clear that the times are drastically changing.

We do not live in the seemingly stable modern world our grandparents did. Their belief in inevitable, comfortable progress has been supplanted by our realization that scientific and technological innovation are relentless and quite ambiguous. Our ancestors' acceptance of the natural limitations of space-time and life and death have been replaced by the fear and hope we feel about space travel, apocalyptic war, immortality, global pandemics, virtual community, ecological collapse, scientific utopias, and cyborgization. The modern assurance that we control our own destiny has been blasted away by horrific wars, ecodisasters, and a proliferation of new scientific discoveries and technological innovations that range from the sublime to the patently evil, as a few hours of television viewing or Internet surfing can easily demonstrate.

At the root of all of this change is that great creation of the modern era: *technoscience*. I use this term advisedly, knowing it will annoy a large number of readers who like to keep science and technology separate, at least conceptually. But while science and technology are clearly different things, they are also mixed together in ways that are impossible to untangle. Their symbiosis is much greater than their respective parts and it is profoundly changing human culture. Humans have always been innovators and makers, but starting around 500 years ago society began to institutionalize scientific and technological discovery. Since then those institutions have grown stronger and more effective, and the small stream of new scientific understandings and new technological inventions has turned into a flood that shows no sign of slackening. In fact it grows stronger all the time. A majority of all of the scientists and engineers who have ever lived are alive right now and they are busy! The hardest thing about understanding this explosion of new knowledge and new things is mentally stepping back from it to ask what its key features are. How is it changing? What is it doing to us?

I will first try to show why it makes sense to think of our time as post-modern. To situate ourselves historically is hard but necessary. Unlike some historians, I believe that history is actually useful. Where we have been is the best predictor of where we are going, yet it is far from infallible. What history can reveal are the choices we have. And we do have choices. We make the future not out of thin air but out of the past and the present. There is also good news about our specific postmodern condition: it is definitely not permanent. Postmodernity is transitory, it is a crisis, and the choices we make will determine what will replace it.

Then, as if explaining postmodernity in one chapter were not hard enough, I will try to convince you that the idea of the cyborg can help us understand what we are and what we might become.

The main argument for the validity of postmodernism is modernism. The label "modernism" is quite established, generally applying to grand narratives that are either irrational (racism, nationalism, high art) or hyper-rational (technoscientific progress). For me modern war exemplifies modernism. Historians define modern war as the development since the 1500s of a war system in Europe, and then the rest of the world, that tends toward total war, that constantly incorporates new technologies into war, and that played a central role in the rise of modern states. Now, because of new military technologies that cannot be used, total war is impossible and the modern state is in decline. Yet, as I will discuss in detail in Chapter 4, war has kept many of its modern elements and so it is postmodern.

The elements that are generally ascribed to postmodernism—a collapse of master narratives, the coexistence as a bricollage of a variety of forms, the centrality of information as metaphor and technology, and a clear instability—certainly apply to contemporary war, as they apply to art, architecture, entertainment, and politics.

Now let us dive a bit more into postmodernism's political implications and we might as well do it in postmodern fashion: glib comments, contradictory ideas, and quotes pasted together, because style itself can be political.

> Postmodernism is more than a buzzword or even an aesthetic; it is a way of seeing, a view of the human spirit, and an attitude toward politics as well as culture. It has precedents, but in its reach it is the creature of our recent social and political moment. In style, more than style is at stake.
>
> —Todd Gitlin

And my style here is certainly political. It says "be tolerant because none of us can know it all." It demonstrates pleasure in life (and therefore ambiguity) but it does not refuse to take a stand, even if principle is performed with an ironic smile.

In politics postmodernism evokes a number of very different responses. Neoconservatives and liberals hate and fear it as a threat to the underpinnings of high modernism and big science.

> [Postmodernism] undermines the social structure itself by striking at the motivational and psychic-reward system which has sustained it.
> —Daniel Bell

For many humanists, the technological and scientific changes that have produced postmodernism physically and qualitatively threaten our very humanity. For self-proclaimed "posthumanists," postmodernism is the door to the future. As N. Katherine Hayles, the brilliant literary theorist, says, "The postmodern may turn out to be equivalent to the posthuman." In *How We Became Posthuman* she explains how posthumanism might recoup the best parts of humanism, by showing that posthumanism is both a social construction of what it means to be human in the present as well as the technological construction of a new type of techno-bio body in the near future through cyborgization.

Some enthusiasts of postmodernism share this radical view of cyborgization as the end of the human and humanism, but deep down they do not really seem happy about it. They describe the transition with smooth bravado and a glib nihilism that claims reality itself is disappearing. Here is Jean Baudrillard:

> It is thus that for guilt, anguish and death there can be substituted the total joy of the signs of guilt, despair, violence and death. It is the very euphoria of simulation, that sees itself as the abolition of cause and effect, the beginning and the end, for all of which it substitutes reduplication.... The cool universe of digitality has absorbed the world of metaphor and metonymy. The principle of simulation wins out over the reality just as over the principle of pleasure.

It is easy to see why postmodernism is often labeled as negative, pessimistic, shallow, and fatally relativistic, even if this is only true of one particular current of postmodern thought, which hides its despair behind wild rhetorical claims.

A different despair haunts radical modernists, such as Jürgen Habermas, who believe the revolutionary promises of modernism can yet be kept. For

15

them, postmodernism represents an abandonment of liberation. Others who put themselves on the left, such as the neo-Marxist critic Fredric Jameson, see postmodernism as a way of achieving the victories denied under modernism. Jameson tries to define postmodernism as a problem of capitalism, not of the contemporary world:

> [E]very position on postmodernism in culture—whether apologia or stigmatization—is also at one and the same time, and *necessarily,* an implicitly or explicitly political stance on the nature of multinational capitalism today...namely that this whole global, yet American, postmodern culture is the internal and superstructural expression of a whole new wave of American military and economic domination throughout the world: in this sense, as throughout class history, the underside of culture is blood, torture, death and horror.

Jameson claims postmodernism will be worthwhile only if it submits to "a dominant cultural logic or hegemonic norm" framed by "Marxian Science" and developing a new "global cognitive mapping" to replace the modernism he blames entirely on U.S.-dominated multinational capitalism. This is not really postmodernism at all, just the return of the modernist myth about scientific liberation through intellectual and physical domination: Marxism.

Postmodernism is the result of social and scientific technologies hegemonic in both the so-called First and Second Worlds. Communism and fascism reproduced the horrors of capitalism with a vengeance. It is industrialization that causes ecological disasters, world wars, mass culture, and the expanded life expectancy that drives overpopulation. It is modern industrialization that must be transcended.

Another major political position is the self-described "constructive" or revisionary postmodernism which, David Ray Griffin claims:

> involves a new unity of scientific, ethical, aesthetic, and religious intuitions. It rejects not science as such but only that scientism in which the data of the modern natural sciences are alone allowed to contribute to the construction of our worldview.

Many intellectuals share this project, especially feminists seeking to shape a "successor" science to the one we have now. However, laudable though their goals are, I do not think it represents postmodernism as much as an attempt to supplant modernism by some new worldview with a somewhat broader epistemology. I do think "constructive" postmodernism will eventually contribute to whatever follows postmodernism, but for now it ignores one of the central insights of postmodernism: totalizing worldviews lead to totalitarianism.

> The nineteenth and twentieth centuries have given us as much terror as we can take. We have paid a high enough price for the nostalgia for the whole and the one, for the reconciliation of the concept and the sensible, of the transparent and the communicable experience. Under the general demand for slackening and for appeasement, we can hear the mutterings of the desire for a return of terror, for the realization for the fantasy to seize reality. The answer is: Let us wage a war on totality; let us be witnesses to the unpresentable; let us activate the differences and save the honor of the name.
>
> —Jean-Francois Lyotard

Out of this understanding of the dangers of total visions, especially the wild dreams of engineers and the cool gaze of science, some feminist philosophers have charted a more usable postmodern politics that seeks to put technoscience into a different context but certainly not to destroy it. One of the best is Donna Haraway. She uses the image of the cyborg to call not for a single dominating worldview but for one of heteroglossia, of many voices:

> Cyborg imagery can help express two crucial arguments...(1) the production of universal, totalizing theory is a major mistake that misses most of reality, probably always, but certainly now; (2) taking responsibility for the social relations of science and technology means refusing an anti-science metaphysics, a demonology of technology, and so means embracing the skillful task of reconstructing the boundaries of daily life, in partial connection with others, in communication with all of our parts. It is not just that science and technology are possible means of great human satisfaction, as well as a matrix of complex dominations. Cyborg imagery can suggest a way out of the maze of dualisms in which we have explained our bodies and our tools to ourselves. This is a dream not of a common language, but of a powerful infidel heteroglossia....

Technoscience is political, socially constructed in part, capable of producing "complex dominations" and "great human satisfaction[s]" both. It cannot be explained through one "mouth" but perhaps it can be communicated with a range of voices. Among these voices are modern ones, and premodern ones, and others still. Tolerance of the other is crucial. Just as necessary, Linda Hutcheon points out, is taking responsibility:

> Postmodernism attempts to be historically aware, hybrid, and inclusive; the...new motto might be "responsibility and tolerance."

Hutcheon argues that we have to take responsibility because we are complicit in postmodern technoscience, no matter if we like it or not. Nobody can escape technology today, whether they live in a cabin in Montana or an ashram in Nepal. Satellites, Nike shoes, Madonna CDs, and automatic weapons are easily accessible. But we can be critical of our complicity because we have the power as participants to shape reality. Jane Flax gives this an even harder edge:

> Feminist theories, like other forms of postmodernism, should encourage us to tolerate and interpret ambivalence, ambiguity, and multiplicity as well as to expose the roots of our needs for imposing order and structure no matter how arbitrary and oppressive these needs may be.
>
> If we do our work well, "reality" will appear even more unstable, complex, and disorderly than it does now.

We live in this postmodern world, and who can deny that it is "unstable, complex, and disorderly"? The political movements that dominate postmodernism set the context for cyborg citizenship, but before we explore that idea in later chapters we need to think a little bit more about cyborgs in and of themselves. Ourselves.

THE IMPORTANCE OF THE CYBORG IDEA

The word cyborg is new but the idea is not, as I discussed in the Introduction. Manfred Clynes minted the term for a NASA conference on modifying the human for living in space. Clynes, a world-class pianist with a knack for inventing computers, melded "cybernetic" and "organism" into "cyborg" to enliven the ideas of a paper coauthored with Nathan Kline, the famous psychiatrist and expert on psychotropic drugs. Clynes and Kline suggested that humans could be modified with implants and drugs so that they could exist in space without space suits. It is not as crazy as it sounds, but even

Clynes would admit today that we will need genetic modifications to make such a transition possible. Clynes, who continues to work on cyborg ideas with his theory of sentics (the physiological basis of emotions) and with a number of startling computer-music programs, now feels that humans will pass through at least four different cyborg stages, culminating in genetic modifications.

The term "cyborg" caught on, but not among scientists, who preferred more specific labels such as biotelemetry, human augmentation, human-machine systems, human-machine interfaces, teleoperators, and—to describe copying natural systems to create artificial ones—bionics. "Cyborg" took off among science-fiction writers who had already recognized the incredible integration of technology into natural systems that was starting to transform society. *Cyborg* is as specific, as general, as powerful, and as useless a term as *tool* or *machine*. And it is just as important. Cyborgs are proliferating throughout contemporary culture, and as they do they are redefining many of the most basic political concepts of human existence.

Steven Mentor and I wrote an article for *The Cyborg Handbook* that notes how the metaphor of the "body politic" has been philosophically important since Aristotle. The Leviathan of Thomas Hobbes, the seventeenth-century English political theorist of the state, is a good example of the power of this idea. Hobbes argued that the king's living body was a model for the nation-state, the body politic. Now the body politic is not mapped by the king's body; instead it is a cyborg in form and fact.

Today's contemporary political communities consist of infrastructure, great armies are made up of human-machine weapon systems, and the world economy is dominated by gigantic multinationals who depend on their own hypercomputerization. The changes that many commentators, from cyberpunk writers to Harvard professors, have noted recently are all signs of a cyborged body politic. First there was the collapse of the simple, and perhaps always artificial, dichotomy of the Cold War. We also see the devolution of nation states into smaller communities and the rise of regional systems, such as the European Community. Nongovernmental organizations proliferate and worldwide institutions grow stronger, from the Web to the World Court.

Steven and I stress that the cyborg body politic is just a metaphor:

There is an arrogance to making these kinds of arguments because they pretend to a coherence that is, at the most, only contingent. The sovereignty of any metaphor, including the cyborg body politic, is illusory, subject to proliferation, hybridization. It should not be prescriptive, so much as descriptive and productive of possibilities, utopian and/or pragmatic.

The metaphor makes the political centrality of technology undeniable, and it reminds us continually that:

> The same technology that will hardwire a pilot into the computer that flies the jet and enables the missiles will allow our friend, hit by a speeding truck, to walk again. There is no choice between utopia and dystopia, Good Terminator or Evil Terminator—they are both here. We are learning to inhabit this constructed, ambiguous body (and explore who constructs it) whether it's the one we walk around in or the one we are told to vote in....

We have to keep in mind that metaphors describe real-world phenomena, flesh-and-steel relationships. We don't need to call it the cyborg body politic. We could call it cyborg power or the informatics of domination or any number of things. But the term "cyborg body politic" links what is happening now to a long tradition of doing and thinking democratic politics.

To understand exactly how our cyborged bodies make for a cyborg body politic, let us start with the source of legitimate political power, according to John Locke and the revolutionaries of the eighteenth century (and I agree): the citizen.

citizenship in the age of electronic reproduction

[I]t is no longer enough to feel represented by a government (if it ever was); now a citizen of the cybernetic political world inhabits various bodies interfaced more or less intimately with various prosthetics, all models for political structures that subject and partially construct us.
—Chris Hables Gray and Steven Mentor

WHO OR WHAT IS A CITIZEN?

In an episode of *Star Trek: The Next Generation,* Data the android is put on trial to determine whether he is property or a citizen. *ST:TNG* is full of cyborgs: Geordi La Forge with his visor, Riker with his transporter clone, Worf with an artificial spine, Pecard with an artificial heart, various holographic characters who come to life, and, in several episodes, the ship itself. And there are the Borg, the evil, black-leather-clad cyborg group mind. But Data is a particularly interesting cyborg because his cyborgization is based on two very unrelated technologies. First, his skin is a biological construction. Second, his consciousness arises from patterns extracted from the memories of humans in the colony where he was built. Technically it is far from clear that Data is anything more than a very sophisticated robot with some borrowings from the organic world. But he longs to be human.

Data's trial results from the machinations of an ambitious scientist from the United Federation of Planets who wants to deconstruct Data to see how he works. Data's friends testify but they are far from convincing. Finally

Data takes the stand. In his testimony he reveals that he keeps a hologram of Tasha Yar, the butch, blonde security chief who died engulfed in an evil ink blot on an earlier episode. Data confesses that he had sex with Tasha once when the whole crew was exposed to an aphrodisiac ("I am fully functional," he told her when she propositioned him), and so he is deemed a citizen after all.

The ability to have sex with a human may seem like a strange criterion for citizenship, but it is actually the ability to have sex *and talk about it* that saves Data. The definition of citizenship is freeing itself from gender-, race-, and class-based criteria and becoming an issue of competent participation in what some philosophers call a discourse community but what most of us would just label a meaningful conversation. The communication need not be speech or writing, as Helen Keller proved, but there must be communication for political participation. This perspective helps us think about cyborg citizenship just as it has helped define intelligence through the Turing test. We will return to the Turing test and the cyborg citizen below, but first a few more things need to be said about citizenship itself.

The idea of citizenship has been growing more powerful as the world transforms into a cyborged society. Consider the alternatives. Would you rather be a subject? An employee? A tribal member? The role of tribal member is much more nuanced than some might think and is quite different from "citizen." But while some coherent tribes remain strong institutions that people gladly subsume their individuality to because of long-standing blood ties and links to specific land, for most people being a tribal member is not an option. And for many tribal members it is an option that is refused. What is popular is citizenship.

The word "citizen" comes from "cities," and the first citizens were in the Greek city-states. They were male, adult, property-owning members who fought in the military; nonmembers, women, children, and the poor were not citizens and had few rights. Originally, in the Massachusetts Bay Colony, a citizen had to be a landowner or ranked as a master craftsman, a member of the Puritan Church, white, male, and an oath-swearer to the Crown. Even now, the U.S. Constitution says that the president must be a "natural-born citizen," which excludes "naturalized" citizens, of course; but does it also mean a test-tube baby cannot grow up to be president?

Some theorists still link the idea of citizenship to membership in a state and, like the Australian political scientist Jan Pakulski, they worry that the postmodern "weakening of the state and the erosion of state legitimacy will ultimately arrest the process of citizenship extension." Pakulski notes that more and more rights are being linked to a person's status as a human being (as in the UN's Declaration of Human Rights) and not to their membership in a state.

For me this is not a problem. I trace my citizenship to my consent to be governed, in the formulation of John Locke, and that stems from my ability to be part of the polis, the political entity that humans and cyborgs (and in the future who knows what else) share through our ability to communicate together about political issues, sex, and whether or not Madonna has talent. Let me stress that I reject the patriarchal and classist assumptions that mar Locke's work and that do not follow logically. But the fundamental premise of Locke (and of the American and French revolutions and many more besides) is that the governed must consent to be governed or the state is not legitimate. Postmodern citizenship is more diffuse and proactive, as consent and allegiance can be granted to more than just nation-states; (bio)regions, cities, and the world as a whole can claim part of the citizen's allegiance. This is not so much a matter of political theory as it is of political practice, and as long as enough of us are willing to put our lives and our sacred honor on the line for this idea of conscious and proactive citizenship, it will remain true.

Pakulski makes much of the state as "the monopolistic enforcer of rights," but it is my reading of history that individuals and groups have to struggle mightily, often against states, to acquire and defend their rights. Sometimes this is to establish or change states so that they are more amenable to human rights, but even then the natural tendency of even the most revolutionary and limited government is to grow in power (the iron law of bureaucracy) and start usurping people's freedoms. Thomas Jefferson stressed that it takes continual effort to keep our freedom. He phrased it in more colorful language, advocating perpetual revolutions every 20 years because: "The tree of liberty must be refreshed from time to time with the blood of patriots and tyrants." Such enthusiasm is probably why I am happy to call myself a Jeffersonian anarchist; after all, his disciple John L. O'Sullivan pointed out that "the government that governs least governs best," which has a nice logic to it.

Since nation-states are contingent, based on belief and history (some political scientists call them "imaginary communities"), there is no reason not to imagine a polity of the world. World citizenship makes much more political and ecological sense than does citizenship in nation-states. Aspects of national citizenship, such as those discussed by Bryan Turner in the premier issue of a journal called *Citizenship Studies*—legal rights, political rights, social rights—can be applied to world citizenship. But global citizenship offers the opportunity of combining human rights with these rights—and the concurrent obligations—of national citizens.

I am in sympathy with Pakulski's call for a "cultural citizenship" that expands the individual's rights and obligations to include economic and cultural dimensions as well as freedom and equality in the political process. Citizenship is clearly changing, as the very ground of politics shifts through the globalization of human culture and the other aspects of postmodernity that our ever-expanding technosciences are driving. But what will citizenship in the twenty-first century look like?

However citizenship may evolve, technology will play a major role. Langdon Winner, for one, has argued that technologies can be autonomous, that artifacts have politics of their own. Thus certain technologies may be inherently authoritarian, and real citizenship might be accorded only to those individuals who gain knowledge, control, or access as a result of their relationships to complex technologies. Those without are doomed to become "technopeasants" or, as my graduate student Katie Meyers wrote in an unpublished short story, "technotards." There is certainly the possibility that the expansion of citizenship might be reversed by differentiated access to technologies, especially health, information, and power. Cyborgization contains this danger as well. Yet the dynamics of cyborg citizenship are more complex than a simple accounting of haves and have-nots.

Engin Isin, a Canadian academic, has explored this issue in his article "Who Is the New Citizen?" He documents the rise of "new knowledge workers" and other shifts in the political landscape, including the development of a new "professional-citizen." This leads him to ask: What are the new political and moral obligations that will inevitably arise with new types of citizenship? The new citizenship must stem not just from the economic changes we are now experiencing but also from the actual changes our bodies are undergoing through cyborgization. We have to think in terms of the cyborg citizen, and that means we have to decide who qualifies.

The complications of cyborg citizenship call for a cyborg citizen Turing test to determine which entities can actually participate in our discourse community and which cannot. The Turing test is a very pragmatic exercise that has long been useful to scientists and writers trying to determine if a computer is intelligent. The test was first proposed by Alan Turing, the homosexual English computer scientist who died mysteriously in the 1950s after apparently biting a poisoned apple; whether it was suicide or the state solving a security risk we may never know. Turing, who played a fundamental role in developing the computer while he was building code-breaking machines during World War II, based his test on a party game called "the imitation game."

In the original "party" version, a man and a woman are given the same set of questions, which they then take to a separate room. One of them replies on a typed sheet, and the party guests try to guess if it is the man's or the woman's reply.

Turing proposed that a machine be substituted for one of the humans, and then argued that since intelligence is an operational concept, not an absolute, the best way to judge it is by testing whether or not the entity in question could carry on an intelligent conversation with an intelligent human for a serious length of time. If it could, then even a machine should be considered intelligent, at least as intelligent as many humans.

The value of Turing's test—and its use for determining cyborg citizenship—is its insight that intelligence, like citizenship, is a working idea, not an abstract universal value. Citizenship is based on assumptions about the consent of the governed, the relationship between responsibility and rights, and the autonomy of individuals. Historically, criteria for citizenship have ranged from gender and class, through literacy, to the current system in which birthright assures eventual citizenship unless it is abrogated through misdeeds. But beneath these shifting rules one can discern that the idea of a discourse community has always been the basic ground. Western political communities may have been limited in earlier days by political goals of racial, gender, or class domination, but among their approved citizens the ideal has always been equal discourse. The polis is a discourse community, after all, and every historical expansion of it has been predicated on arguments about the participation of new individuals in that discourse. Today, as we are faced with a whole range of complex and difficult decisions about who should be and who can be citizens, it seems wise to stay within this framework.

Currently, judgments about the suitability for citizenship of individual humans and cyborgs are made on the grounds of their ability to take part in the discourse of the polis, either by assumptions about age or by the evaluation of experts. Many of the more difficult cases are of actual cyborgs: humans linked to machines that keep them alive or humans who maintain autonomy only through drugs and other technointerventions. Instead of a jury of one's peers, the decision usually results from a negotiation between doctors, social workers, lawyers, and judges. Even in such cases, the criterion is operational. For example, in the United States, the National Council of State Boards of Nursing defines competence as "the application of knowledge and the interpersonal, decision-making, and psychomotor skills expected." If people are going to be judged on what is "expected," maybe that determination should be made by their peers.

Let us take such power away from the "soft" police and return it to the polis at large, in the form of juries of peers conducting their own rough Turing tests. An entity must convince a simple majority of twelve other citizens that it can be part of their conversation. This requirement should prevent refusals of citizenship on the basis of racism or other prejudices. The point is not to exclude those who are already citizens, as literacy and property laws were designed to do. And the point is not to include pets or fetuses or corporate entities. If such entities deserve rights and protection, they can be granted in other ways than citizenship.

The beauty of the Turing test is that it escapes the straitjacket of arbitrary standards and static definitions. Flexible though it is, it does not cast out all values; instead it focuses on the core of politics—communication—and enshrines that as the ultimate value. Also it implies strongly that citizenship is embodied, whether the body be organic, machinic, or both, ambiguous or not, constructed or not.

THE CYBORG BILL OF RIGHTS

Donna Haraway's "A Manifesto for Cyborgs" is the founding document of cyborg politics. Republished dozens of times since 1985, it has inspired, outraged, and befuddled countless readers. Since then there has been a proliferation of cyber-manifestos. It almost seems as if most things written now about "cyber" anything are in the style of a manifesto. Which would be appropriate, since, according to Steven Mentor:

> All manifestos are cyborgs. That is, they fit Donna Haraway's use of this term in her own "A Manifesto for Cyborgs"—manifestos are hybrids, chimeras, boundary-confusing technologies. They combine and confuse popular genres and political discourses, borrow from critical theory and advertising, serve as would be control systems for the larger social technologies their authors hope to manufacture.

Among the more interesting cyber-manifestos are the "Mutant Manifesto," Stelarc's "Cyborg Manifesto," "The Magna Carta for the Knowledge Age," and a number of proclamations from the Extropians. Many of these are based on earlier manifestos from the late 1700s. Other manifestos include

"The Declaration of the Independence of Cyberspace" announced by cyber-libertarians in 1996, and the "Bill of Gender Rights" from the Second International Conference on Transgender Law and Employment Policy in 1993. This bill of rights includes "the right to control and change one's own body," the "right to medical and professional care," and the "right to freedom from psychiatric treatment." Manifestos seem to break the ground for new rights, which are sometimes then codified into texts that seem like technologies.

Bills of rights, and the constitutions they are prosthetics for, are technically called "written instruments" and they are indeed technologies. They are supposed to help us govern ourselves. While my particular Cyborg Bill of Rights is designed as amendments to the U.S. Constitution, the ideas in it are relevant to all postmodern democracies. Many constitutions draw from the U.S. version, as Japan's and South Africa's do. The U.S. Constitution comes out of English common law, French political thinking, and Greek, Roman, and Native American governing traditions. This is not a proposal aimed just at the United States. All cyborg citizens need their rights defended. So, in the hope of making a modest improvement in the human political condition, I propose this *Cyborg Bill of Rights.*

One last point. Despite some strange rulings in the past by the U.S. Supreme Court, it is explicitly stated in this new Bill of Rights that:

> Business corporations and other bureaucracies *are not* citizens or individuals, nor shall they ever be.

As it is now, corporations have many of the rights of citizens but few of the obligations. In the future there might be "corporate" cyborgs with multiple or distributed intelligence. Without some level of unitary identity, such a cyborg will not have the ability to act coherently. But, perhaps some cyborg of the far future will be multiple but coherent enough to be capable of casting one vote. Still there is no reason to allow business corporations to keep their quasi-citizen status. Even without it they have too much power.

The ten amendments are as follows:

1. *Freedom of Travel.* Citizens shall have the right to travel anywhere, virtually or in the flesh, at their own risk and expense.

2. *Freedom of Electronic Speech.* Electronic and other nonphysical forms of transmitting information are protected by the Constitution's First Amendment.

3. *The Right of Electronic Privacy.* Electronic and other nonmaterial forms of property and personhood shall be accorded the protection of the Fourth Amendment.

4. *Freedom of Consciousness.* The consciousness of the citizen shall be protected by the First, Fourth, and Eighth Amendments. Unreasonable search and seizure of this, the most sacred and private part of an individual citizen, is absolutely prohibited. Individuals shall retain all rights to modify their consciousness through psychopharmological, medical, genetic, spiritual, and other practices, insofar as they do not threaten the fundamental rights of other individuals and citizens, and that they do so at their own risk and expense.

5. *Right to Life.* The body of the citizen shall be protected by the First, Fourth, and Eighth Amendments. Unreasonable search and seizure of this sacred and private part of an individual citizen shall be absolutely prohibited. Individuals shall retain all rights to modify their bodies, at their own risk and expense, through psychopharmological, medical, genetic, spiritual, and other practices, insofar as they do not threaten the fundamental rights of other individuals and citizens.

6. *Right to Death.* Every citizen and individual shall have the right to end their life, at their own risk and expense, in the manner of their own choice, as long as it does not infringe upon the fundamental rights of other citizens and individuals.

7. *Right to Political Equality.* The political power of every citizen should be determined by the quality of his or her arguments, example, energy, and single vote, not based on his or her economic holdings or social standing. Congress shall permit no electoral system that favors wealth, coercion, or criminal behavior to the detriment of political equality.

8. *Freedom of Information.* Citizens shall have access to all information held about them by governments or other bureaucracies. Citizens shall have the right to correct all information held on them by governments and other bureaucracies at the expense of these bureaucracies. Institutional and corporate use of information to coerce or otherwise illegally manipulate or act upon citizens shall be absolutely forbidden.

9. *Freedom of Family, Sexuality, and Gender.* Citizens and individuals have the right to determine their own sexual and gender orientations, at their own risk and expense, including matrimonial and other forms of alliance. Congress shall make no law arbitrarily restricting the definition of the family, of marriage, or of parenthood.

10. *Right to Peace.* Citizens and individuals have a right to freedom from war and violence. War shall be a last resort and must be declared by a two thirds vote of Congress when proposed by the president. The Third Amendment shall not be construed as permitting citizens and individuals to own all types of weapons. Freedom from governmental tyranny will not be safeguarded through local militia or individual violence. Only solidarity, tolerance, sacrifice, and an equitable political system will guarantee freedom. Nonetheless, citizens and individuals shall have the right to defend themselves with deadly force, at their own risk and expense, if their fundamental rights are being abridged.

These amendments are important, but alone they cannot protect us. We need active citizens and new political technologies to protect our rights from the relentless changes that cyborgian technoscience is producing.

I have assumed here that cyborg citizens are real political bodies and therefore they need real political rights instantiated in technologies such as constitutions and operational tests of citizenship. The individual needs real political protection in this age of new powerful technosciences and the systems they make possible. Without such protection, corporations, parties, bureaus of police, governments, and wealthy families will achieve hegemony, and the vast majority of us will lose all political power.

Citizenship will always be embodied in some sense, although not necessarily in living flesh. Many theorists, and I am one of them, think intelligence itself is inherently embodied. A disembodied intelligence, if it were even possible, might very well not be interested in our definition of citizenship. Our political system (indeed our existence) is based on embodiment.

It is feminist philosophy that has made the embodiment of citizenship undeniable in the postmodern era, through an examination of the dangers of disembodied philosophies that make hyperrationality the measure of all things and through many case studies of the role of bodies in real politics. For example, Elaine Scarry's *Bodies in Pain* details how bodies are the ground for both war and the coercive power of government. Different philosophies have put forward many other possible bases for political principles—the soul, the race, the nation—but in real terms it is the action of, and on, bodies that is the basis of politics. This explains the crucial political importance of cyborgs.

Donna Haraway points out that cyborg politics are not inevitably liberatory. Far from it. They offer a chance for sustaining, even extending, democracy, but also the equally real chance of ultimate oppression, especially if we subscribe to illusions of "total theory," "pure information," and "perfect communication" and deny the messy reality of machinic and organic bodies and their rights.

An example of where such illusions might lead can be found in Bruno Latour's political thinking, especially in his 1993 book *We Have Never Been Modern*. Latour, an aristocratic French scholar, has argued that science is a collaborative construction involving alliances between institutions, rhetorics, technologies, artifacts, and humans. On the surface it might seem that his argument parallels the one here. He denounces totalitarian rationality-is-everything narratives and urges a reconciliation between nature and technology. But Latour's advocacy for granting rights to nonhuman, nonliving objects and implementing a "Parliament of Things" is profoundly problematic on several levels. First, the argument is couched in abstract and symbolic terms. Secondly, it depends on a series of oversimplified dichotomies, such as the alienation of modernism from nature and the domination of human(ism) over the rest of reality. Finally, it is based on illusions about agency and causality that in actuality would make working politics impossible.

That artifacts have politics does not mean that they have agency. Certainly, cyborgs (or "hybrids," in Latour's formulation) demonstrate that organic embodiment is not the final arbitrator of agency, but that does not mean that anything can be an actor ("actant" for Latour). That everything can be called a system does not mean that all systems can think, or act, or practice politics in any real way.

The dangers of Latour's schema becomes apparent when one looks closely at his Parliament:

> Let one of the representatives talk, for instance, about the ozone hole, another represent the Monsanto chemical industry, a third the workers of the same chemical industry, another the voters of New Hampshire, a fifth the meteorology of the polar regions; let still another speak in the name of the State; what does it matter, so long as they are all talking about the same thing, about a quasi-object they have all created, the object-discourse-

nature-society whose new properties astound us all and whose network extends from my refrigerator to the Antarctic by way of chemistry, law, the State, the economy and satellites.

All of this "speaking" for others reminds me of vanguard parties speaking for the working class. Elites have a funny way of helping themselves while they speak for others. This diffusion of representation based on Latour's totalizing theories about binary reality and his assumptions about perfect communication and pure information (both necessary for all this "speaking for," unless the meteorology of the polar regions suddenly does become articulate on its own) paves the way for the end of real representative government.

Citizens need representation, holes in the ozone layer and chemical companies do not. Chemical companies will look after themselves, unfortunately. That is why we have an ozone hole that threatens us, after all. It is living intelligence (whether human, cyborg, or purely artificial as may someday happen) that must be empowered, not every quasi-object we can count dancing on a pinhead.

"Lives are at stake," Donna Haraway reminds us, "in curious quasi-objects like databases...." *Lives,* not objects, quasi or otherwise. Of course it is in the long-term interest of citizens to recognize how interdependent we all are, how much a part of nature we are. And it is in our interest to do more than theorize about old and new dichotomies. We have to get political, down and dirty, and mess with the cyborgian machinery of government. As Haraway also says:

> Undoubtedly, we will have to do more than mutate the stories and the figures if the cyborg citizens of the third planet from the sun are to enjoy something better than the deadly transgressive flexibility of the New World Order.

Accepting ourselves as cyborgs can be liberating and empowering. We can choose how we construct ourselves. We can resist. But we must go beyond resistance. The long degradation of representation can be reversed if we reject calls such as Latour's for its elitist reconstruction. If autonomy is to avoid becoming automaton, we must make cyborg citizenship real, and defend it and expand it, in every way we can. Hence my ironic but serious proposal for a Cyborg Bill of Rights and a Turing test for citizenship. The threat to our freedoms and to justice from the megacyborgs of governments, corporations, and the superwealthy is very real indeed.

CYBORGIAN JUSTICE: PANOPTICONS VERSUS
CYBORG DEATH CULTS

> I believe the fundamental bioethical imperative for behavioral scientists
> today is to have the courage to renounce all collaboration with forces
> seeking to "control" or "modify" or "engineer" human responses.
> —Dr. Richard Restak

He would carry a gold-plated ice pick in a velvet case. After applying a mild local anesthetic, he would drive the ice pick into the patient's skull through the edge of one of the eye sockets, severing the nerve connections to the thalamus and producing, in many cases, zombielike behavior along with convulsive seizures, intellectual impairment to the point of severe retardation, and the loss of all emotions. He did this more than 3,500 times. He was Dr. Walter Freeman, a neurologist at George Washington University Hospital in Washington, D.C., and was, along with James Watts, the inventor of the lobotomy.

Controlling human behavior through psychosurgery or other means is an old dream dating at least back to the ancient Romans, who noticed that sword wounds in the head sometimes cured mental illness. But only in the late twentieth century did it become a massive industry with a tremendous amount of government support, often framed in the language of cybernetics, the science of control.

Ice picks and other surgical implements passed out of favor with the advent of powerful drugs that offered the potential for "chemical" lobotomies. Thorazine and other tranquilizers are used massively today to control violent or just annoying mental patients, even though their long-term effects are sometimes just as damaging as the gold-plated ice pick. Behavior modification scientists have gone much further, researching electrical brain implants, studying military brainwashing techniques to see how they can be applied to criminals, and even inventing their own torture devices.

In the 1960s, the staff at Atascadero and Vacaville, prisons for the criminally insane in California, used the drug succinylcholine to "modify" patient behavior. Since the drug paralyzes the whole body, including the lungs, but leaves the victim conscious as they suffocate, it was considered ideal for convincing prisoners to change their behavior.

Fortunately, legal interventions stopped these "experiments" and also ended other programs, such as the one where doctors coerced patients to agree to psychosurgery by administering brain shocks and then forcibly operated on them even though they had later recanted their earlier approval. The U.S. courts ruled that prisoners and patients could not be forced to undergo irreversible treatments and that in many cases noncoerced consent was impossible. However, reversible interventions, illegal experiments (some no doubt undertaken by the government), and studies outside North America and Europe, where patients' rights are protected to some extent, undoubtably continue.

In his book *Pre-Meditated Man*, Richard Restak reviews this history and looks at a number of other areas where biotechnology is impacting society, such a genetic engineering. The key issue, he decides, is power. Who has the power to decide? Transplant programs, kidney machine use, and behavior and genetic modifications "are not questions of 'ethics,' they are questions of power." As a physician and scientist himself, he stresses that we cannot rely upon scientists to be the ultimate judges. Society must decide in general, and individual patients must have the power in particular. And, he warns, we cannot assume the government is a disinterested mediator of what the people want. It has interests of its own. He also argues that the power of new technologies for behavioral and genetic modification and the ever-quickening rate of innovation in these areas means that the amount of time society has to respond to them grow shorter while the consequences of mistakes grows heavier. Every time we do not get it right there is a wave of deaths, deformations, and other horrific consequences, as with the thalidomide babies.

Some people just aspire to control people directly. Consider Dr. Jose M. R. Delgado, author of *Physical Control of the Mind*. A distinguished professor at Madrid University, UCLA, and Yale, he implanted electrodes in the brains of animals to control them. Donna Haraway describes Delgado's joint project with Nathan Kline and leading primatologists to manipulate gibbons through brain stimulation:

> The proposed research was a straightforward extension of work Delgado had done for over twenty years. He had been instrumental in developing the multichannel radio stimulator, the programed stimulator, the stimoceiver, the transdermal brain stimulator, a mobility recorder, chemitrodes, external dialtrodes, and subcutaneous dialtrodes. These were cyborg organs within cybernetic functionalism.

The cyborgs are animal-machines, experimental objects for perfecting cybernetic control. Along with the animals, the behavioral observations were automated as much as possible using a mobile telemetry system that, when analyzed by computer, would produce suggested medication levels. As Haraway notes, the "structure of a command-control-communication system pervades the discourse of Delgado and his community, whether or not explicit military metaphors or social ties appear." Command, control, and communication do not apply just to military units now; they are what governments want to exercise on citizen-subjects who otherwise might run out of control.

It is an old fear of rulers. How do we control the masses? More subtle approaches than those discussed here often work, but sometimes the powers-that-be feel that extreme measures are necessary. Technoscience has gifted us with incredible destructive powers. What do we do when they are used by small groups of clever nuts who have been driven insane by society's rapid transitions?

Today's body politic is clearly uncomfortable when it contemplates its progressing cyborgization. There is good reason to fear that there will be pathological reactions. The Aum group from Japan, famous around the world for its nerve gas attacks, was in many ways the first cyborg death cult. Along with the typical trappings of insane death cults (a guru, a bizarre eschatology, and an internal dynamic of oppression and conformity), cult members had also totally embraced the idea that they were cyborg supermen who would save the world from the apocalypse of the current world ecological crisis.

Aum's worldview was shaped equally by science fiction (the work of Isaac Asimov), Buddhism, and its leaders' dreams of commanding and controlling its members though perfect communication. World domination was their goal, nothing less. Aum devotees wore special six-volt electrode shock caps (four volts for children) that were meant to synchronize the wearers' brains to their guru's brain waves, which were continuously broadcast into their heads. They were called Perfect Salvation Initiation machines and they cost initiates about $7,000 dollars a month to use. Aum's security/medical team treated dissenters with electroshock and psychopharmacology. The executed were literally microwaved into ash. Cult members were told that they were superhumans capable of resisting nuclear blasts and plasma rays, thanks to a combination of cyborg technologies (such as the shock caps and drugs) and meditation. Aum's many young scientists not only manufactured small arms but also produced a wide range of biological and chemical weapons, including the sarin used in the Tokyo subway attacks that killed 12 and injured thousands. They had been trying to buy nuclear weapons and develop laser and microwave weapons as well. Fortunately, this particular cyborg microculture collapsed into self-destructive paranoia before it could effectively incorporate mass-death weapons.

The danger of groups like Aum is real. But perhaps the "cure" for such terrorism is just as dangerous as the disease. Using high technology to combat the threat of high-technology terrorism has tremendously corrosive effects on our freedoms, especially from government coercion and surveillance. Video systems have proliferated. They can be found in most stores now, in many workplaces, and on thousands of street corners. The government installs them not only to capture street crimes on tape, but traffic violations as well. Less obvious but perhaps even more intrusive is the explosive growth of databases full of information about the average citizen. A whole range of companies, from marketing to insurance, are creating profiles of millions of potential customers to maximize their advertising budgets or vet potential insurers. Much of this information is illegally acquired, inaccurate, or both.

Meanwhile, new surveillance technologies are introduced all the time. For example, police now possess a device that can detect electromagnetic radiation with such sensitivity that they can tell who is carrying a gun—or wearing a colostomy bag—without a direct search. There are also thermal-imaging devices that can track large mammals from the sky, gamma-ray scanners that can look inside trucks, X-ray technology and computer-aided metal detectors that can reveal items hidden under clothing up to 60 feet away, and ion sniffers that sample the air around someone's skin for chemical traces of cocaine and other naughty things.

Drug tests are used by many corporations and government agencies, from the short-term and inaccurate (but cheap) urine tests to the expensive hair analysis that can detect drug use from years before. Despite the many false-positives such tests produce (do not eat poppy-seed muffins before hand!), their popularity is increasing. Managers find the superficial clarity of such measures reassuring, and for this same reason they have begun to use various personality profiles to cull potentially bad employees and even resort to lie-detector tests for important positions.

A universal infallible lie detector such as the one imagined in James Halperin's novel *The Truth Machine* might seem like a beneficial development at first glance, but not upon reflection. No machine would be 100 percent accurate, only 99.999 percent at best, because there will always be a few sociopaths who can beat it. In the story, the inventor, who programmed it, can also outsmart it. Who watches the watcher? Then there is always the problem of people who are mistaken. They think they are telling the truth but they are wrong, which actually happens with many eyewitness identifications today. Even if the machine were perfectly accurate, is it really what we want? Sure, most of the criminals would be caught and most of the innocent freed, and most politicians and lawyers would be out of a job. But every insincere compliment, every stray politically incorrect thought, every incomplete self-deception could potentially be exposed. In the novel no wedding, no hiring, no contract, no graduation takes place without a truth test, and it fundamentally reorganizes society.

While a perfect truth machine might never be possible, more accurate lie detectors will eventually be built because our understanding of cognition and physiology continues to improve. Do we want a lie detector of 98 percent accuracy, for example, admitted into court? There is always that 2 percent, but most people do not seem to care. Even now, the use of our current horribly inaccurate lie detectors is spreading. Society loves technological solutions to political problems; look at the popularity of "electronic" arrest.

Since 1983 many convicted minor criminals, such as habitual drunk-driving offenders, have been held under "house" arrest by electronic "leashes" that are cuffed to their wrists or ankles and linked to their phones. A simple call from the probation department can verify if the convict—or at least the leash—is at home.

The system is being adapted for more dangerous criminals, such as Wesley Miller, who killed and mutilated a high school classmate in 1982. Three different systems monitor Miller: the ankle cuff, a global positioning system (GPS) satellite link on his other ankle, and a pager that he must answer immediately so that a computer can verify his identity with voice-recognition software. The satellite link insures that he will not go to any forbidden locations. Texas monitors over 1,000 high-risk parolees using these systems, but Miller is the first to have all three. He will not be the last.

A whole range of such cyborg containment technologies are being developed, including chips to be implanted in the flesh. They give the government and other big bureaucracies unprecedented power to control the population. Private security firms sell much of the actual equipment and expertise to the highest bidder, so we are beginning to experience a privitized version of *1984*. "I want to thank George Orwell for having the depth and foresight to plan my career," remarked Richard Chace of the Security Industry Association, an organization that promotes closed-circuit television security systems.

But is privacy overrated? David Brin, a physics professor and brilliant science-fiction writer, has explored the idea that privacy may be a problem. In his novel *Earth*, the nations of the world have attacked Switzerland in a nuclear Helvetian War to expose the secrets and the fruits of governmental and corporate abuse hidden in Swiss banks. His novel explores the politics of privacy in great detail (along with a dozen other fascinating themes, some of them quite cyborgian), and, to his credit, he does not simplify the issues. Surprisingly, he comes down unequivocally *against* privacy. He argues that "secrecy has always favored the mighty." Today the powerful benefit from secrecy; they can buy the most impenetrable privacy and they can also "get around whatever pathetic barriers you or I erect." So "privacy laws and codes will protect those at the top."

His answer is not "more fog, but more light: transparency." He admits that the average citizen would sacrifice something, but "we'll have something precious to help make up for lost privacy: freedom." Brin proposes to do away aggressively with privacy altogether. No secret bank accounts, no hidden files, free access by anyone to any camera anywhere! If the police have a surveillance system, the citizen should be able to view it. The weakness of this proposal is that it would take a world war to implement. Until then, do we really want to live in a totally surveilled society, inside the panopticon?

Jeremy Bentham coined the term "panopticon" for a prison he designed with his brother in which jailers could always observe the inmates. A key to the success of the panopticon is that the inmates would not know if they were being watched or not, just that they might be. The same can be said of the ubiquitous video cameras spreading through contemporary society. You can never know if someone is watching the monitor or might view the tape later.

The effect of this uncertainty is very wearying. Have you ever been watched? During my years as a political organizer, I was photographed at scores of demonstrations, visited by the FBI and Secret Service, had my phone tapped more than I probably know, and was jailed 10 times. Once, when asked how it felt to get out of jail, I replied: "It feels the same out here"—which was an exaggeration, of course. Still, I have seldom felt that the outside world was fundamentally different from jail. Our culture disturbingly resembles *The Truman Show*, where the unsuspecting Truman had his whole life broadcast live on television. As the actor who plays the actor playing Truman's best friend explains, the set of the Truman Show is "real, it is merely controlled." Our real world seems quite controlled. It is becoming more and more like the panopticon designed by the Bentham brothers. The difference between the two is shrinking at an alarming rate.

Is this what cyborg society inevitably leads to—a commanded and controlled body politic? A consumer-friendly police state? Do cyborg technologies offer only potential threats to our freedoms? Many people would argue that the reverse is true. Cyberdemocracy is true democracy, they claim. We shall see.

cybocracy, mobocracy, and democracy

THE MANUFACTURING OF CONSENT

There's no way William A. Cozzano can lose the upcoming Presidential election. He's a likable Midwestern governor with one insidious advantage. An advantage provided by a shadowy group of backers. A biochip in his head hardwires him to a computerized polling system. The mood of the electorate is channeled directly into his brain. Forget issues. Forget policy. He's more than the perfect candidate—he's a special effect.

—Cover blurb for the novel *Interface*

The cyborged presidential candidate in Stephen Bury's *Interface* represents the logical outcome of the current political system in the United States, the United Kingdom, and other postindustrial democracies: the candidate as conduit. During the election he conducts the latest poll information and feeds it back to the populace in order to obtain enough votes to win. After the election he is a conduit for his backers and delivers to them the political decisions they have so carefully paid for. Today the process is mediated with many human experts, from spin doctors to lobbyists, but in *Interface* it is automated. As voter participation drops and cynicism rises, as soft money and corporate cash continue to buy laws, as politicians slavishly twist their public stances to fit polling data, it is hard to believe in citizenship at all. But some people still do, and some actually look to cyberspace as the place to make a stand.

There are dozens of projects seeking to use the Internet to improve political participation, including, in the United States, the Civic Practices Network, Minnesota E-Democracy, Open Meeting, the Political Participation

Project, the Public Communication Technology Project, WebActive, and Vote Smart Web. The e-zine *Democracies Online* documents other groups around the globe, such as United Kingdom Citizens Online and Malaysia.Net. All these projects seek to "cyberize" traditional (and in many peoples' view, failing) representative democracy formats. They organize petitions, meetings, and voting. But as Richard Sclove of the Loka Institute (established to raise a public voice around technoscientific issues) points out in *Democracy and Technology*, people deeply involved in the Net are likely to lose connection with their own communities and so their ability to influence the forces that dominate their lives will erode even more.

Representative democracy is melting under the acid rain of special-interest money and a shallow and manipulated mass media that, since it is fundamentally an entertainment product, must amuse before it informs. Noam Chomsky and Edward S. Herman have analyzed this disturbing development and they call it "the manufacturing of consent." The French Situationists termed it the Society of the Spectacle. The writer Benjamin Barber calls it McWorld, and argues that its cynicism and consumerism has provoked a counterresponse from fundamentalism, which is why much of global politics is McWorld versus jihad, in his view. Together consumerism and fundamentalism have colonized the attention and allegiance of many people. Hope, autonomy, and tolerance are all under siege. So how is consent manufactured? We are seduced by products that offer empowerment through the elimination of body odor or that will makes us high through what we buy.

In a society that officially says "Just Say No to Drugs," how can every soda pop and snack food promise psychedelic and ecstatic experiences? You are what you buy is a lie. No matter how many cars and deodorants you purchase, beautiful blondes will not drape themselves on you because of a brand name. But it is not a total lie. The car is part of the extended "you," and the deodorant even more so. They could marginally influence someone, maybe even a blonde, to want to meet you. And in the near future, when it becomes possible to purchase bodily augmentations, you might really become what you buy.

The ultimate consumption is to cyborg yourself, as the French performance artist, Orlan, demonstrated when she underwent a series of cosmetic surgeries in order to resemble the ideal of beauty represented by the Mona Lisa and other famous art works. Interesting, but great art would be cosmetic surgeries to make oneself ugly, which is not likely. Even cyborgs want to be beautiful. And they may be more likely to believe that technology can make them not only beautiful but empowered as well.

TECHNOFIXES: FROM TELEVISED COMMUNITY
TO ELECTRONIC VOTING

There is a growing school of thought that certain technologies will inexorably produce positive political changes. Electricity, radio, and television were all supposed to lead to better communities and stronger democracy. Lately the computer in general and the Internet in particular have inspired even wilder claims. This theory is called "cyberdemocracy" and there actually might be something to it. After all, the Internet differs from television because it fosters communication between people, and that is what politics is about.

The Open Society project of the Soros Foundation, the philanthropic arm of the Hungarian-American billionaire George Soros, has put a great deal of money into Eastern Europe for everything from opening a cybercafé in Slovenia to installing the Internet connections of every university in the old Soviet Empire, in order to foster democracy. This approach is informed by theories about civil society, technological change, and communication infrastructures that are based in part on our historical experience.

Many historians argue that the printing press had a tremendous impact on grassroots politics. It started with the mass production of Bibles in the languages of Europe, a major demand of many Protestant reformers. Once average people had access to the "word of God," they often felt they did not need the Catholic Church to act as an intermediary. More people became literate in order to read the Bible, and then they began to read other things, such as broadsides, newspapers, and books. Often, these texts were arguing that just as everyone had their own direct and equal relationship with God, everyone should have a similar unmediated relationship to their government. By the 1700s, radical democratic tracts such as Thomas Paine's *Common Sense* were best-sellers. In the English colonies of North America, only the Bible was more widely read. In a very real sense, participatory democracy as we know it would be unthinkable without the printing press.

There are growing indications that computer technology might have the same cascade effects on politics. Research for the Political Participation Project, founded by Mark Bonchek at Harvard University, has confirmed that computer networks can greatly help grassroots organizing by reducing "communication, coordination and information costs, facilitating group formation, group efficiency, member recruitment, and member retention."

But changes will not occur simply by automating present processes. In 1998 Costa Rica experimented with electronic voting. But as Steven Miller

41

argues in an article in the Computer Professionals for Social Responsibility's newsletter, "Electronic voting is *not* electronic democracy." CPSR, one of the most important groups in this debate, stresses that democracy depends more on an informed and active citizenship than on any particular technology. Technology will help only if it shapes "an informed and engaged electorate."

Some who laud cyberdemocracy's potential seem to have hidden agendas or to expect too much from one technology. Is self-interest behind Republican advocacy for electronic voting by everyone on everything, even trials? Special interests and mass media would dominate this kind of mobocracy. Many U.S. citizens do not even approve of the Bill of Rights when they are asked about its provisions in blind studies. To hand power directly over to the simple majority would lead to horrible abuses and probably another civil war.

Less dangerous but still wrongheaded are those who think that cyberspace maps neatly over into material reality. Take the group called the Electronic Disobedience Theater (EDT), which organizes support for the Zapatistas in Chiapas. They do a tremendous amount of great work involving technical support for indigenous people, art actions, and embodied protests. They are also exploring the potential of so-called "cyber sit-ins," where people around the world try to jam targeted Web sites and e-mail addresses with continual visits and mailings, sometimes using automated means. These are technically called "denial of services" attacks, although EDT has not actually tried completely to crash any targeted sites.

While I agree with EDT's goals, I believe that with this tactic we risk more than we might gain. The Web is a great resource for the politically marginalized; for big business and big government it is still a toy. The large organizations have the resources not only to win any hacker challenge (hacker talent can be bought pretty cheaply, actually), but also to counterattack the protesters much more effectively and deny them use of the Net. This has already happened in the EDT campaigns. Some of the Web sites that were used to stage electronic protests against Mexican institutions in the spring of 1998 came under cyberattack themselves, and they do not have the money and equipment to resist as well as banks and embassies do. The virtual sit-ins of June 10, 1998 were met with a program that responded to the automatic "sit-in" script, Floodnet, that blocked any disruption.

On September 9, 1998, EDT planned to try to jam the Web sites of Mexican President Zedillo, the Frankfurt Stock Exchange, and the Pentagon. What happened instead was that the U.S. Department of Defense complained to New York University, which was being used to host some of EDT's programs, about its Web site being used to support the attacks. Ricardo Dominquez, an EDT principle attending the Ars Electronica conference on infowar in Austria, received death threats ("We know who you are. We know where you are. We know where your family lives.... This is not a game."). And when Floodnet protests were launched, all the messages were bounced back, often crashing the protesters' computers and, in at least one case, overloading and destroying someone's badly configured hard drive, thanks to some clever programming someone has done for the U.S. Department of Defense.

But my main disagreement with this part of EDT's efforts is philosophical. Their goals with these type of protests seem to be to deny freedom of speech to the people they oppose. There is nothing on these Web sites that is integral to the repression in Chiapas, so the protest is only symbolic. This is fine, except the symbolism is wrong, and it is a bad precedent besides. It will certainly boomerang eventually, when anti-imperialist and other alternative Web sites are besieged in their turn. In fact, in the great hacking attacks on e-businesses of February 2000 the dangers of these kind of disruptions were clearly revealed.

Someone launched denial of services attacks against the Web sites of Yahoo, eBay, ZDNet, Amazon.com, and several other prominent Net businesses or sites by hacking into and hijacking dozens of machines and using them to send literally billions of "hits" to the targets. There is no evidence that these attacks were political; they were really vandalism. While some young men go down to the local school and break windows, this group apparently desired a larger stage. Because how-to guides on breaking into poorly secured networks are easily available and programs like Floodnet are offered up free as well, it did not take a great deal of sophistication to carry off this hack. But the results were impressive.

Several of the targets suffered a serious degradation of services and, even more disturbing, the Net as a whole was seriously slowed by the attacks. By the third day, the average time to access a Web page was 26 percent slower than it should have been. In many respects the Net is just a part of the real world. Protests happen there, capitalism happens there, vandalism happens there. But it is also a particularly fragile part of the world. It completely depends on technology and it also relies on the mutual agreement of its participants not to destroy it. You can totally disrupt the fabric of the Net without risking your actual body at all. To do the same in the real world is impossible.

This is why this type of electronic civil disobedience is not good politics so much as it is mischief, low-grade sabotage, and an effective generator of publicity. I am all for good publicity, but one has to be aware of the costs. Civil disobedience involves putting oneself on the line, not one's Web site.

The kind of protest that has the potential to make fundamental political change is embodied. It is a rich and frightening sensual experience. It is a sacrifice and a commitment that even your opponents must recognize, respect, and listen to. Gandhi called it *satygraha*, "truth force." You testify to the truth with your body. Our rights must be paid for with real sacrifices; this is the obligation of citizenship.

This is not just a philosophical discussion, either; it is an argument about how nonviolent social change is made. To work on all levels, a demonstration needs some theater to entice the media and some logic to the protest for it to make sense to the public; face-to-face communication with people you are trying to convince makes it better and, most of all, you need to put bodies on the line, or no one will listen. Hakim Bey, the postmodern political theorist, has stressed this in his brilliant essay "The Information War." He proclaims: "The body is still the basis of wealth." The greatest wealth is freedom, and you can earn it only with your body.

But this does not mean there is not a tremendous amount that can be done using technology. Groups such as The Critical Art Ensemble and Bread and Puppets Theater use a hybrid of new and old technology to inspire people to action and thought. Even more important, perhaps, is what computers can do to improve communication among the disempowered. During the Velvet Revolution in Czechoslovakia, computers were used extensively both to network within the country and to get information to the outside. They are still important there today for those without much power.

The large, vibrant, Czech environmental group, Duha ("rainbow") is, as of this writing, involved in a long-term civil disobedience campaign against the ongoing construction of a nuclear facility at Temelin, near the Austrian border. A project of the communist regime, the facility is still being pushed forward by the privitized power company supported by the conservative "free market" parties, often in power. The power company has hired the top surveillance experts of the old Czechoslovakian secret police. So Duha does its sensitive internal communications using e-mail encrypted with the Pretty Good Privacy (PGP) program. This widely available software allows average people to send messages that can be decrypted only with a great deal of effort and computer power.

The U.S. government tried to keep PGP, invented by an American who gave it to the world, from being exported, claiming it was a "weapon." This was all part of the Clinton administration attempts to make sure that the U.S. security apparatus can always intercept and decrypt any communication it wants. After the failure of the "clipper chip" plan to put a component in every U.S. computer that would allow government access, and as T-shirts with the PGP code became best-sellers, the U.S. government backed off a bit. But electronic transparency *for the government* is still the government's goal.

The power company was eventually exposed for illegally wiretapping the environmentalists (and the Czech president), yet Duha continues to use PGP internally and to communicate with other East European antinuclear groups. Not only does the program assure privacy, but the computer communications are clearly more robust than phone or mail links. Still, Duha has learned that computer communication alone is not enough. Meeting in person every few months is worth the effort. When Duha communicates only through cyberspace there is a continual degradation of the quality of understanding. Small miscommunications become massive on-line arguments (flame wars) that a few minutes of face-to-face meeting can dispel, thanks to all the nonverbal cues humans have evolved over the last million years. Real communities are better than virtual communities, but the Internet and other prosthetic communications can make real communities better.

The Internet played a remarkable role in the 1996–1997 public protests in Serbia to force the government to install legally elected local officials. The right-wing Yugoslavian rump government, run by old communist bosses, had crushed the widespread Serbian resistance to the civil war against Croatia and Bosnia, in large part due to total control of television and radio. When they rejected the elections of 1996, they were confident that their stranglehold on mass media would again suffice. But they were wrong. Using the Internet nodes at a university and a radio station, the opposition managed both to coordinate massive protests within the country and to mobilize international support. The only way to shut down the opposition's communications would have been to arrest every computer (and there are tens of thousands even in Serbia-Macedonia) or shut down the phone system. By the time the government was even aware of this tactic, however, they had lost.

David Bennahum, a *Wired* magazine reporter, went to Serbia straight from a conference touting cyberdemocracy and he was dubious of the whole concept, but the Serbian experience changed his mind:

Now, with a real case study at hand, it appears clear that access to the Internet is incompatible with authoritarianism, that regimes around the world that want the benefits of the information age while maintaining a lock on information control are facing a paradox.

Just as faxes and videotape figured largely in the protests in China at the end of the 1980s, computers offer yet another way to circumvent central government control. China is actually struggling with Bennahum's paradox now. Industrialization depends on computerization, and yet China's leaders do not want the Web to be used politically. It may be impossible to stop. As the Web grows stronger, its political effects may grow greater still.

David Brin, in an interview with *Wired*, insisted that the WorldNet of the future would foster democracy, but he warned it would be painful:

> In all history, humans found just one remedy against error—criticism. But criticism is painful. We hate receiving it, though we don't mind dishing it out. It's human nature. We've learned a hard lesson—no leader is ever wise enough to make decisions without scrutiny, commentary, and feedback. It so happens those are the very commodities the WorldNet will provide, in torrents. Try to picture multitudes of citizens, each with access to worldwide databases and the ability to make sophisticated models, each bent on disproving fallacies or exposing perceived mistakes. It's a formula for chaos or for innovative, exciting democracy—if people are mature enough.

We can hope people will opt for "innovative, exciting democracy," but even tired old democracy fixed up with technology has strong allure—perhaps too strong. The temptation is to count on technology to fix much more basic problems. There are fundamental weaknesses in most simple technofixes. Arthur and Marilouise Kroker, for example, attack Newt Gingrich's belief in automatic deterministic polling:

> He wants to break down any notion of democracy based on collective discussion. His is in fact a push-button democracy: 53 percent of people want Congress to do this? Adopted. Power to the pollsters! That's the *antithesis* of digital democracy.

The Krokers also point out that "digital solidarity" for the Zapatistas can have only limited effectiveness:

> How can people outside Mexico really intervene decisively against the Mexican government's fascist policies of exterminism? This is a peculiar-

ity of life in the '90s. At the same time digital media encourage a global consciousness, parts of the world recede into darkness.

But it is still one world, after all and the right uses of technology can help us understand that. There is a group called Witness that started by providing human-rights activists around the world with video technology so they could record abuses in their countries. In February of 2000 Witness began putting reports from these activists onto the Internet. When every potential victim of government repression or of ethnic cleansing can broadcast live directly to the Net, then cyborg technologies will have fundamentally changed our political reality. Until then, we need to carefully think about how the Net, and the political philosophies it fosters, organizes our thinking and our choices.

BIOREGIONS, INFOSPHERES, NETS, WEBS, TAZ, AND COMMUNITY

We've spoken of the *Net*, which can be defined as the totality of all information and communication transfer. Some of these transfers are privileged and limited to various elites, which gives the Net a hierarchical aspect. Other transactions are open to all—so the Net has a horizontal or non-hierarchic aspect as well. Military and Intelligence data are restricted, as are banking and currency information and the like. But for the most part the telephone, the postal system, public data banks, etc. are accessible to everyone and anyone. Thus *within the Net* there has begun to emerge a shadowy sort of *counter-Net*, which we will call the *Web* (as if the Net were a fishing-net and the web were spider webs woven through the interstices and broken sections of the Net).

—Hakim Bey, 1996

In 1985 Hakim Bey analyzed what he called the Temporary Autonomous Zone (TAZ), an area of real but temporary freedom within the bosom of the Spectacle/Informational State. Since then, both the Net and the Web have exploded through years of geometric growth. The distinction is valuable—one that, if used regularly, would add to the clarity of political discussions about cyberspace—for there is a "web" lurking in the "net." Bey's intuition that the Web would continue to thrive and that interlinked computers would be the perfect technology for fostering the TAZ has already been confirmed. Radicals like to point out that the Net itself is the biggest working anarchic system the world has seen, all the more ironic in that its origins were so profoundly militarized and its present is so capitalistic.

Although some historians insist on ignoring or rewriting the history of the Internet, there is no doubt the U.S. military created it to do two things: first, test the concept of decentralized networks organized around the distribution of "packets" of information so that such a system could control the military in the case of a nuclear war; and second, link military researchers at labs and top universities for better intercommunication. The Net grew out of control, was turned over to the National Science Foundation (while a pure military net—Milnet—was set up for the Department of Defense), stayed out of control, and was then handed over to a strange conglomeration of volunteer groups and fast-buck artists.

Some people are so in love with the Net that it colors the way they think. *Wired* magazine is a good example. It has promoted the idea of the "netizen" as a successor to the citizen. It is an incredibly empty concept, focusing more on the Net hookups and pagers of young entrepreneurs than anything else, and does much to confuse the real political issues.

One of these real issues is invoked by another favorite *Wired* word, "digerati:" the digital illuminati, or the elite of the digital economy with all the pretentiousness of the literati and none of their depth . . . but some cool machines. The digerati are an info-aristocracy lording over the techno-peasants and technotards who cannot figure out how to boot up—the "tired" versus the "wired."

There are certainly haves and have-nots in terms of cyberspace but they tend to be the same people in "meatspace." The Net and the Web are just part of a larger worldwide system that is the ultimate political unit: the infosphere, Gaia, Metaman, the world. The favored term of ecologists, the bioregion, is part of the same set of concepts. It is based on the cybernetic thinking that is the heart of the science of ecology. Bioregionalism stresses decentralization and advocates that decisions be made within the ecosystems that those decisions impact, but since the Earth itself is a bioregion, some decisions are global. That democracy works easiest on a small scale is one of many good reasons for bioregionalist thinking to supplant the bizarre nation-state arrangement history has gifted us with. But two things cannot be forgotten: 1. that bioregions are everything from microecologies to vast watersheds to the planet as a whole; and 2. that bioregions are made up of "nature" and "civilization"—they are cyborg systems.

There is a strange new pseudo-biosystem emerging that is particularly cyborged: cyberspace. The political struggle for its future is crucial. Is it going to end up as just another drug for the alienated, as "television land" has become, another profit center for the megacorporations that wax so strong? Or will it be a place for people to communicate and even build community—a virtual region that can encourage autonomy and democracy?

Computer Professionals for Social Responsibility (CPSR) has crafted a very important initiative, a set of principles around the theme "One planet, one Net." They are:

1. There is only one Net.
2. The Net must be open and available to all.
3. People have the right to communicate.
4. People have the right to privacy.
5. People are the Net's stewards, not its owners.
6. No individuals, organizations, or governments should dominate the Net.
7. The Net should reflect human diversity, not homogenize it.

CPSR has one of the strongest voices on the future of the Net, all the more powerful as it represents a consensus among a number of political tendencies including liberals, socialists, anarchists, libertarians, and even some tolerant Republicans. While there is surprising unity now among computer professionals and cyberactivists about many key issues dealing with the autonomy of the Net, it cannot last. Eventually there will be a parting of the ways based on the differences between the various political perspectives. One of these is particularly new, incredibly prevalent on the Net (especially among the digerati), and, for many people, is especially confusing: Libertarianism.

So this is a good a place to analyze Libertarianism, which must be dealt with in any serious discussion of politics in cyberspace and, indeed, cyborg citizenship. Libertarians are all over the Net in organized groups such as the Extropians (discussed below) and as individuals writing for *Wired*, haunting the chat rooms and posting to newsgroups. By Libertarianism (with a capitalized L) I mean the mainly U.S. political perspective (including but not limited to the Libertarian Party) that is fanatically pro–free market but also incorporates many aspects of classical liberalism, including a very harsh view of the nation-state. This is not the libertarianism of Spain and Italy, where it is just another label for anarchists. Procapitalist U.S. Libertarianism is actually spreading around the world, slowly in most places but quickly through the Net, where it is a major perspective, and among young business folks everywhere. As an anarchist I am very sympathetic to certain aspects of Libertarianism but at its heart it is very unimpressive. There seems to be an incredible faith in the magic powers of Adam Smith's invisible hand, updated lately by claims that complexity theory mandates capitalism, a major theme of *Wired*, although some Libertarians have rejected complexity theory because in their reading it runs counter to Adam Smith's "leveling hand." Yes, economies are systems. Yes, they follow certain rules. Yes, they are "out of control" in the sense that they have their own built-in dynamics. But this does not mean that the blind pursuit of profit and advantage by everyone will lead to the best possible world. In fact, it is an insane idea. It just *seems* possible in the never-never land of cyberspace, where nothing is real and Libertarian fantasies of perfect information, flawless meritocracies, and invisible hands washing each other seem on the verge of fulfillment.

There is no natural law that says that unbridled self-interest (greed) will lead to the perfect economic system. A look at economics in action shows otherwise to all but the true believer. Complex system dynamics do not lead to the "perfect" system automatically. Often systems collapse. Often the stability is achieved in a form that is less than perfect. So where do the Libertarians get their faith? How does Libertarianism come down in favor of capitalism but against the capitalist state? How can it believe in both absolute individual freedom and the freedom to exploit both nature and people? I will endeavor to explain.

There are two central premises of Libertarianism. In Murray Rothbard's book *For a New Liberty*, it is put quite directly:

> The central core of the Libertarian creed . . . is to establish the absolute right to private property of every man: first in his own body and second, in the previously unused natural resources which he first transforms by his labor.

Libertarians then try to prove that property rights follow from the individual's right to control his or her own person. We shall look at those mental gymnastics in a moment. But the first thing to note is that the "civil" libertarianism of Libertarianism comes from the principle of individual liberty. The defense of capitalism, of inheritance, of the domination of nature by "Man," and of the right to exploit the labor of other people springs from the second principle—the absolute right to property.

At the core of Libertarian property rights is what I call the "magical labor theory of appropriation." Libertarians believe not only that you do deserve the fruits of your direct labor in the everyday sense, but that anything and everything "previously untouched," once affected by your labor, or affected by something once affected by your labor becomes in perpetuity the property of you and your heirs.

Rothbard approvingly quotes John Locke when he claims:

> Thus, the grass my horse has bit, the turfs my servant has cut, and the ore I have digged in my place where I have a right to them in common with others, become my property without the assignation or consent of any body.

Exactly how the turfs ol' John Locke's servant digs become his is never explained, although one can imagine it is because the servant, like the horse, belongs to Mr. Locke. In a similar way, the value that workers bring to an enterprise belongs not to the workers but to the capitalist, since he or she "owns" them and their work at the price of a wage.

Several simple ideas lie at the core of this pleasant hubris. The first is that property rights are monolithic and perpetual. Rothbard sees them in absolutist terms—all or nothing. There is no division of property rights—only limits where your rights (like the right to burn down your forest) run into someone else's right (for their air to be smoke-free).

Who gets ownership of this indivisible bundle of rights? Rothbard argues coyly that either: 1. "the creator" gets it, or 2. "another man or set of men…appropriate it by force," or 3. "every individual in the world has an equal quotal share." This leaves out a host of other possibilities: property rights held by smaller units than the whole world—villages, or cities, or worker collectives; certain property rights held by one group and others by a separate group; use as a part of ownership criteria; or need as a part of ownership criteria.

Such complexity may be disconcerting but it is also more realistic. A lack of natural realism is at the core of the Libertarian position toward property rights—the idea that every last thing in the natural world could and should be completely owned by individuals.

This old idea of "Man's" natural right to conquer and own nature can be found throughout history, from the Bible through Karl Marx all the way to Exxon. It is one of the major reasons that *Homo sapiens* has brought the whole planet to the edge of destruction. If we do not cease to see nature as an object to exploit and realize it is an organic/cybernetic whole that we are part of, we will soon go over that edge.

The Libertarians' attitude toward society is incredibly reductionistic. They argue that there is no such thing as society, there is merely a collection of "interacting individuals." The Libertarian Frank Chodorov says: "Society is a collective concept and nothing else. . . . When the individuals disappear so does the whole. The whole has no separate existence." Of course one cannot have society without people. That does not mean society is only atomistic individuals multiplied. Thinking in terms of systems theory, the same theory that justifies the Libertarian faith in the invisible hand, it is obvious that the whole is often greater than the parts. That is the whole point. The real world has many examples, not just society. Any individual Libertarian's body could be deconstructed into a bucket of water, a pile of protein, a jar of cholesterol. Would they be equal to the living body?

The Libertarians' faith in capitalism and naïveté about business directly undermine their principled stand against an intrusive national state. Libertarians should confront the fact that profits and the "free market" have led to the present government-business alliance. If there was not a state, capitalists would invent one. The best way to maximize profits is to regulate your market, eliminate or join with your your competitors, repress similar or superior products, and ignore so-called externalities such as the pollution you produce or the occupational diseases of "your" workers. The "free" in "free market" is free to get away with all these things at the expense of everyone else.

To paper over the many fundamental contradictions some Libertarians have proposed desperate solutions. Rothbard has argued that a massive privitized legal system could handle all disputes from murders to the environmental destruction of the oceans. Now there is a nightmare—replace the government with pure lawyers.

At its core Libertarianism appeals only to those who think they might have the talent or luck to get rich. Every Libertarian sees him or herself as a swashbuckling entrepreneur inventing wonderful products and selling them to an admiring public for vast profits. Is this the natural human condition? It has not been my experience. Most people work, hour after hour, year after year, at deadening, killing, meaningless labor in order to buy food, shelter, and drugs (from sugar to heroin). Libertarians choose not to be exploited but they do not understand that for this to happen, they must choose not to exploit as well. In the Libertarian world of owners, there will always be the owned. It is time to go beyond all that. It is time to say with Camus: neither master nor slave.

We also must say we will not be a slave to technoscience and, indeed, we must be its master. That is easier said than done. One of the key sets of political fault lines in our cyborg society is not recognizable because it is hidden by old political categories. These fault lines divide those who completely hate technoscience from those who uncritically love it, and all the rest of us who fall somewhere in between. The haters include anarcho-primitivists and Neoists, whose writings can be found in the Detroit quarterly *The Fifth Estate*. This wonderfully written survivor of the 1960s advances an incredible analysis of technology, including almost convincing attacks on such basic "inventions" as writing, language, and numbers, not to mention industrialism and more recent outrages like computers. *The Fifth Estate* also publishes analysis by neo-Luddites and others who hold that many but not all new technoscientific achievements are a bad idea. Kirkpatrick Sale, a leading neo-Luddite, estimates that about 25 percent of the U.S. population are "techno-resisters" on this side of the spectrum.

The Extropians (from extropy, the opposite of entropy) fall on the other extreme with their belief in "Boundless Expansion, Self-Transformation, Dynamic Optimism, Intelligent Technology, and Spontaneous Order." This techno-utopianism translates into a fanatical belief in immortality (through cryonics), uploading consciousness into machines and other cyborgizations, space exploration, and the perfection of the free market and the Libertarian philosophy.

Slightly less extreme are most of the writers for *Wired* and the many technophiles in business and computing who rhapsodize about a digital nation. They fetishize technology and see it as the solution to all the problems earlier technology has caused, but they do not expect to live forever, do not want to be turned into popsicles trying, and do not expect technology to lead to a perfect world, though they admit it may cause decades of prosperity in the near future. Jon Katz, the main promoter of the "digital citizen" idea, estimates that the superconnected and connected account for about 10 percent of the population. Another 62 percent are semiconnected, and for him, this population constitutes the potential digital nation.

However, even Katz would admit that most of the techno-resisters are probably from this group (such as CPSR's membership) and not from the 29 percent who are not connected at all. It is not just a matter of who has a beeper and an Internet account, it is how they feel about these technologies. In between the digital nation and the techno-resistors is the rest of society— maybe half of it.

Several academics and writers have attempted to organize this middle population by founding a school of thought called "technorealism." Their positions on cyberspace issues include:

- Information wants to be protected.
- Wiring the schools will not save them.
- More private use of public property.

Their main point is that government must play a major role in cyberspace. In this they are breaking with most of the active political voices in cyberspace debates who, coming from anarchist or Libertarian assumptions, have tried to keep government's role at a minimum.

Actually there is little danger (or hope) that government will stay out of cyberspace and other cyborg issues since the government has played a major role in creating cyberspace and cyborgization. The government's most significant contribution to cyborgization has been in the arena it monopolizes: war—which is, appropriately enough, the subject of the next chapter.

cyborg warriors

In these "post-modern" times we often behave as if we were cybernetic organisms—confusing the mechanical and the organic, the inner and the outer realms, simulation and reality, even omnipotence and impotence...such cyborg worlds are structured by military paradigms of power, in particular through the military constitution of information technology.
— Les Levidow and Kevin Robins

POSTMODERN WAR AND PEACE

Our conception of citizenship is intimately tied to war. Victor Hanson has shown in *The Western Way of War* that in Classical Greece and republican Rome the citizen *was* the soldier. Women, slaves, foreigners, and the very poor could not be citizens because they did not serve in battle. The Norse had a similar tradition, and it is from these two currents that the contemporary institution of citizenship grew. Origins are not determining but they are crucial. Citizenship and war are still intimately linked, although not in the same way as in ancient times. War is changing now, maybe dying, and it seems to me that citizenship should be divorced from war as we know it, but not from the obligation to sacrifice. To make citizenship work in the long run we need at least the moral equivalent of war, as William James called it. For now, we must understand postmodern war as it shapes the future of citizenship. Understanding postmodern war begins with defining modern war.

Modern war can be differentiated from ancient war by its commitment to technological and scientific innovation, its acceptance of the complete mobilization of a society for war, its belief in the fundamental usefulness of war as a political instrument, and the combination of these factors in a drive for total war. With the advent of superweapons, the most obvious being atomic bombs, total war became an impossible end for modern states to pursue, yet the other central ideas of modern war live on. Out of this develops postmodern war, full of paradoxes, struggling to survive.

There are two characteristics of postmodern war that are directly relevant here. First, postmodern war depends on a new level of integration between soldiers and their weapons, what are called human-machine weapons systems or, in other words, cyborg soldiers. By maximizing computerization and perfecting the warrior-weapon interface, military analysts expect to make war useful again. Second, the rise of modern war corresponds with the rise of the modern state and modern science, as well as the spread of Western colonial systems throughout the world. The end of modern war, which is marked by the atomic bombing of Hiroshima and Nagasaki, also corresponds with the beginning of the end of European colonialism and the initiation of profound changes in contemporary science and of the modern nation-state, and the institution of citizenship.

These changes mirror those usually ascribed to postmodernity. There is a proliferation of different, even contradictory, factors (bricollage); a collapse of a universal belief in single explanatory systems and ideas (the end of grand narratives); and a recognition of the centrality of information and its sub-categories (simulation, computerization). In politics we see new forms of organization and complex loyalties, all in the context of a world knitted together by new communication and travel technologies. Science, which in one respect is fracturing into thousands of fields, is also uniting around informatics. Cybernetic principles have become central to most disciplines theoretically, even as computers have become indispensable in practice. This means that primary engine of modernity, technoscience, is more important than ever and that we must confront its most important product: a relationship between humans and our technologies that can best be termed cyborgian.

Lewis Mumford argued that the very first machine was an army, consisting of the soldiers and their weapons as the moving parts. This early protomachine looks suspiciously like a cyborg, as does the twentieth century "megamachine" that Mumford railed against. The special status of weapons, the disciplining of individual soldiers into cleanly working parts, and the military's fostering of industrialization and automation have all contributed to the drive to integrate humans and machines into effective complex systems. World War II culminated this process with the genesis of computers and the elaboration of incredibly complicated human-machine systems: ships, fleets, planes, wings, weapon teams, armies. The cyborg was born.

The military has looked to technology for a solution to the identity crisis of postmodern war. Smart weapons and bloodless infowar are only dreams, but the cyborg soldier is the new reality. But cyborg soldiers die like normal humans, so the basic problem at the heart of contemporary war remains. Besides, even cyborg weapons systems can go horribly wrong, as the destruction of Iranian Flight 655 by the USS *Vincennes* demonstrated. A regularly scheduled civilian airliner climbing into its normal flight path was shot down by the United States's best cruiser. This tragedy occurred because the navy relied upon a state-of-the-art computer system, the Aegis, to "manage" a U.S. incursion into Iranian territorial waters. But where the humans and the computer system interfaced, there was failure. Fear (always present in battle), faith (in the Aegis system), and scenario fulfillment led to fundamental errors of judgment and analysis and directly to the death of hundreds of innocent civilians. There are no technological solutions to the problem of war, not even cyborgization.

HUMAN-MACHINE WEAPON SYSTEMS

Recall that it is not only that men make wars, but that wars make men.
—Barbara Ehrenreich

In *Male Fantasies*, Klaus Theweleit examines the psychology of World War I German veterans who fought in the right-wing paramilitary Freikorp. He charts the emergence among combat veterans of a new type of man, one with a deeply erotic and ambivalent relationship toward mechanization. This new man, Theweleit postulates, was a creature "whose physique had been machinized, his psyche eliminated—or in part displaced into his body armor." This self-mechanization performs a crucial and pleasurable function for the soldiers—it allows them the release of killing others and risking their own death. In Theweleit's words:

The crucial impulse behind the regeneration of the machine seems to be its desire for release—and release is achieved when the totality-machine and its components explode in battle.

A bloody catharsis indeed, a built-in obsolescence for the living machine, soldier or army. It is an analogy that has only grown more literal through the years. In World War II, the man-machine system was institutionalized through operations research and scientific management practices, and then irrevocably changed by the computer. In the postmodern military, cybernetics is the dominant metaphor, computers the most important force multiplier, and the cyborg man-machine weapons system the ideal. The military expends vast resources to transform soldiers into cyborgs. Already human-machine interfaces have improved incredibly, and now information is displayed on windshields, visors, or even directly into the eyes of weapon operators. The field of virtual reality came out of this research. There are also projects studying psychopharmological modifications that reprogram soldiers so they can fight without fear in the hyperlethal battle space of postmodern war. Other research seeks to develop direct mind-computer communications for infantrymen wearing exoskeletons, as well as for tank drivers, submarine steersmen, and aircraft pilots.

These technological interventions, along with the shift of focus from war-fighting to peacemaking and from warriors to managers and technologists, have profoundly changed the social construction of soldiers themselves, especially in terms of gender. As soldiers become more like cyborgs, their gender identity shifts. Cyborgs in general can be masculine or feminine, although they have the potential to be more cyborg than either or neutered or even something new. Military cyborgs, on the other hand, are still pretty masculine in our cultural coding. But since most postmodern soldiers are also technicians, the new "masculine" identity of soldiers is constructed more around mechanization—fixing machines and working with machines—than the traditional masculine identity of the user of physical force, easy access to violence, and the direct subjugation of other men and all women. Women had a nearly impossible time fitting into the old masculine category, but the "new male" version seems somewhat easier to adapt to. It is as if the female soldier's identity is collapsed into the basic soldier persona, a creature that is vaguely male in dress and posture, vaguely female in status, and vaguely masculine-mechanical in role and image.

Killing directly, as opposed to killing through computers or just getting killed, is still a domain rhetorically preserved for male bodies, as can be seen by the restriction of women in most militaries to "noncombat" roles. But it is a shrinking preserve, threatened by the possibility that open homosexuality can be allowed in place of the overwhelmingly homoerotic subculture of secret gays, masculine friendships, and the displacement of homoerotic desire into a virulent mix of misogyny and homophobia. The old link between citizenship and soldiering explains why feminist groups such as the National Organization of Women have pushed for gender equality in the military. The realities of postmodern war and cyborg soldiering explain why they have largely succeeded.

The U.S. military is perhaps the most cyborged in the world, and so it reflects the many political crises of postmodern war, including the struggles over women and gays in the military, the resistance of the military and political leaders to suffering any casualties, and the resulting emphasis on high-tech semiautonomous weapons, as well as the division of military personnel into countless technical specialities, few of them with any direct role in killing. In the near future, conflicts will evince both this confusion over soldierly identity and the horrible destructive potential of postmodern human-machine weapon systems.

This confusion over identity, the growing reliance on a technologically sophisticated professional military, and the instability of postmodern war itself can only increase the alienation between the civilian world and the military sphere. In the twentieth century many countries had their elected governments swept away by military establishments with their own goals and worldviews. As these trends continue, there is no reason to think that North American and European democracies are automatically immune to military coups. In Robert Heinlein's novel of future cyborg soldiers, *Starship Troopers*, only military veterans are allowed to be voting citizens. Considering the horrific potential of future conflicts, this is an idea that some soldiers and their leaders are sure to find prudent and just.

FUTURE CONFLICTS: NUCLEAR, CHEMICAL, BIOLOGICAL, INFORMATIONAL, NANO

War in the future will be shaped by the forces sketched above. War will become less human where weapons of mass destruction are involved and less like war (and more like politics) in the ever-expanding realm of peacekeeping operations and so-called information war. These two trends—toward apocalyptic war and away from it—are directly relevant for future citizens. The danger of wars of mass destruction indirectly corrodes democracy, as the Cold War did, and it directly threatens our survival. Information war and similar theories of low-intensity Cool War, even non-violent conflict, also directly militarize politics by imposing a continual state of confrontation. Even the militarization of peacemaking and peacekeeping degrades the idea of peace into merely the absence of war. The only long-term solution is to take war out of politics, but that will prove to be extremely difficult.

Three aspects of future conflict will be particularly important: weapons of mass destruction, the idea of information war, and the advent of nano-technology, which gives rise to totally new technological approaches to war that attempt completely to integrate humans and machines.

In 1989 Iraqi troops attacked the Kurdish village of Halabja with mustard gas and a nerve agent because it supported Kurdish autonomy. Five thousand men, women, and children died immediately. If you have ever seen the pictures of this massacre you will never forget the dead babies cradled in the arms of their parents. A 1998 medical analysis (the first since the attack), covered on the U.S. TV news show *60 Minutes,* revealed that the mutagenic and carcinogenic effects of these poisons continue to kill people to this day, and the fields nearby remain poisoned and barren.

Halabja is history and it is the future that concerns us; a future that may well hold worse horrors. The problem is twofold. First, at the heart of post-modern war are the existence and proliferation of mass destruction weapons that cannot really be used militarily. Nuclear, chemical, and biological weapons all offer vast killing potential, but historically the only really effective armaments in this class have been nuclear, and they are very hard to make. Even with nuclear material for sale to the highest bidder in the states of the old Soviet Empire, it is still not easy to put together a nuclear "gadget."

Because of this, only nation states have the resources to make an effective nuclear weapon. Until such a state uses one, or until a nonstate terrorist buys or steals one, the most likely use of a nuclear weapon would be a dirty bomb without much explosive potential. Its nasty effects could just as easily be accomplished by detonating a conventional (high-explosive or even fertilizer) bomb at a nuclear plant. However, unless international politics change fundamentally, eventually nuclear weapons will be used. The most likely scenario is a "limited" nuclear war in the Mideast, perhaps starting with a terrorist strike at Tel Aviv followed by an Israeli response of five-eyes-for-an-eye, taking out Tripoli, Teheran, Baghdad, Damascus, and maybe Cairo. Another possibility is a conflict between India and Pakistan; antagonistic fundamentalists (Hindu and Moslem) are powerful in both states. There are other danger zones as well, but horrible as nuclear war seems, for now at least it is not the most likely nightmare we face.

Halabja shows that chemical weapons can be terribly effective, but even despite scientific and technological improvements, chemical weapons remain limited by weather and chance. Still, on a good day, the danger of nuclear and chemical weapons seems manageable. The same cannot be said of biological weapons. The biological revolution in genetic engineering that has produced cloning and other wonders presents an even greater danger than other weapons of mass destruction.

People do not realize the progress that is being made in genetic engineering. Even those involved are often amazed at the pace of the field. Newspaper headlines capture such feats as inserting jellyfish genes into mice to make them glow in the dark, engineering mice with human ears on their backs, and developing animals with human genes so they produce natural medicines (which is the purpose of Dolly and the other cloned animals, all discussed in Chapter 8). But behind these freakish breakthroughs is the relentless improvement of genetic engineering technologies, including gene splicing-and-dicing-and-linking machines, and related increases in our understanding of genetic and other biological processes. The development of more effective and specific biological weapons gets easier every day. Soon (if not today), a competent graduate student with the right equipment (which is available at most good colleges) will be able to make the stuff of nightmares.

Terroristic postmodern states and postmodern terrorists pose the clearest threat, but the underlying problem is the way contemporary societies make political decisions. Before war truly became total, it may have made some sense to work out many disagreements in blood. Now, when mass death is available to more and more smaller and crazier groups, it will not work. The only way to end the threat of weapons of mass destruction is to realize the dream of true democracy and international cooperation. However, the military response has been to seek yet more advanced and dangerous technological and theoretical solutions to this crisis. The latest solution is the idea of information war.

In military discourse, infowar is an attempt to save war by reconfiguring it in part as a bloodless conflict in cyberspace and, in part, as all of culture. This is a doomed and dangerous effort. No real conflict can stay limited to hacking attacks on computers. So in reality this part of infowar will just become another aspect of real war. Attempts to crash radar systems or confuse communications will all be in the service of actual combat. War is about killing and maiming human bodies, and if that does not happen, it is not war. Information can serve these ends, as has been recognized since Sun Tzu, but it cannot replace the macabre role of embodiment. But the illusion of bloodless infowar could well lull decision-makers into committing a horrible error in judgment and starting a real war thinking they were only indulging in its simulation. An equally dangerous part of infowar doctrine is to argue that all manipulations of information are legitimate aspects of war. Propaganda and disinformation would then have no limits. This makes all of culture into the battleground, including the domestic media, and it turns every conflict into a war. This is the ultimate logic of postmodern war: the militarization of everything.

On a deep level, infowar manifests society's confusion about the incredible transformations information technologies are bringing about. This confusion is particularly evident in debates about such concepts as information, knowledge, and art and the tensions between such simple dichotomies as human versus machine, natural versus artificial, and real war versus infowar. Infowar doctrine hides the fact that there is actually a real chance for various (post) human survivals and even utopias, including the most important of all: real peace.

Infowar is a sexy term for a very unerotic set of concepts. While the idea benefits military budgets and mass-market magazines, it does not actually describe a new type of war so much as it disguises the crisis of contemporary war itself. The increasing power of weapon systems has led to the system of postmodern war that now frames international relations. In large part this has resulted in returns to older forms of war, limited and even terroristic, and conflicts through proxies, as the Cold War was fought. But it has also produced in the military an incredible technophilia. There is a raging desire for new weapons of science-fictional powers and for new types of war without the political costs of traditional conflicts.

Infowar doctrine presents a strong argument by linking itself to fundamental changes in human culture. There are all sorts of schema, including one that focuses on four epochs defined by power sources, but the vast majority of military theorists look to the work of the futurists Alvin and Heidi Toffler, who argue that human culture moved through primitive, agricultural, and industrial ages into a new informational age. To their credit, in their own book on war the Tofflers focus almost as much on the need for peace (antiwar, they call it) as they do on the new opportunities the information age offers conflict.

Many antiwar activists believe that the information revolution favors peace and democracy over war and authoritarianism. Perhaps. It has yet to be proven. Cyberdemocracy initiatives and the interlinking of the global community through various technologies (space exploration, telecommunications) and theories (from ecology mainly) are certainly positive, but many peace activists seem to think that peace is now inevitable. Hardly. The war movement is still much stronger than the peace movement and has embraced the information revolution just as ardently (if perhaps even more clumsily). Clearly, the future of war and peace is not yet written, as the new superfield of nanotechnology demonstrates.

Nanotechnology is engineering on the microscale. It is making machines, including machines to make smaller machines, that are too small to see in many cases. As a technoscience it has many civilian cyborg implications that are explored in Chapter 13, but this startling new field might also change the scale of war. Military nanotechnology is not entirely new—biological, chemical, and nuclear war have all arisen from nanotechnologies, as has the electronic battlefield—but it is on the cusp of some incredible breakthroughs.

The most interesting nanotech weapons are the cyborg insect warriors that are under development. The Japanese have already created "roboroach," the grandfather of such weapons. These weapons will not be aimed just at people. A spider that spins conductive webs would be great to "bug" computers. Most proposed nanoweapons aim at machines. Biological weapons are the ideal nanoweapon for killing humans, after all, and people have been working on them for some time.

In the far future, if war survives, one could imagine a complex nanowar fought entirely by beautifully sophisticated machines capable of everything our current human-machine weapon systems are. But this will not solve war's basic problem. The same paradoxes that bedevil weapons of mass destruction apply to nanowar, and it is also beset with the same ironies and illusions that information war specifically, and computer war in general, face.

Among the most salient are:

- The transformation of the soldier into a cyborg, a part of a weapon system.
- The insanity of total war. The most effective nanoweapons can no more be used (except by the insane, and eventually they will get such weapons) than can nuclear or biological weapons.
- The shift in casualties from soldiers to civilians.
- The expansion of the territory of the battle(space). Now it is not just world war, it is war at the bottom of the oceans, war in the upper atmosphere and in space; it is also war at the microlevel. As the high ground (space) and the deep sea (for boomer subs and secret passage) confer great military advantages, so does the supersmall. Does he who controls the microworld control the normal world?
- The more highly technological the army and/or culture, the more vulnerable it is to attack by nuclear weapons, by infowar assaults, and by

nanotechnology. As with infowar and biowar, building effective defenses will probably be a major motivation for the growth of a nano capability.

- Offense has the advantage over defense.
- Postmodern war is transitory. Postmodernism itself is clearly just a short period between the modern and the future: the same is true of postmodern war. War will either destroy us (so nano is irrelevant), or be outlawed (and nano could play a large role in this through sur-veillance especially), or it will transition into a lower-level kind of con-flict of sabotage and well-disguised info and bio attacks. "Cool War" is what it is called in Frederik Pohl's SF novel of the same name. Cool War will not be just for city- and nation-states. In Cool War, corpo-rations will be major players, probably as important as most, if not all, of the nation-states. The stealth potential of nano- (and its cousins bio- and info-) technologies could make Cool War possible. The dan-ger of nanowar could lead to One World Government; perhaps a horribly effective one, otherwise what is the point?
- Fear of technological surprise will encourage the military to throw money at all potentially deadly technosciences, including nano. It is happening already.
- Illusions about the effectiveness of state-of-the-art weapons lead to disasters, such as Vietnam and Afghanistan, especially by those states that feel these weapons have conferred a great advantage. Techno-things do not work perfectly in real life (in jungles, urban or not, or deserts, or space, or anywhere) like they do in Tom Clancy novels. Weapons fail and war is still politics, even nanowar. The culture that has the most to gain and is willing to lose the most will win most wars. But not all; if it has stupid leaders, it can still lose easily.

Some of the analysis of nanowar I've seen argues that nanotech will allow for fightable/winable wars. No. How many times have I read this about computers? All things being equal, the army that effectively inte-grates the new weapon(s) into its battle systems will win in the beginning. This is why the Germans won the first half of World War II. They did not spread their tanks out; they made Panzer armies. They did not use the best part of their air force for strategic bombing; they used it to support the ground armies. But in the end they still lost because wars are not won by technology.

Anyway, we can expect that most effective nanomachines will be sur-veillance or targeting devices, not weapon platforms. Many will be inert, waiting for something to come to them, not mobile. Small, but not nano, machines will become more common, some will have the potential to kill, and many will be teleoperated.

As with so many cyborg technologies, nano will be driven in large part by military desires and paradigms. This will shape what kinds of cyborgs and cyborg soldiers are possible in the future. These possibilities, and the polit-ical and military dangers that this type of war poses, will invariably impact cyborg citizenship.

Today, postmodern war is starting to blur the line between business competition and politics/war and crime. Nano- and infowar will only increase the confusion. So many of the things I have claimed about nanowar also clearly apply to the war on crime. Companies and domestic govern-mental institutions can easily deploy nanosurveillence technologies and nanosabatoge. But there is a good side to nano: longer and better lives. Next, in Part II, we will explore this aspect, because many of the break-throughs in cyborg medicine are happening through nanotechnology.

promulgating cyborgs

infomedicine and
the new body

THE DIGITAL BODY

Convicted murderer Joseph Jernigan transformed from Dead Man Walking to Dead Man Digitalized when he donated his body to science. In 1993, the Texas convict became the Visible Man, now on total display in books, on CD-ROMs, and through the World Wide Web. Jernigan has been immortalized as 15 gigabytes of data not for his life of crime, which culminated in the murder of a 75-year-old man who interrupted one of his burglaries, but because he was a fit 39-year-old killed neatly with chemicals. Lisa Cartwright describes his execution:

> prison workers attached an IV catheter to Jernigan's left hand and administered a drug that effectively suppressed the brain functions which regulate breathing...the catheter...functioned as a kind of prosthetic disciplinary hand of the state of Texas....

After his execution, his body was quickly flown to the Center for Human Simulation in Colorado, where it was frozen in a block of gel at -70 degrees centigrade (-160 degrees Fahrenheit). He was chosen as the best corpse from a number of candidates, then was quartered, an old medieval punishment but in this case just a stage in his immortalization. The four blocks were shaved into 1,871 thin slices that were filmed, digitalized, and entered into a sophisticated database that allows 3D reconstructions of his body so accurate that viewers can admire the dragon tattoo on his chest. This murderer is the archetypal human, anatomically speaking.

The Visible Woman was not a murderer but a 59-year-old Maryland housewife. When she died, she was treated in the same way, except that technological advances allowed her body to be sliced into 5,000 sections. The Visible Man and the Visible Woman are prime examples of the ongoing digitalization of the body. Every aspect of the human is being converted into computer information, whether it is blood gas compositions, heart rates, brain waves, or the genetic code itself.

Contemporary medicine depends on this mathematization of the human body, and this process will only increase as scientists perfect real-time scanning instruments and delve deeper and deeper into the nanoprocesses that vitalize our flesh, power our feelings, and make our thoughts possible. All high-tech medicine is cyborg medicine, for it involves this digitalization.

Modifying ourselves through medicine is also becoming more and more common. Every year millions of interventions are performed to suck out or insert fat, carve better facial features, modify the immune system, or otherwise "improve" the natural body. All these procedures raise important political issues, from the nature of informed consent to the wisdom of using medical resources to improve someone's buttocks while others die for lack of basic care. Another set of key cyborg political issues is linked to the ancient cycle of reproduction, decline, and death (see Chapters 6 and 7, which track the cyborg life cycle). Thanks to medical advances such as penile prosthesis, the vibrator, and transsexual surgery, sex has also become a cyborg issue, as I explain in Chapter 7 (penile prosthesis) and Chapter 9 (dildonics and transsexuality). But let us first look at one of the fastest-growing aspects of cyborg medicine: the increasing use of drugs to modify behavior and bodily processes on a massive scale.

The explosion of psychotropic and other drug use stems from three breakthroughs. First, there is the intimate understanding of body chemistry as a balancing act of hormones and other chemicals. The mathematical modeling of the biochemistry of consciousness, for example, means not only that drugs can be designed to produce specific mental effects, but that their production in the body can be controlled efficiently. The second breakthrough is innovations in monitoring the brain and the body in action. Real-time three-dimensional brain scans are now possible, and that means the testing of drugs can be improved and accelerated, even if the scientists do not yet fully understand what they see. Finally, society's supposed hatred of "bad" illegal drugs is matched by its love of officially sanctioned "good" drugs. It has become socially acceptable to medicate oneself not just for bone loss or incontinence or headaches, but also to achieve sanity or even just happiness.

Since before there was institutional medicine, when there were just pla-cating the spirits and healing, drugs have been used to modify human con-sciousness and the body. Medicine, with its ability to reprogram the immune system (see Chapter 6) and many other pharmacological interventions, has built on this history with a vast array of drugs that block pain, kill invading viruses and bacteria, and modify bodily processes. Some of these interven-tions have very dangerous ramifications that could have been avoided if the complex and permeable cybernetic relations between human bodies and other organisms were better understood. Antibiotics are a case in point; their overuse in treating humans and animals has produced microenvironments that effectively evolve new resistant strains of the very organisms we have tried to kill.

New understandings are leading to whole new generations of active drugs. Prozac and Viagra are good examples. Viagra, the hit of 1998, is just one of a new wave of "baby boom" drugs that are supposed to make life longer and better. These boomer drugs include Propecia (baldness), Lipitor (cholesterol), Evista (bone density), and Detrol (bladder control). Their extreme marketability stems from the common human desire for immor-tality, the ubiquitous cult of youth, and capitalism's relentless pursuit of profit.

Pharmaceuticals are big money. Over $20 billion was spent on research alone in 1998 by just U.S. companies; Pfizer realized $2.2 billion in profits in 1997, *before* Viagra. Pharmaceutical profits are growing at an incredible rate. The relationship between drug production and profitability is not always obvious. For instance, the big companies withdrew from research into new antibiotics because they assumed that there was not going to be a mar-ket for such drugs. Since common bacteria are developing resistance to the most powerful antibiotics, largely because drug companies have supported the massive overprescription of the antibiotics they already produce, this assumption has already proven incorrect. But there are no new antibiotics ready. What may turn out to be a major health crisis of the early twenty-first century will have resulted directly from the imperative to maximize profits. Economics are always political, especially when medical policy is deter-mined by profits, even if the causal chain is complicated by bacterial evolu-tion and other exotic factors.

Many drug-related political issues are more predictable. Some HMOs refused funding for Viagra and were immediately attacked. This is an issue that legislators—overwhelmingly male and aging—have great enthusiasm for, yet it is no surprise that they have not found the same energy for forcing HMOs to supply birth control and other reproductive services to women. Medications are not free, and so their distribution involves class as well, especially when it comes to government health policy. As more cyborgian technologies become available, who will have access to them? Only the rich and well-insured?

The new class of psychotropic (mind-affecting) drugs also has a number of surprising political ramifications. What can the drug wars possibly mean in the context of a whole raft of mood-elevating drugs such as Prozac? What is the line between treating depression and getting high? If mild depression can be treated chemically, should it be classed as a mental illness? Is there such a thing as cosmetic personality surgery for mild behavioral quirks? The vast increases in our understanding of the biochemistry of the body mean that the range of possible interventions increases apace. The temptation to medicalize everything from grumpiness to aging will be very powerful indeed. Already, when one looks at the extraordinary range of direct cyborgian interventions, it is clear that the whole body is open for improvement.

THE MEDICALLY MODIFIED

If you watch TV with an obsession about cyborgs, as I do, you will notice that one place they appear almost weekly is on medical shows such as *ER* and *Chicago Hope*. Episodes have focused on almost all of the typical cyborg medicine issues, from genetic engineering to xenotransplants. But sometimes they focus on things that surprise even me, like *Chicago Hope*'s story of the "half-man," a racist firefighter with a cancerous lower body and the desire to die. Then the kindly doctors of Chicago Hope Hospital bring in his estranged son and he decides to undergo the radical surgery they offer: the amputation of the lower half of his body, enabling him to live, hooked to machines, to see his son grow up into... a racist? The show even hints that because of the help of a black doctor, the fireman might grow out of his racism. Maybe as a cyborged half-man, race will come to seem less fundamental to him. In any event, his worldview will certainly change.

This half-man option is just one of many ways cyborg technologies can modify people. A quick tour of the human body from the head to the toes will offer some idea of how many other ways medicine can reengineer humans.

In the head, the most advanced artificial implants are platinum or glass electrodes used as cochlea replacements in the ears. They pick up sound waves and relay them directly to the auditory nerve. Researchers are also learning how to interface this information with implanted computers for speech processing. Neural probes are installed semipermanently in trauma victims to monitor the pressure of cerebral fluids and to administer medications directly. There is also significant research on "brain pacemakers" to treat neurological dysfunctions with electrical and biochemical stimulations.

Researchers also hope that work on artificial eyes will result in tiny cameras that supply visual information through an electronic patch laid directly on the visual cortex of the brain. Artificial tracheas have been implanted, and there is currently extensive research on an artificial thymus and artificial lymph glands.

The heart is one of the major sites for biomechanical interventions. Not only are there millions of pacemakers and artificial valves installed in hearts around the world, but there are also tens of thousands of cardioverter-defibrillators. These miniature heart resuscitation machines apply immediate electric shocks to the heart if sensors note the possible onset of a heart attack. Although the fully artificial heart has been successful only as a temporary bridge to allow patients to survive until a human heart transplant is available, there are also various other cardiac assist devices, many of which include feedback loops, that are used as permanent implants. Artificial hearts will be discussed below, as will artificial kidneys and artificial livers.

Moving further down the body, there is significant research on artificial bladders and sphincters. Inert testes prostheses are given to transsexuals and males who have been injured, and there is a great deal of work on penile implants, described in the following chapter. There are also literally millions of artificial joints implanted in hips, knees, ankles, elbows, and wrists.

Implanted electrical stimulation systems are growing in sophistication. They are used to stimulate diaphragms to combat sleep and breathing disorders, induce micturition, improve defecation, facilitate penile erection in paraplegics, and stimulate atrophied muscles in paraplegics and quadriplegics. In combination with exoskeleton legs, gait sensors, and computer walking programs, paraplegics can sometimes even walk. Treating facial and other paralysis with nerve, muscle, and electromechanical stress gauges implanted together shows promise in initial experiments.

Complex biomaterials, especially polymers, are being developed that mimic biological tissues such as glands, cells, vessels, skin, bones, and cartilage. They are often "hybrids" that allow growing transfected mammalian cells into polymeric gels or scaffolds. Since 1969, when charcoal granules were put in ultrathin membranes and then injected into the bloodstream for blood detoxification, there has been an increasing development of artificial cells including prototypes containing insulin, antibodies, anticholesterol compounds, enzymes, and urea converters. Research on artificial red blood cells and full artificial blood continues as well.

To understand the possible implications of this wave of prosthetic medicine, a few specific technologies will be considered in turn: artificial limbs, the artificial kidney, the artificial liver, and the artificial heart. In many ways, the use of prostheses is a search for wholeness not of the human but of the system.

Only recently has there been real improvements over the prostheses of the Middle Ages. In 1967, one leading researcher, Dr. D. S. McKenzie, predicted:

[I]t seems to me that significant progress in externally powered limbs will be made only when it becomes possible to link the central nervous system "on line" with the prosthetic control system.

Dr. McKenzie admitted that "a well-designed hook is more functional than any of the many so-called functional hands" and that it was "very doubtful indeed" that self-powered cybernetic limbs were any better than "conventional body-powered prosthesis." However, he foresaw that work on position-controlled servos and pressure-demand pneumatic valves would be regarded "as among the first breaches in the man-machine interface." He was right. By the 1990s not only had powered prostheses become much more effective, but the human nervous system had been brought "on line" through electrical stimulation and monitoring that allow amputees, paraplegics, and even quadriplegics to control limbs through muscle or nerve activity, or both.

Sensors on and in muscles can now pick up electromyographic signals and convert them to specific commands for the powered prosthesis. While direct electroencephalographic signals from the brain are not as easily controlled or understood, they are also being tested experimentally, especially by the military.

Less invasive are projects to use head motions (tracked by accelerometers) and voice commands to initiate preprogrammed actions that control computer-directed prostheses and slave robot arms for the disabled or for military pilots and drivers. The disabled can call up eating motions, telephone dialing, and any number of other small domestic tasks. The military has focused on targeting and launching weapons, flying and driving, calling up visual displays, and damage control activities. Unlike artificial organs, which currently seek simply to restore the natural organ functions to a level that permits the patient's survival, new interfaces and prosthetic technologies have the potential for enhancing human abilities, not just restoring them.

Some functions, such as cleaning the blood in the case of total kidney or liver failure, require a real organ or a close simulation. But the development of such organs is not always a clear-cut case of life over death. Sometimes there is an ongoing tension between prolonging death and prolonging life. This is certainly true of the artificial kidney and its development. Dr. Nils Alwall, a famous researcher, admitted about one early case: "The technical result of the treatment was satisfactory, but the patient died the following day."

The artificial kidney was the first artificial organ. Originally, however, it was not that effective. While research started in 1913, a successful artificial kidney was not made until 1944, when Willem Kolff made his rotating-drum dialysizer in the Nazi-occupied Netherlands. Almost all of Kolff's first patients died. In the early days of dialysis, other treatments for uremic poisoning offered a much better success rate than kidney machines. In 1949 the *British Medical Journal* compared the 50 percent success rate of a diet treatment with the 5 percent success rate of hemodialysis. That year the *Yearbook of Medicine* challenged the wisdom of working on artificial kidneys, and in Great Britain and the Netherlands hemodialysis was suspended. In this case proponents of artificial organs were correct in their promise that eventually their work would lead to the most effective treatment of kidney failure.

While researchers are working on portable artificial kidneys, most dialysis requires the patient to be attached to the kidney machine for some time. This kind of intermittent or temporary human-machine symbiosis could be termed a *semicyborg*. This category of cyborg is bound to increase as home dialysis becomes more common and as other techniques for feeding, medicating, or blood cleaning (such as with artificial livers) are developed.

This traffic between the organic and the inorganic also includes animals. The artificial liver presents a clear case of machine-human-animal symbiosis, though it has yet to produce an effective artificial organ.

Motokazu Hori, a leading researcher on artificial livers in Japan, notes in his insider history that there have always been three "streams of development" of the artificial liver: the biological, the artificial (or inorganic), and the hybrid. Because of the incredible complexity of the liver, the biological and the hybrid approach have been the most successful. Nonorganic blood-purification techniques sometimes return patients to consciousness from their hepatic comas, but they do not save patient lives because as yet they cannot perform the various metabolic functions that only living liver cells can manage. Hori concludes somewhat apologetically that:

> Because it is not possible to play the "Almighty" in the development of a complete artificial organ whenever a difficulty is encountered, a way must be found to apply the concepts and specific technologies of a hybrid system.

Indeed, the first artificial liver in 1956 was a hybrid arrangement in which a human was hooked up to a living dog's liver "incorporated in a cross-hemodialyzer." Every successful artificial liver system since has also been of a hybrid form, almost all of them developed in Japan, which in 1979 launched a national project to develop the artificial liver.

The direct use of animals for organ transplants or in hybrid systems only deepens their role as research animals. Animal experimentation has been and still is crucial to artificial organ research. Rabbits, sheep, pigs, calves, dogs, rats, hamsters, and others have all been used to test and retest artificial organs. Calves have been especially central to artificial heart research, and many of the prototype hearts are judged by how long they can keep a calf alive. Such work is, by necessity, often very cruel, involving much animal suffering and sometimes horrible deaths, such as the literal explosion of calves whose artificial hearts produce too much pressure.

Animal research and xenotransplants demonstrate that cyborg medical solutions are not free of organic suffering even when they work perfectly on humans. Nor are they economically, psychologically, or politically free. There is no better proof of this than the story of the artificial heart.

THE ARTIFICIAL HEART

[T]he mechanical heart borders on science fiction and wishful thinking....
— Dr. Denton Cooley, nine months before performing
the first human artificial heart implantation into Haskell Karp

On or about April 8, 1969, Haskell Karp died as a result of surgical experimentation performed on him by Dr. Denton A. Cooley, Dr. Domingo S. Liotta, and others in St. Lukes's Episcopal Hospital in Houston Texas....

Defendants, using devices approved only for animal experimentation, after removing the human heart of Decedent from his body, implanted an experimental mechanical device in Haskell Karp.... The mechanical heart, in fact, had not been tested adequately even on animals, had never been tested on a human being....

From the Wrongful Death Lawsuit filed by:

—Mrs. Haskell Karp

Because of its mythological and metaphorical resonances, the artificial heart has received the most publicity even though its medical impact has been significantly less than that of the artificial kidney. The first use of a totally implantable artificial heart (TIAH) was in 1957 at the Cleveland Clinic. Willem Kolff and Tetsuze Akutsu replaced a dog's heart with two compact blood pumps. The dog survived for about 90 minutes. Since then there has been continual research on TIAHs, including thousands of operations on calves, pigs, sheep, dogs, and people, using dozens of different designs. This work has overlapped with the development of different "assist" devices, especially those for the heart's left ventricle, which does most of the pumping. Various power sources have been considered, including nuclear radioisotopes to produce steam, the body's own skeletal muscles, and most successfully, lithium and other improved batteries. There has also been a great improvement in blood-compatible artificial heart materials and artificial heart valves, which have benefited many thousands of heart patients even if they have not yet led to a perfect TIAH. Most recently, miniaturized control systems have been developed to synchronize the heart to the body's needs, either through biofeedback, outside programming, or both.

Much of the funding for artificial heart research has come from the U.S. government's National Institutes of Health (NIH). Independent medical nonprofits (such as the Cleveland Clinic), foundations, and university medical programs (especially at Baylor, Rice, and the University of Utah) have also devoted significant resources to artificial heart research, as have several medical conglomerates and start-up companies formed by artificial heart researchers themselves.

The artificial heart has been marked by a great deal of economic calculation as well as political and psychological forces. As Michael Strauss details in his article, "The Political History of the Artificial Heart," the artificial heart itself came out of the biomedical revolution that "was in large measure political in nature" and driven by "an alliance of interested congressmen, powerful NIH directors, and eloquent science lobbyists." By the late 1970s the artificial heart project "had acquired a degree of autonomy and a momentum that was both scientific and political."

Another factor often ignored is local cultural dynamics. Renée Fox and Judith Swazey argue that Utah is a center of artificial organ research in part because it is the spiritual home of Mormanism, which Thomas O'Dea has called "the most American of religions." It is a religion with a very proactive attitude toward problems, a great faith in traditional ideas of progress, and a belief in the perfectibility of the body. William DeVries and many of the other main players in the artificial heart program are Mormons.

There are two main economic issues to note about the artificial heart and most other high-tech cyborg interventions. First, the money spent on developing and using it could save many more lives if spent elsewhere, especially on preventive medicine or medical services for the impoverished. While artificial heart advocates have often tried to defend the program with straightforward (and unusually crude) calculations about the supposed benefits of returning artificial heart recipients to the economy, they avoid, for obvious reasons, comparative calculations with, for example, preventative medicine. If resources were infinite, a crash program to develop the artificial heart might well make sense. Medical resources are far from infinite.

The second economic factor is the possibility that artificial organs will be very profitable. Hence start-up companies financed by researchers and medical corporations proliferate. Even if there are no immediate profits forthcoming, the benefits of publicity make the promotion of spectacular artificial organ research well worth the effort. For example, Humana, Inc. recruited Dr. William DeVries, the University of Utah heart surgeon who performed the famous operation on Barney Clark, for their own research center. After he performed his first transplant for them, the number of enrollees in the chain's health maintenance organization more than doubled in the next six months; as *Business Week* pointed out then, the hiring had "already paid off in spades."

Humana's president, William Cherry, insisted that profit-making was not their incentive. "My heart is as ethical as anyone's heart," he promised. But DeVries's move from the University of Utah to Humana does not appear to have been motivated by ethics. DeVries had become disenchanted at Utah because the Institutional Research Board (IRB), which must approve all experiments with human subjects, criticized the Barney Clark transplant on several grounds. Even though the Federal Drug Administration (FDA) had preapproved six transplants at Utah, Utah's IRB approved them only one at a time. The Chairman of Humana, David Jones, asked DeVries during his recruitment: "How many hearts do you need to find out if it works? Would ten be enough?" When DeVries said that it would, Jones replied: "If ten's enough, we'll give you 100." Soon after DeVries moved, Humana's IRB granted him permission to perform six more transplants, although he performed only three, none of which were successful. So is economics the only motivation for doing experimental transplants? Absolutely not. There are real psychological reasons as well.

The major motivator for artificial heart research is probably death. As Willem Kolff said:

> People do not want to die, and no government committee, no FDA regulations, no moral or theologic, not even economic considerations are going to change this.

Death motivates funders, especially geriatric politicians with heart disease; it motivates physicians who do not want to give up on patients and probably fear death as much as anyone; and it certainly motivates many of the patients who end up as experimental subjects.

The desire for "fame and fortune" is probably just as important among artificial heart researchers as the desire to conquer death. Dr. Denton Cooley offers a clear example. His lust to be the first surgeon to implant a TIAH in a human led him to violate numerous NIH and other regulations and even to appropriate a heart from another research team. In 1969 Cooley implanted an artificial heart into his patient, Mr. Haskell Karp, ostensibly as a "bridge" until a transplant heart could be found, but actually so Cooley could become a footnote in history. Mr. Karp died after three unpleasant days with the artificial heart and one with a donated heart, which was wasted on Mr. Karp as the artificial heart had practically finished him off.

Diana Dutton notes that Cooley's actions were "ethically dubious, as there was no reasonable expectation of scientific advancement or benefit for the patient." Cooley was forced out of his position at Baylor University by Michael Debakey, the leader of the team that produced the heart Cooley hijacked. But Cooley's career did not suffer. He moved to a new position at the Texas Heart Institute, and he even received a standing ovation from his peers at the next annual meeting of the American Society for Artificial Internal Organs.

Over ten years later, after learning that the University of Utah team was soon going perform another artificial heart transplant, Cooley rushed into another one of his own, also as a bridge for an organic transplant. His patient suffered for a week (two days with the artificial heart) before dying. Again Cooley had failed to gain approval of the local IRB and had violated FDA regulations by using a new medical device without approval. He was given a warning by the FDA, which he mocked in public.

Cooley is a remarkably unprincipled and arrogant man; no other artificial organ researcher has so nakedly displayed a lust for publicity and disregard for patients' welfare, although others have violated FDA and other regulations. But Cooley's hubris and drive are present in lesser amounts in all researchers. As one informant said about the Cooley controversy:

[A]nybody who gets involved in the artificial heart has to be a very ambitious man...because if things work out well [it holds forth] the possibility of instant immortality.

The same can be said for transplanting organic organs, whether from humans, living or dead, or animals, as in the case of xenotransplants.

NATURAL TRANSPLANTS

Of course, in an entirely concrete sense, organ transplantation *is* a form of nonoral cannibalism, that is, the taking of the flesh and blood from one person into another.

—Stuart Youngner

In 1992 the two leading researchers of the social implications of organ transplants left the field. Renée Fox and Judith Swazey explained that:

[W]e are intentionally separating ourselves from what we believe has become an overly zealous medical and societal commitment to the endless perpetuation of life and to repairing and rebuilding people through organ replacement—and from the human suffering and the social, cultural, and spiritual harm we believe such unexamined excess can, and already has, brought in its wake.

After years of observing transplant doctors and recipients, Fox and Swazey noted that three "themes" dominated the transactions: *uncertainty, gift-exchange,* and the *allocation of scarce resources.* The interplay of these three forces is profoundly political. Uncertainty represents the mathematical realities of cutting-edge cyborgian practices. Since outcomes cannot be predicted with certainty, who decides? The inclusion of "gift-exchange" as a central factor brings to the fore the oft-neglected social reality that politics determines the allocation of scarce resources.

There will always be uncertainty with transplants. The number of successful "solid organ" transplants has been steadily climbing since the first successful kidney transplant (1951), liver transplant (1963), heart transplant (1967), and lung transplant (1981), but they still often fail. In the early stages of the procedures' development failures often approached 100 percent. This is why the scientists who pioneer these operations need "the courage to fail." Their patients do not need the courage to die, for they are dying already. They do need the courage to suffer and to hope.

Until there is a complete understanding of the immune system, all organs transplanted will eventually be rejected unless they are from one identical twin to another. But Fox and Swazey observed that the "transplant community" avoids discussing this and often allows recipients to assume that rejection only occurs in bad matches. The rejection rate for kidneys is 50 percent within 10 years, and for hearts roughly the same rate within five years.

Since possible transplants (which also include pancreas and combined heart-lung transplants) are severely limited by the number of donors, doctors are continuously exploring new sources for organs, such as repairing damaged organs for reuse as bridges or doing domino-donor operations where the old organs that are taken out of one patient are transplanted into someone else. All of these procedures are uncertain. What is certain is that whether or not the transplantation is successful, the donation of organs, either from living donors or from dead, is one of the great gifts one human can give to another.

The importance of the gift dynamic is especially clear in the case of "live" donors of whole kidneys and liver or lung lobes. Most live donors (usually relatives) offer their organs "upon hearing of the need," without any deep reflection. So strong is the desire to make this gift of life that when doctors must reject a donor for psychological or sociological reasons, they commonly report instead that the potential donor is biologically incompatible. In these "live" donor cases, however, severe consequences might befall the donor, including death. In the face of such risk, many bioethicists worry about whether consent can be considered uncoerced when a parent donates to his or her child, for example.

In the case of bone marrow transplants for drastic cancer therapy, there is a growing trend of parents having a new child in the hope that he or she will be a biological match for their ill child. Between 1984 and 1989, there were at least 40 babies conceived and birthed in order to help dying siblings, and eight of those infants became donors. The most famous case was of baby Melissa Ayala who saved her 20-year-old sister's life with a transplant. The Ayalas wanted the baby in any event, but these cases raise a number of issues that worry many people. Fox and Swazey wonder about the possible impacts of the "tyranny of the gift" and how a family might feel if the gift fails. In a way, the new child is a type of biological factory, whatever else she or he might be. This issue becomes clearer as researchers realize advances in bio-"pharming" (see Chapter 8), which will soon make such roundabout production of bone marrow obsolete.

Gift-accepting is also complicated by the transformation of the recipient. Biologists are engineering organisms with tissues from multiple genetic donors and organisms made with genetic material from two species; they call these organisms "chimeras," after the mythical monster with the head of a lion, the tail of a serpent, and the body of a goat. In successful transplants, cells from the organ migrate to the body of the recipient and vice versa. So transplant patients are also chimeras. There is a growing body of urban legends that tell of recipients acquiring the attributes and desires of the organ donors. This kind of "animistic, magic-infused thinking about transplanted organs" disturbed the medical establishment so much so that in the 1980s they started downplaying the "gift of life" aspect of organ donation and cut back on the participation of psychologists and psychiatrists in transplant teams. Fox and Swazey argue that this is a mistake, and that the surgery still involves intense emotions even if the procedure is now routine. But, for policy-makers the only problem is a lack of organs, and many of them seem to think the market might solve this problem.

Since transplant organs have become so desperately needed, reports have surfaced of the poor selling eyes or kidneys and even of mass murders to provide the black market with organs. The most frightening examples of this so far have been from Bangladesh and Argentina. In 1992 the Argentinean police uncovered an extensive slaughter-for-organs scheme run at a mental hospital near Buenos Aires. Hundreds of patients were killed and harvested. In 1994 the respected periodical *Asia Week* reported that police in Chittagong City, Bangladesh, thought that 400 disappeared children had been murdered for their kidneys.

There are dozens of urban legends about kidnappings and murders-for-organs for every confirmed case. The historian Ruth Richardson, an expert on the history of grave-robbing, has warned that in the early 1800s similar reports of mass murders to provide dissection corpses were also labeled legends, but they turned out to be horribly true, as I describe below. We should not feign surprise when more cases like those from Buenos Aires and Chittagong come to light.

Richardson also argues that attempts to coerce organ donation through laws or bribes will fail, just as similar attempts to produce corpses for dissection a few centuries ago led to extensive resistance and a severe decline in donated corpses. The legalistic route is called, euphemistically, "presumed consent." It stipulates that unless there is evidence to the contrary, doctors can assume that the dead consent to donate their organs. Of course, it is the corpses of the poor that are usually picked for this honor. Schemes for financial inducement vary from a totally open market, to buying organ futures (you would be paid now for your organs later), to providing burial expenses to the survivors of donors. All of these will destroy the gift relationship of organ donations and also contribute directly to the commodification and desacralization of the human body.

Richardson notes that between 1675 and 1725 in the United Kingdom: "the human corpse began to be bought and sold like any other commodity." This led to a "class of entrepreneurs" known as body snatchers or resurrectionists. Eventually some of them graduated from stealing corpses to manufacturing them: mass murder. In the early 1800s several cases came to light that changed the economy of corpses drastically.

At a Halloween party in Edinburgh, some of the guests discovered a real dead body. It was the last of 16 victims killed by the infamous duo Burke and Hare to supply a Dr. Knox with dissection corpses. Hare turned state's evidence and Burke was executed (and dissected). A few years later, another case of so-called *burking* was uncovered, this time in London, with 60 victims. Richardson explains: "It had suddenly dawned on society that poor people had become worth more dead than alive."

Finally the open market in corpses was outlawed but the parliamentary solution was to give institutions (workhouses, hospitals, mental asylums) the rights to the corpses of anyone who died in their care without provision for burial. Resistance to this early version of "presumed consent" led to an actual decline of available corpses, with many spontaneous fund-raisers and riots resulting.

The current system relies on people donating their organs, usually after death. But on the receiving end it still seems to favor white males with high incomes, because they have the resources to circumvent the system by getting on numerous regional donor lists or to cheat it by buying black-market organs. In the Third World, and maybe in North America and Europe, income often determines who gets transplants. This is the "green screen," so-called because if one cannot pay for the exams, treatments, and the organ, or get someone else to, then one cannot have a transplant.

There is evidence that up to 5 percent of all donated organs are being exported from the United States to wealthy patients abroad. Sometimes these are held to be inferior organs, but the transplant success rates indicate nothing of the kind. Other controversies swirl around such practices as giving one patient multiple organ transplants and giving a patient with a failed transplant a new organ (one third of the cases, sometimes up to five retransplants).

Finally there is the problem of "eligibility criteria." In the 1970s the committee that distributed dialysis opportunities was called "the God Squad." While there has been a move away from psychosocial criteria, there are still many hard judgments to make because the number of available organs is not anywhere close to meeting the demand.

All these factors have helped turn patients into experimental objects, transforming organ donation from a gift to a commodity. For Renée Fox, it is "a profanation." For some, death itself is being profaned by this process. Others point out that the line between the living and the dead is growing very blurry indeed.

And so is the line between humans and animals, thanks to xenotransplants. The use of animal organs and tissue in humans is a growing part of the contemporary proliferation of cyborgs. Cyborgism can be seen as a full-scale assault on traditional divisions (such as machine, human, animal) with an inevitable proliferation of cyborgs and other monsters. The rhetoric adopted to discuss such procedures uses the metaphor of "repairing" rather than "healing." When animal organs or tissue are used for transplants, that tissue is conceptualized as a machinic element, not as organic matter, and integrated into the machine-body of the recipient using an array of tools and attachments. Unsurprisingly, as the "programming" of organic immune systems becomes easier, the number of xenotransplants will certainly increase. They will easily surpass the number of human transplants now performed, because the major constraint on human transplantation is the availability of organs.

None of the attempts, which started in 1905, at using whole animal organs in humans has yet been successful, although pig cartilage, heart valves, and lenses have been successfully transplanted. Perhaps the most famous xenotransplant was the "Baby Faye" case in 1984, where a baboon heart kept a small girl alive for 20 days. In 1992 a team led by Dr. Thomas Starzl transplanted a baboon liver into a man, using a new anti-immunization drug known as FK-506 combined with three older drugs. While it was not successful, eventually an effective regime of immunosuppressive therapy or breakthroughs in genetic engineering will open the door for the widespread transplantation of various animal organs, especially from pigs and baboons, into humans.

For Fox and Swazey this is a nightmare:

> The number, variety, and combination of solid organs and other body parts transplanted during the 1980s, along with the array of extracorporeal and implanted devices in regular use, being tested, or being designed has brought our society closer to the world of "rebuilt people" classically portrayed in science fiction, in which humans are more and more composed of transplanted parts of one another, and of "man-machine unions" that "prosthetize" humans and humanize man-made organs. It is the "spare parts" pragmatism, the vision of the "replaceable body" and limitless medical progress, and the escalating ardor about the life-saving goodness of repairing and remaking people in this fashion that we have found especially disturbing.

And transplants are not the only cyborg medicine that is rapidly growing in scope and effectiveness. As the next two chapters demonstrate, there is now a whole cyborg life cycle that mimics the natural human life cycle, from technoscientific conception to machine-mediated death.

cybernetic human reproduction

CYBORG CONCEPTIONS

It begins with an egg and a sperm. You would not think that the human egg and the human sperm could be mechanized, digitalized, commodified, and cyborgized, but that is just what has happened. For most of human history the dance of the egg and the sperm has been sorely misunderstood. People once believed that little babies crouched in sperm ready to feast on eggs; or conversely that the egg held the child and the sperm was for sustenance. Even once it was discovered that both egg and sperm merged to make the new baby, most experts assumed that the sperm was the active participant, the egg merely waiting to be fertilized. Finally the actual details unfolded revealing that the egg is active after all.

Emily Martin has written a beautiful account of all this in her article "The Egg and the Sperm," showing just how much cultural attitudes shape "scientific" explanations. But now it is time to worry about the influence going the other way: science shaping culture. Science's story—Martin calls it the "romance" of the sperm and the egg—now more accurately describes, predicts, and intervenes in the reproductive process than it did just a few decades ago. This means that technicians can now remove eggs, insert new nuclei, and stimulate them to divide; they collect, sort, wash, and insert sperm at their will. Both egg and sperm can be typed, frozen for later use, or discarded if judged inferior. It seems the romance is over.

Or is it? Maybe there can be romance in cyborg reproduction, at least where there is love among the machinery. Robbie Davis-Floyd and Joseph Dumit explore this question, and other cyborg issues, in the collection of essays they edited on technoscientific human reproduction called, appropriately enough, *Cyborg Babies*.

In their introduction they make important distinctions about cyborgs that are directly relevant to the cyborg citizen. First, they use the word "codependence" instead of "interdependence" when discussing reproductive cyborg technologies. They explain that the more popular term, interdependence, "does not sufficiently connote the compelling, addictive quality of our relationship to cyborg technologies...." Just how much choice is involved when people choose technoscientific interventions? It requires more than setting up cyborg twelve-step groups: "Hello, my name is Chris and I'm addicted to cyborg technologies." No, it necessitates an awareness of the danger of mindlessly using every possible high-tech intervention and asking: "Do I really want this drink...uh, this cyborg technology? Do I really *need* this cyborg technology?"

In a related warning, Davis-Floyd and Dumit ask us to watch carefully the line between "improvement" and "mutilation":

> We are immersed in cyborgs; they saturate our language, our media, our technology, and our ways of being, posing questions we cannot answer about the exact location of the fine line between "mutilating" a natural process in a negative and destructive way and "improving" or "enhancing" it.

Even though this line "may be impossible to locate," we have to keep looking for it, and not just where cyborg technologies are directly used, but wherever they have an impact—on the environment, on those not cyborged, and on those who are changed by cyborgization—because each specific technology is a choice. The details matter tremendously.

Davis-Floyd and Dumit cite the work of Barbara Katz Rothman, who has shown that "the more technological options that exist, the less possible it is to choose options that do not involve technology." This is a reflection of society's addiction to these technologies. When a new technology becomes possible, it automatically has a constituency: its developers, its implementors, anyone who might be able to banish some small part of life's uncertainty by believing in the technology (whether it really works as advertised is another matter). We all fear uncertainty, from the doctors and patients who want results to the doctors and lawyers who fear lawsuits.

The great appeal of cyborgization is that it often works. It does more than make us feel good: it saves lives; it brings to life babies who would not have been born; it allows biologically impossible parenthood. While it is true that the "subversive potential of these technologies is often subverted into the service of the dominant cultural mode," every time a gay couple has a child, for example, that dominant cultural mode is undone. The evidence is growing that in some areas, such as our binary gender system, the overall effect of cyborgization is inevitably subversive. Simplistic male/female categories cannot stand against the polymorphous desires of so many people mobilized by so much cyborg technology.

But in many areas the end results are far from clear, because, cyborg "is a tricky term, a wily subject," as Dumit and Davis-Floyd remark. They note how four different perspectives deploy "cyborg" in actuality: 1. good cyborg ("positive technoscientific progress"); 2. bad cyborg ("mutilator"); 3. unmarked cyborg ("neutral analytic tool"); and 4. sign-of-the-times cyborg ("signifier of contemporary, postmodern times"). Analyzing these different meanings, Dumit and Davis-Floyd raise several points worth keeping in mind as we develop criteria for our own cyborgizations:

- Faith in cyborgization as purely positive progress leads to the overly hasty conclusion that we should use "all the resources of science and technology," and if we do not, a good outcome (as with natural childbirth) is merely "lucky."
- Peter Reynolds's concept of the "one-two punch of technocracy" described in *Cyborg Babies*, shows how dynamic the cyborgization-is-mutilation perspective can be. First, according to Reynolds, technology does something, such as makes it possible for older women to conceive—punch one. Then the mother and the baby need even more technology to have a successful pregnancy and birth—punch two. Reynolds calls this dynamic "mutilation and prosthesis." Technology is both the problem and the cure.

  Linked to this is the common belief that technology gives us more control over our lives, even if things are already out of control precisely because of technology. Consider the driver going 80 miles-per-hour in his car, which goes into a skid. He wants anti-lock brakes. They may save him, they may not, but technology got him into danger in the first place. The only real safety would be in not being in the speeding car at all, but we are not going to give up our cars. Even if technology does not really give us more control in our lives, it at least gives us the illusion of more control.
- One of the most significant ways the cyborg can be deployed as a "neutral analytic tool" is as a metaphor. Dumit and Davis-Floyd point out that the anthropologist Clifford Geertz used the "metaphor of cul-

tural evolution in which humans as biological animals use culture as a prosthesis in order to begin participant evolution." To use the concept of the cyborg as a metaphor is not to argue that it is intrinsically good or evil, simply that it bears a relationship to known reality. Since metaphor is one of the basic ways we understand the world, this is a more important point than it might seem at first. Still, metaphors can never be more significant than actual technologies.

- Viewing the cyborg as a "signifier of postmodern times" utilizes what Dumit and Davis-Floyd, drawing on Donna Haraway's work, call the "tactic of science fiction." It allows us to tell stories about the here and now that do not paint the present as an inevitable product of the past. This means that the future is not determined either.

They conclude that:

Cyborgs thus represent a paradox: they are potentially better than human *and* they threaten the loss of our identity—if we become too much the cyborg, will we no longer be human? Serving as both enhancers and mutilators of what went before, cyborgs—and especially cyborg modes of reproduction—represent, in another of Haraway's potent phrases, a "promise of monsters."

This "promise," as Adele Clarke argues in her sociological work on medical reproduction, is a postmodern one. Clarke's research on the cyborgization of medically mediated human reproduction shows that the modern paradigm of "achieving and/or enhancing *control over* bodies and processes" has been supplemented by postmodern approaches "centered on re/de/sign and *transformation* of reproductive bodies...."

She points out, citing Nancy Scheper-Hughes and Margaret Lock, that the body in question is always three actual bodies: the individual's lived body, the social/symbolic body, and the body politic. The shift from modern to postmodern entails a concordant shift in the level at which power operates on individuals, meanings, and society itself. The power partially to shape transformations is a type of control but it is specific, indirect, collective, and limited, as opposed to the command-and-control power of the military paradigm.

An example of this postmodern control is the technology of technosemen, whose original goal was simply to make the reproductive process work when it did not function normally. But very quickly, as the medical sociologists Matthew Schmidt and Lisa Moore demonstrate in their article

"Constructing a 'Good Catch,'" in *Cyborg Babies*, the goal became to breed superior children for a superior society, thus radically changing the definition of masculinity and how race and class prejudices are reified by high technologies. Instead of impacting only the sterile, the process divides all men into strange "hierarchies of potency":

> Only some semen is good enough to be made cyborg; thus at its very essence technosemen is divisive. Only elite semen samples are allowed to undergo the disciplining process of new reproductive technologies. Through the construction of semen as cyborg, hierarchies of potency are established across categories of men.

The semen is in a sense constructed. The treatment it undergoes, including cleaning and sorting, certainly transforms it from a natural body fluid into a processed product. The same thing happens to the eggs that are extracted for artificial fertilization. Then, after the sperm and eggs have been culled once, fertilized ova are often culled again before or after implantation.

The entire process of artificial reproduction is technologically mediated to an incredible degree, and it drastically shifts how we think about creation—and by extension, women as creators—in ways that are not clear yet. Inevitably, it changes what we think of fetuses and babies as well.

POSTMODERN PREGNANCY

Now that conception has been achieved, we move on in this cyborg life cycle to consider the fetus. Cyborg technoscience has given scientists the tools to develop a full theory of the fetus. The fetus is now manipulated through so many cyborg technologies that Monica Casper, another sociologist of medicine, says "science and medicine have made possible the emergence of a plethora of fetal cyborgs and technomoms." Some technomoms are legally dead, as are some fetal cyborgs. There is not space here to detail all the monsters, hopeful and otherwise, that fall into these categories, but some of the implications of fetal-cyborg technology are crucial.

The case of ultrasound is particularly striking. What are the effects on families and society in general of the ability to see images of the fetus in utero? It seems having a visual relationship with the child in the womb helps establish the "personhood" of the fetus before it is even born. This can contribute to the right-to-life claim that the fetus should have equal status to the mother. In essence, the prenatal stage, has become a cyborg stage, and the

91

family communicates with the child, at least partially, through a machine. This means the ultrasound machine not only represents the child, it helps make a child of a fetus, something that used to happen at birth. This is true of all fetal monitoring and fetal surgical interventions.

Although the communication system is quite limited, it is interesting that a machine that shows a representative image—a sort of shadow— becomes the symbol for the child and to some degree, the family interacts with that machine as though it were the child. Actress Dierdre Hall commented that the first time she saw the ultrasound image of her first child, who was being carried by a surrogate mother, it was as if an "incredible experience of life had just entered the room." All someone had done was to turn on a machine. And Hall was only the legal mother, not the biological one.

Fetal tissue itself offers a number of special properties. When doctors operate on a fetus, the wound heals without a scar. Fetal tissue also sometimes lacks immune response. In its fetal stages, brain and other tissues do things they do not do when mature, such as grow. These qualities have led scientists to try many strange experiments. In Casper's words:

> fetal tissue is like Play-Doh™ for many scientists, easily manipulated and shaped into all sorts of baroque cyborganic configurations.

The political implications are potent indeed. Abortion is an extremely volatile political issue and fetuses are an inevitable part of this debate, so in many places fetal research is outlawed partially or completely.

A more subtle political question is how cyborg interventions might shift the meaning of both fetuses and mothers. Casper observes that "technologizing fetuses, turning them into cyborgs, may serve to make them seem more 'naturally' human." On the other hand, the fact that dead mothers can be kept alive as cyborg wombs until their babies are born can lead to the devaluation of women's rights when compared to the right of fetuses to be born. If the courts can order a dead mother be turned into a cyborg womb, then it is only one more step to insist that living mothers be defined as primarily wombs.

Each family involved must decide how much they want medicine to intervene when a pregnant women is in danger or dead. Hospitals assume that they will use a certain amount of technology even though many families offer resistance. The medical establishment has a well-cultivated image of expertise and legitimacy. Though medical interventions, particularly those that take place in the hospital, are quite costly and often carry serious risks, they are routinely prescribed because doctors believe that they offer the best possible outcome. This is not always the case. One medical intervention often leads to another, warns Dr. Robert Mendelssohn, especially with labor and childbirth in a hospital. Dr. Mendelssohn urges women to have home birth if possible and avoid unnecessary medical interventions, because he believes the less cyborgian interventions, the healthier for the child:

> There is ample evidence that the medical technology, drugs, anesthetics, surgery, and other obstetrical slings and arrows employed in most hospitals expose mothers and babies to needless risk.

Although he believes that the medical establishment is too technologically oriented, he acknowledges that most doctors are not evil, greedy people; instead he blames medical education for indoctrinating them into intervention-centered practice. Doctors, not patients, are the first to be impaired by medical schools' preoccupation with intervention rather than prevention, by its infatuation with drugs and technology, and by the indefensible rituals, mores, and egotistical attitudes that are burned into the brain of every student who survives the rigid curriculum and training. Once locked into the interventionist philosophy of the medical establishment, most doctors uncritically believe in the superiority of intervention (cyborg) techniques. Those who do question this risk being professionally ostracized and exiled.

Dr. Mendelssohn believes that scientists develop and use new procedures too quickly, without measuring the long-term effects, and that they misrepresent data in order to maintain the appearance of positive results. Although many routine procedures used during pregnancy, labor, delivery, and in the first few moments after birth (silver nitrate, phenylketonuria tests, hexachlorophene soap, bilirubin lights, circumcision, antibiotics) are unnecessary and have serious risks, doctors present them to the parents as routine practices.

Medical treatments are often administered on the slim chance that they will succeed. Sometimes, if one hospital refuses treatments because the chances for success are deemed too small, the parents can find another hospital willing to treat the patient. Profit usually figures intimately in such decisions, whether it is in the form of knowledge and prestige or money.

Angela and Amy Lakeberg were twins, born on June 29, 1993. During the pregnancy, the parents were told that the babies were conjoined and they were offered the option of abortion, but they declined. When the babies were born at Loyola University Medical Center, doctors determined that because the twins shared a damaged heart and liver, surgery to separate them was not an option. The Lakebergs then found another hospital, Johns Hopkins, that would separate the twins.

Amy was weaker than Angela, so the doctors and parents decided that Amy would be sacrificed in order to give Angela a chance at life. No such surgery had ever been successful; all previous patients had died within five days. Donations began pouring in for the two girls. The twins were separated in a five-hour operation. Amy died in the first few minutes of the surgery, and some of her tissue was used to repair damage to Angela's organs.

Ten months and $1.3 million later, Angela finally succumbed to heart and lung problems. She had never left the hospital except to be transferred to another one for surgery, and she had never been removed from the respirator. She had lived a painful, heavily cyborged existence. When she died, Angela was surrounded by her surgical team, who described themselves as her "surrogate parents" and Angela as a "sweet little girl." Her father had recently been arrested and her mother was downtown bailing him out when the baby died. The surrogate parents reported that the natural parents had not visited the child in weeks. Angela's new family, her surgical staff, described her as a cheerful and affectionate little girl whom they loved very much. This is a good example of the technologically created cyborg family, which I discuss in detail in Chapter 10. Angela's legacy is to be the longest-living separated conjoined twin in which the heart and liver were shared. She was buried next to her sister. The uninvolved observer (as opposed to the parents, the practitioners, and the hospital) must ask whether Angela and Amy would have been better off left alone to a short life and death together.

It is interesting to note how the press covered this story. In the Associated Press article that the New York Times ran, the operation ("surgical wizardry") was portrayed as the decision of loving parents who could not let go and were willing to try anything to save at least one of their babies. In the same paper ten months later reporting Angela's death, the Lakebergs were described quite differently. No longer the devoted parents presiding over a tragic decision, the Lakebergs were now neglectful parents who rarely visited their child. The press loves to make parents in such cases into heroes when they opt for high-tech treatments, and villains when the children die.

A different example of cyborg medicine is the case of Baby Ryan. When he was born six weeks premature with kidney and possible neurological damage, physicians at Sacred Heart Hospital in Spokane, Washington proclaimed him "too badly damaged to save." Two other hospitals repeated that diagnosis. But Ryan's parents took one hospital to court to force it to continue kidney dialysis. The doctors argued that the procedure was futile and painful and that it was cruel to continue to treat the child. The parents accused the hospital of throwing away their child's life, and the hospital accused the parents of cruelty. Eventually, a doctor at Emanuel Hospital in Portland, Oregon, read about Ryan's case and agreed to treat him. He discovered that Ryan's kidneys were not as badly damaged as was first thought. Extreme cyborgian intervention was not needed and Ryan is still alive, though he suffers bowel problems and brain damage. No one yet knows how normal Ryan's life will be, but he clearly was not the "lost cause" that many doctors thought. In Ryan's case, the perseverance and willingness to embrace any possible medical procedure paid off, while for Angela Lakeberg, a new cyborg family of medical technicians and technologies was constructed around her suffering, which at least offered some solace during her short existence.

PROGRAMMING CYBERCHILDREN

It is not just unusual children like Angela or very sick ones like Ryan who undergo intense cyborg interventions. Parents feel tremendous pressure to program their children's immune systems as well. Although vaccines are not the first medical intervention children encounter, they are one of the more potentially dangerous and the most widely accepted. They are fundamentally a soft technology, aimed at "improving" the body's immune system.

The evidence strongly suggests that while some vaccines have great public health benefits, other vaccines are ineffectual, dangerous, and stupid: ineffectual because they often do not provide the expected immunity; dangerous because they cause illnesses and death instead of preventing them, as with the swine flu innoculation and some whooping cough vaccines; stupid because they protect against childhood diseases such as measles, rubella, and chicken pox that are not generally dangerous unless they infect adults, which is much more likely if the vaccines prevent the acquisition of natural immunity. Doctors do not fully understand the general effect of vaccines on the immune system, and there is strong evidence of a relationship between vaccinations and various immunological disorders.

Despite these issues, the pressure on parents to allow injecting their children with numerous complicated and little understood vaccines when they are just weeks old is enormous. The assumptions are that the natural immune system is in some way flawed, medical science has invented ways to improve it, and we must alter the immune system to battle disease. Thus has intervention in the immune process become routine. Walene James describes the attitude of the medical establishment toward vaccines:

> Vaccines are miracle weapons that rout the invaders [diseases] and save us from being conquered by them. They are one of the heroes in man's eternal struggle against the terrifying threat of disease, disability, and death.

Some claim that these vaccines have virtually eliminated most of the deadly childhood diseases, but most evidence shows that drops in the rate of polio and diphtheria occurred *prior to* the widespread use of vaccines, probably due to improvements in hygiene and sanitation. In fact, there was a slight increase in the incidence of polio after the introduction of the Salk vaccine in 1952.

There have also been some clearly disastrous vaccination programs, such as the swine flu fiasco and the smallpox vaccine, which proved to be "the only source of smallpox related deaths for three decades after the disease had disappeared."

Some doctors believe there is a host of potentially devastating problems that could be caused by immunization programs. Dr. Mendelssohn summarizes this perspective:

> There is a growing suspicion that immunization against relatively harmless childhood diseases may be responsible for the dramatic increase in autoimmune diseases since mass inoculations were introduced. These are fearful diseases such as cancer, leukemia, rheumatoid arthritis, multiple sclerosis, Lou Gehrig's disease, lupus erythematosus and the Guillain-Barré syndrome.

Immunization publicity campaigns, sponsored by governments, imply that parents who do not vaccinate their children are neglectful mothers and fathers who do not care about their children's health. Proimmunization rhetoric calls for keeping your child "safe" through immunizations, implying that those who do not immunize are endangering their children.

Walene James's daughter Tanya was ordered by the Virginia Department of Child Services to immunize her child. When she refused, they took her to court. Tanya had to prove to the judge that immunizations posed a threat to the child's health before she finally won the "right" not to vaccinate her son.

After the trial, their doctor nearly lost his license for supporting them and he was cited by the Virginia Beach Medical Society for unethical conduct for supporting the child's exemption from immunizations.

The trial, the invasion of privacy, and the denial of a parent's right to choose the appropriate care for her child resulted from a very powerful campaign by drug companies, government agencies, and the medical establishment. This alliance has also enabled a key part of the vaccine industry's profit structure—drug companies' limited liability for the harmful effects of vaccines.

Technological solutions can certainly be effective, as antibiotics and vaccines often are, but the long-term implications of such interventions sometimes become clear only much later. There exist no clear criteria for how to use these technologies. Children's antibiotics may cure infections but also might compromise their immune systems, and in the long term they certainly contribute to the evolution of antibiotic-resistant infections.

A related cyborgian ethical problem of vaccination is the tension between what is best for specific children (and adults) and what is best for the "herd" (general population). If the herd has established immunity (a certain level of effective vaccination and/or natural immunity that precludes an epidemic of the disease), it is often safer not to vaccinate oneself or one's children, since the the dangers of the vaccine can be avoided and yet we can reap the rewards of the herd's immunity. This is a hard political choice, balancing the risks that immunizations pose for the individual with the community's perceived need to have a certain threshold of vaccinated children and adults. What are the parents' rights? What are the parents' responsibilities?

This tension between an individual and a societal good is found wherever cyborg technosciences are at work. This is especially true, as we shall see in the next chapter, for the large class of humans who are fundamentally transformed by cyborgization, whether it is the restoration of lost bodily functions or the creation of new creatures who aren't quite dead or alive: neomorts and living cadavers.

enabled cyborgs, living and dead

(DIS)ABLED CYBORGS

In 1992, I met a rotund, bearded, psychedelic biker who had a deformed hand with only two vestigial fingers. Sometimes he wore a prosthetic but often he did not, especially when he performed weird puppet shows for the kids. The puppeteer's name was Bandit and he was an accomplished sound engineer, computerist, and motorcycle mechanic. His hand had been "different" since birth, so he had made a number of artificial attachments for it. There were special ones for working on machines, for handling electronics, for riding his hog, and for partying. Bandit had an interesting theory about prosthetics and the disabled. He had observed that people born without limbs or parts of limbs had a very secure relationship to their prostheses. The prosthesis was not something they resented; it was a part of them that was all the more interesting because it was removable, adjustable, and interchangeable. In Bandit's experience, people who had suffered traumatic amputations had much more trouble accepting and appreciating their prostheses.

Later, while on a fellowship, I worked with someone who had suffered just such a loss, and while he did not exactly say he hated his prosthesis, he sure did not think much of my research. In fact, he hated the whole idea of cyborgology and always said there was nothing of value in it. This seemed like denial to me. When one looks at the research and anecdotal evidence about the relations between people and their prostheses, it is clear that some very significant psychological dynamics are occurring that are relevant to cyborg politics.

Consider some of the transitions Christopher Reeve underwent. After his initial anger and denial, he adapted to helpful technology. He says: "I'm so accustomed to the chair now, it's like a part of my body." Still, he wanted his bodily autonomy. When he got an ulcer on his lower back, the wound was so bad it "penetrated to the bone . . . so big that you could put a hand inside it." Doctors recommended an operation with skin grafts, but he "hated the thought of one more invasion of my body, one more manifestation of helplessness." At another point he suffered several bad episodes of dysreflexia, an overloading of the kidneys and bladder leading to high blood pressure that can be fatal. "I was forced to become a serious student of myself," he remarks. Reeve progressed through fear and denial to the struggle for autonomy and self-knowledge.

Researchers have studied the psychology of people living as enabled cyborgs in hospitals, dependent on life-allowing technologies (especially polio patients on iron lungs, kidney dialysis patients, and terminal patients on respiration and other support equipment), as well as the disabled (also including some polio and dialysis patients along with amputees and paraplegics with various medical histories) who live outside hospitals with the help of various machinery.

The dying and the legally dead who are kept alive through painful and expensive cyborg machinery represent a serious problem of ethics and resource allocation. According to Bruce Hilton, director of the National Center for Bioethics, an incredible "70 percent of hospital deaths now involve the decision to withdraw some kind of support" machinery. More than a third (36 percent) of people who have lived symbiotically with kidney machines, for example, reject the option of cardiopulmonary resuscitation in case of heart failure. Many (8 percent in one study) terminal kidney patients who live on dialysis machines choose to terminate their treatment, which is a form of suicide.

Dr. Willem Kolff, the acknowledged "father" of artificial organs, has advocated a policy of deferred consent among artificial heart recipients, so that patients who wake from surgery to hear the "clicking of the pump" where once there was the beating of their heart could not disconnect their mechanical pumps until 24 hours had passed. To put such a decision in perspective, he reminds his colleagues that: "there are also people with normal kidneys and normal hearts who commit suicide because they cannot cope with life." Cyborg technologies such as these and the more widespread life-support machinery have led to a sea change in the public's attitude toward suicide, which is now seen by many as an exercise of individual autonomy and a right.

Numerous studies have shown that kidney transplant recipients do better than patients on dialysis and that patients who successfully use home dialysis fare much better than those who use the hospital. Clearly, the more normal the patient's life can become, the happier they are. Patients sometimes reject even life-sustaining machinery if the quality of their physical or psychological life becomes too low. As a German researcher, Dr. Zimmermann, notes: "Therapeutic dependence on technical devices represents a major intrusion into the life of the patient." Other important factors are: 1. the age of the dialysis patients (the older the patient, the less willing to continue living); 2. whether they are working; and, significantly, 3. their gender. Several studies indicate that men have more difficulty than women in adapting to an invalid status, especially because of the role reversal (from provider to dependent) and the new body image (a human dependent on a machine) this change involves.

A study of polio victims and their relationship to life-support technology reveals that many medical cyborgs go through several stages in coming to terms with their mechanical prostheses and that mechanical systems can be liberating. The researchers Joseph Kaufert and David Locker carried out a study that followed the rehabilitative experiences of ten victims of the Manitoba poliomyelitis epidemics of the 1950s.

A number of different "careers" followed the patients' original illnesses. First came the "acute" phase, the fight to live, involving tremendous physical effort and reliance on the iron lung for survival. Then came "rehabilitation," where they viewed dependence on the iron lung and other machines as an impediment to independence. This was followed by "stability," entailing constant exercise and conscious breathing to minimize or eliminate reliance on medical machinery. As many of these patients grew older and entered a "transitional" stage, setbacks in their health were offset by the development of newer equipment such as portable respiration machines, which could fit on wheelchairs. Patients who could not maintain themselves without machinery could nonetheless grow more independent with the help of portable machines. Even patients who could breath on their own (albeit with great effort) discovered an improved quality of life with the use of portable respirators.

Ironically, this independence required increased reliance on machinery and on friends and family who were prepared for mechanical, and therefore medical, emergencies. Patients needed to overcome the extreme work ethic of the rehabilitation and stability phase, since it was linked to a rejection of machine dependence. As Kaufert and Locker note: "Within rehabilitation ideology, virtue lay in resisting the temptation of the machine: dependence on equipment rather than the self was depicted as idleness and having given in to the disease."

The most difficult surrender, for some patients, was accepting the creation of a permanent tracheal airway for the portable respirator. It necessitated quite a change in "body image" because it involved a "direct physical connection to a machine." However, the patients who underwent the procedure often considered it a "small price to pay." Accepting the machine was not a simple process. The patient had "to adapt to the rhythm of the machine." One patient explained: "Nobody can tell you, nobody can teach you, you have to learn the machine." Even more, patients had to live with great awareness of their machines for the rest of their lives. They had to listen to its functioning, feel its operations (the air pressure and vibrations), and be prepared to repair or adjust it:

> As a consequence, the machine, and tending to the needs of the machine, become the central focus and activity of everyday life. Moreover, the problematic aspects of living with the machine did not detract from its role of promoting a quality of life of more than minimal tolerability.

The machine became part of even the most intimate moments of the patients' lives. One recently married woman described what this meant to her and her husband:

> When we received our marriage vows the doctors didn't tell us, they didn't know themselves, about the intercourse, that your respirations increase. The machine just gives you your ten or eleven breaths per minute, so I need sixteen breaths per minute, during that time I need more air. My husband and I had to interpret this as another experience— turn the rate button up, increase the pressure, turn this up, and he was paying more attention to the respirator than he was with...and trying to keep his mind on everything. All of a sudden as you're enjoying intercourse you have to turn the rate button up.

Still, humans are adaptable. Kaufert and Locker found that:

> All those respondents who had made the final transition to a ventilator with a tracheal airway readily agreed that it had a positive impact on their

lives. The differences in quality of life were so dramatic that portable ventilator users often tried to persuade other post-polios to make the transition too.... A transformed sense of self accompanied the new dependence upon machinery and the changed relationship to the environment and the people in it.

For the patients, the choice of a cyborg existence made them more independent. Overcoming traditional fears of machinery and their learned rehabilitation ethic allowed them to become free of the hospital and to become active citizens again. As Kaufert and Locker conclude, this new cyborg ideology is as important as the medical condition of the patients themselves.

> The nature and extent of the gains and losses experienced by the respondents appeared to be influenced by variation in individual functional status and degree to which people were able *to successfully modify culturally grounded beliefs about dependence upon technology.*

Significantly one of the patients became a leading advocate for disabled rights in Canada after she adopted the portable respirator. This dynamic of independence through dependence on improving technologies is a key factor behind the growing disabled rights movement.

These polio victims confronted a new technology after years of working to free themselves from an older, more intrusive, and limiting technology. Amputees have long benefited from workable artificial limbs. In one of the first major studies of how wearers of prostheses felt about their artificial limbs, carried out by Jerome Silber and Sydelle Silverman in 1958, a surprising number (61 percent) claimed that they forgot they were an amputee "most of the time," and 7 percent even claimed they forgot "all of the time." Careful psychological testing subsequently revealed that these numbers were somewhat exaggerated but that amputees (in this case war veterans) do have a tremendous ability to adapt to their new situation by maintaining feelings of "bodily integrity and adequacy" through denial. More surprisingly, almost half the amputees claimed to be able to do "as much" as non-amputees and 14 percent claimed to be able to do "somewhat more." In what the authors considered a similar pattern of denial, 61 percent of the amputees said that though hooks were "mechanical-looking," they were not unsightly, while 13 percent said they were "as natural looking as any hand":

The amputee's preferences in artificial limbs, and his habits in using them, are evidently not based entirely upon his objective assessment of his functional and social needs. They are influenced also by emotional factors arising from the meaning he attaches to the wearing of artificial limbs.

This survey demonstrates once again that body image and cultural attitudes toward technologies are relatively flexible, constructed and reconstructed in society and its subcultures again and again.

Contemporary medical cyborgs view technologies pragmatically and then construct their ideologies. Attitudes toward human-machine integration are plastic. Quality of life is subjective but, as the different decisions of all of these patients show, it is acted upon. Machine integration and a declining quality of life might lead to suicide, while machine integration and an improving quality of life can lead to growing independence and activity. There is no clear line between survival and pleasure, so it is not surprising that the responses of penile prosthesis recipients follows the pattern of other medical cyborgs; performance precedes politics.

PENILE PROSTHETICS

Patients' needs drive the development of new cyborg technologies, but the doctors, bureaucrats, and businessmen control it. And I use the term "men" deliberately. Of the hundreds of key players named and described in the research, virtually *none* are women. Women play a role in judging the social impact of the technology and certainly they are present as patients and wives of patients as well as nurses and technicians, but as doctor-inventors, surgeons, NIH bureaucrats, or corporate leaders they are almost entirely absent. This gendering of the invention of and the surgical interventions in the body supports feminist analysis of the patriarchal underpinnings of contemporary technoscience. Therefore it should come as no surprise that the malfunctioning penis has been a major focus of these interventions.

Early attempts at curing this specifically male malady were limited to the use of internal medicines such as potions and herbs and the use of surrogate partners (preferably virgins, at least according to the *Bible*, which describes King David's unsuccessful treatment). In 1688, Regneri De Graf discovered that he could induce erections in a dead man by injecting the penis with fluid using the forerunner of the modern syringe, which he invented.

Little noticeable progress was made until the 1900s, when various doctors began direct surgery on the penis. Between 1908 and 1935, doctors made a number of attempts to reconstruct damaged organs using implants of human or animal bone and cartilage. In 1936, they achieved the first success with rib cartilage. In 1950, the first artificial implant was successful, and in 1960, Dr. Pearman improved such implants with the use of perforated acrylic materials. "Pearman's Penis" inaugurated the charming tradition of naming artificial penises after their inventors.

The next great advance in prosthetic penile technology was a vacuum penis that users could inflate by squeezing a small pump hidden in the scrotum and deflate by pressing a release button on the pump. Dr. F. Brantley Scott and his team at Baylor Hospital designed their "implantable, inflatable prosthesis" as a modification of an "implantable, dynamic, artificial sphincter." "Scott's inflatable prosthesis," Dr. Domeena Renshaw commented in an editorial for the *Journal of the American Medical Society*, "confirms that phallic worship is alive and well in the United States today."

Despite this proliferation of artificial male genitalia, some theorists argue that the penis is disappearing and a crisis of masculinity is upon us. The Canadian postmodern philosophers, Arthur and Marilouise Kroker, for example, have announced that this "panic penis" is part of the "panic sex" system in contemporary America:

> No longer the old male cock as the privileged sign of patriarchal power and certainly not the semiotician's dream of the decentered penis which has, anyway, already vanished into the ideology of the phallus, but the *postmodern penis* which becomes an emblematic sign of sickness, disease, and waste ... the penis, both as protuberance and ideology, is already a spent force.

Yet the penis continues to rise, and fall, and rise and fall again (sometimes thanks to a little pump), and patriarchy hardly seems to have dissolved, although there are indeed signs of panic. Perhaps simply "decentering" the penis is enough to make some people fear the end of the world. But not to worry; technoscience has come to the rescue. Even for men whose "manhood" has been weakened by alcohol, stress, age, and other injuries of time, contemporary biomedicine offers a prosthesis sufficient for lust, perhaps even love, and certainly for the signification of power. The cyborg penis is quite the fitting sign for postmodern patriarchy: threatened, inconsistent, yet in the end adaptable and bolstered by technology, and so still functioning. But how is the pomo penis working out for the individual cyborg man?

Studies of the recipients of penile implants have uncovered some interesting outcomes. A very large percentage do not reveal to others, even their sexual partners, that they have an implant. There are secret cyborgs among us! One patient admitted that when his sexual partners asked him why his penis was so large, he would tell them "It's just the way you make me feel." In one study, almost 20 percent of recipients tried to hide their penis from strangers while using rest rooms, because a rigid implant makes it semierect. Somewhat more surprising, 10 percent became exhibitionists; some men even partially inflated their vacuum implants before going out. While men reported a fair amount of satisfaction in many studies (up to 90 percent in one), more careful research that included interviews with partners as well as patients revealed that actual rates of satisfaction may be much lower. For example 40 percent of one study reported malfunctions, dreams about the prosthesis "blowing up," and anxiety about having a foreign object in the body. Even one patient who was very outspoken about his vacuum prosthesis displayed a great deal of distress. According to the study: "He seemed to relieve his anxieties through bragging, telling other men to 'eat their hearts out' and saying he was called the 'pump man.'"

But perhaps the doctors were projecting and he was not really distressed. Dr. Richard Manning (a pseudonym) described his transformation into a cyborg lover as a regaining of control, masculinity, and harmony. Here he recounts a discussion with his doctor before the operation:

> But wait. Once its done, how will I feel? Will I be different? "Lets hope so!" was his reply. He said that after about a month I would feel that I could have an erection any old time I wanted to—for as long as I wanted to. That's more dependability and staying power than most men enjoy. So the implant can't be all bad. Thinking back, I knew there were times even when I was young that I simply could not produce an erection at the moment when I wanted to. . . . Aha! Once you've had the implant, there are very few excuses available. But who needs or wants excuses then? A mighty pleasant thought.

After the operation the good doctor takes to calling himself "The Implant Man" and "a hard man to love." In describing his first night of cyborg sex with his wife, he remarks that many "first-time" sexual encounters are far from perfect, since they are "fraught with anxiety, fumbling and even loss of erection on the man's part." But this is not the case "for the man with the silicone helper" because he has control of himself:

> First, the Implant Man starts with a lot of confidence that he will be a fully adequate lover for as long as his lady is interested. He will not wilt, and

that's a given. This increases *her* confidence and relaxation level. Having hopefully been a successful lover before his impotence set in, he will not waste his energies now on performance worries. The Implant Man makes sure he has a tube of water soluble lubricant such as KY handy. He remembers that love-making takes time—the more time the better. He inflates and deflates discretely—not secretly, but discretely. He concentrates fully on his partner. Success likely follows.

Just how one is supposed "discreetly" to handle the complex technology of cyborg sex, especially one's own technological apparatus, while concentrating "fully" on one's partner, I do not know. No doubt this is just an ideal to strive for as the technodocs quest to create the perfect penis. Unfortunately, as it is with many of the pump or implant men, perfection remains unreachable, but pleasure is possible at least.

Penile prostheses have allowed many men to share *le petit mort* (the "little death," as the French term orgasm) with their partners again. And again. But while cyborg technologies enhance life for some people, for others, they painfully extend death instead. Death lies at the end of the cyborg life cycle just as it does for humans, despite our fantasies of immortality.

NEOMORTS, LIVING CADAVERS, AND IMMORTALS

The true marriage of human form and technology is death.
—Mark Pauline

What will it even mean to be "dead" in the future? Some predict it may soon be possible to cool living human bodies down to near (or even past) freezing, suspending life processes, perhaps so people could be revived at a later date. In fact, by primitive standards, it's already happened—for example, in cases of extreme hypothermia. The can of worms this might open is boggling to consider. And yet, enthusiasts for this nascent field of "cryonics" answer moral quandaries and strict definitions of death by asking, "Why pass *binary* laws for an *analog* world?"
— David Brin

Linda Hogle's graduate work involved watching people die. In the United States and Germany she waited in the rooms of terminally ill patients who had decided to donate organs, observing what happened to them and their organs. It was both fascinating and scary. While the patients were alive, the nurses would talk to them encouraging them to keep living. But as soon as the heart and lungs stopped, everything changed. A new team of medical personnel, called procurement specialists, would replace the intensive care team. They would bring in special equipment and cover the donor's face and genitals with cloth. Now there were more people working on the body than when it was alive. If problems arose at this stage, the medical personnel would talk to the machines. The cyborg is now what is called "single dead."

Chemicals and machines keep the body running in order to preserve the organs. At a certain point there is legal brain death; harvesting may begin, though it is now much harder to keep the organs viable. This is "double dead." Finally the system collapses and the organs begin to decay. They can no longer be harvested. This is "triple dead."

Cyborgization has radically refigured death, creating a whole new class of medical and ethical issues: the conversion of the patient to a donor-cyborg and the resultant dehumanization, the management of the differing needs of the organs, and how the "spare parts" of the donor-cyborg are seeds for new cyborgs. The line between living and dead, human and not human, has never been vaguer.

Stuart Youngner, a leading commentator on the "new" death, describes the treatment of a patient he calls Janet in his article, "Some Must Die." Twenty-two weeks into her pregnancy a blood vessel burst in her head ("spontaneous ruptured cerebral aneurysm"), and she was, for all intents and purposes, dead. Within 24 hours doctors had declared her brain-dead, but her fetus still lived. The hospital picked an elite team of nurses to care for Janet and her child until a birth was possible.

Although Janet was legally dead, the nurses were convinced that she could hear music (her heart rate seemed to change in response), and some believed that her "soul" was still there. As one nurse explained, they knew she was dead but "*felt* she was alive." Her hair and nails grew. Her baby grew. What is death if, as in this case, healthy life can spring from it?

Youngner points out that some health care professionals do not like the term "brain death" because it implies that there is a difference between brain death and death. But is that not the case? In one sense, Janet's body was not dead, thanks to the machines that sustained it. Her intelligence was gone, but maybe not her soul. As a cyborg she was less than human, more than dead.

Some people today, if facing death, would probably gladly sacrifice their humanness for a semilife such as Janet's, but many more people fear that their death will be delayed unnecessarily by medical technology; thus the popularity of right-to-die laws such as the ones in Oregon and the Netherlands.

There are three different definitions of death: when the heart and lungs stop; when the whole brain ceases activity; and the end of activity in the higher brain. The drive for donor organs pushes society toward the more liberal definitions. Organs are now being harvested "from non-heart-beating cadavers whose hearts could in some cases be started again." Inevitably we have to ask: Are we taking organs from people who are still technically alive?

The " brain death" definition became prevalent in the 1960s in the United States and most of Europe to facilitate organ harvesting and justify turning off ventilators. Many brain-dead people's hearts beat naturally. They are called "heart-beating cadavers," or "neomorts." Sometimes when a heart stops it can be restarted, or machines can take its place, and this is called by some doctors a "non-heart-beating cadaver. But if doctors use this "heart stops equals death" criteria, they can harvest organs even if the brain is still active.

At least one hospital, the University of Pittsburgh Medical Center, has tried to implement this standard. Their protocol permitted full-code responses to help preserve organs even when the patient had specified that he or she did not want such measures taken. So a person who wanted to die naturally could, upon being declared dead because her heart has stopped beating and her lungs have stopped breathing, find herself partially resuscitated so that her organs would be optimally fresh for transplant. The University of Pittsburg wanted to use two minutes of heart stoppage as the criteria for death, instead of the more common six to seven minutes. This meant that some patients could "be subjected to invasive, potentially distressing and harmful procedures. . . ." For Renée Fox, this is "death by protocol." She quotes Paul Ramsey in saying that such policies make every single one of us merely "a useful precadaver."

Eventually the university changed its protocol to allow patient-donors to die in peace with their families present before their organs were harvested. This change resulted not because of the dubious ethics of the original approach, but merely because the revisions would produce just as many organs but less "stress" for (that is, complaints from) families.

The pressure to produce more and better organs will always conflict with the health and dignified death of potential organ donors. Other scandals have surfaced, such as hospitals administering drugs to dying patients to preserve organs. The Regional Organ Bank of Illinois tried to implement a protocol that would have severely limited informed consent by allowing hospitals to treat the kidneys of newly dead patients in a solution to make them better transplant organs before obtaining permission for the organ's use. The bank withdrew the policy under sustained criticism.

That great crusader for death, Dr. Jack Kevorkian, has linked his campaign for euthanasia with organ transplantation. He advocates allowing condemned criminals to donate their organs for transplantation, and a specific goal of his physician-assisted suicide program is to increase the number of available organs.

In 1994 the American Medical Association (AMA) supported the harvest of organs from anencephalic infants (infants born with brain stems but no brain). To quote the AMA:

> It is normally required that the donor be legally dead before permitting the harvesting of organs. The use of the anencephalic infant as a live donor is a limited exception to the general standard because of the fact that the infant has never experienced, and will never experience, consciousness.

Stuart Youngner notes that the AMA does not define the infants as dead, simply that they are not human and so can be killed for their organs.

We can see that the politics of death and the politics of transplantation are becoming closely intertwined. Death for some determines life for others. Should convicts be able to donate organs? Should patients be able to choose suicide and donate their organs? Should doctors be able to choose definitions of life/consciousness and death/nonhuman in order to maximize the production of usable organs?

Yet death can be appealing on other levels. As the artist Mark Pauline notes, many people love technology because it seems to promise a way "through" death by "marriage." The futurists of Italy—fascist sympathizers—also made this link between death and technology:

> We will conquer the seemingly unconquerable hostility that separates our human flesh from the metal of motors.
>
> —F.T. Marinetti

This is echoed in the Spanish fascist cry of "Long Live Death!" and in some fundamentalists' (Christian and Islamic) love of death as the only way to heaven. Freud thought that thanatos, the love of death, was a psychological aberration particular to modern man, which may be so, but hatred and fear of death seem much stronger these days than love or even acceptance. As one British commentator, Derek Morgan, notes in his discussion of legal definitions of death: "What appears to be an instinctive fear of death seems to be reflected in an eerie silence on the part of the law. This dread of death shapes much of what is done."

Dread often inspires action. Whole movements, such as the Extropians, have turned immortality into a fundamental political position and they depend on cyborgian technologies to realize it. Our culture passionately dreams of immortality, as with the ever-popular vampires and the *Highlander* movies and TV show. Immortality is a staple in science fiction, although SF is also particularly good at demonstrating the downside to immortality.

One story shows how, if people were immortal except for accidents, we would all become incredible cowards. It is one thing to go out for a drive and risk shortening one's life by a few decades; it is another thing to risk losing thousands of years. Needless to say, in the story rock climbing and war both became very unpopular.

The lust for immortality certainly has its limits, as Peter Alldridge observes:

> A fear which has for years affected many people, and which is the basis of many legends, is the fear of becoming "undead." A person who is "undead" lacks qualities both of the live and the dead. The combination of advancing medical technology, cruel courts, and the fanaticism of the protoplasm obsessed, *soi-disant* "pro-life" school have made the prospect of being numbered among the undead very much more of a reality than any vampire or werewolf ever had.

Renée Fox and Judith Swazey have been particularly concerned that the drive for immortality is based less on an appreciation of life than on a fear of death. They cite the work of the theologian Paul Ramsey, who argues for "a religious sense that death is not an evil that ought always to be opposed." Ramsey quotes Socrates:

> Now it is time that we were going, I to die and you to live, but which of us has the happier prospect, is unknown to anyone but God.

He says that understanding death in this way might save doctors from the "triumphalist temptation to slash and suture our way to eternal life." But can scientists resist the temptation to splice their way to eternity? The technoscience most likely to produce immortality is genetics, the topic of the next chapter.

FIGURE 1. Diego Rivera's beautiful mural, Pan American Unity, graces San Francisco City College. It expresses the liberatory potential of cyborgization by showing Goddess and Machine in productive harmony. On one level Rivera was calling for a synthesis of North and South, but clearly the mural cries out for transcending all simple dichotomies. *Pan American Unity* by Diego Rivera.

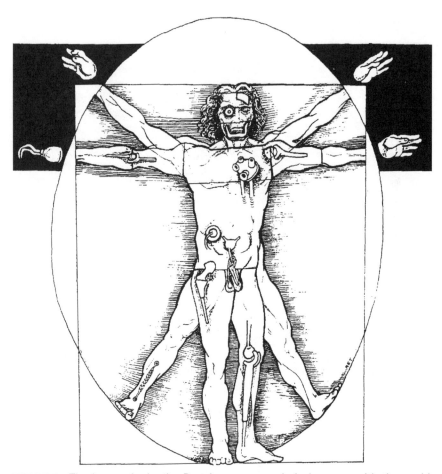

FIGURE 2. The human body, the Renaissance man, is in harmony with the world geometric. As natural "man" we put ourselves at the center; so to as cyborg. Here the artist Bob Thawley has updated Leonardo de Vinci's famous drawing with a catalog of contemporary medical prosthesis. The proliferation of effective artificial body parts and the resulting prolongation of many people's lives is one of the success stories of cyborg medicine. The expensive prolongation of death and the reduction of the singing body electric to a rather inefficient mechanical system, and a source of commodities, is part of the story as well.

FIGURE 3. Here I have reworked part of the front piece illustration, which is also pictured, for Leviathan by Thomas Hobbes. *Leviathan* is itself a cyborg creature made up of many people. The idea is an old one, going back at least to Aristotle. The postmodern nation-state isn't just people, of course. It incorporates a whole range of technologies including laws, bureaucracies, and many different types of machines, especially computers. Citizens are cyborg citizens now, and territory is infrastructure.

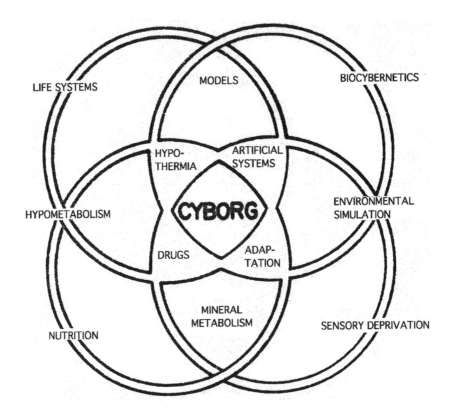

FIGURE 4. This diagram is from the only NASA report that focused on the idea of the cyborg. It shows that even though the term cyborg makes many a bureaucrat nervous, the concept of the cyborg is situated at the heart of a number of engineering, scientific, and medical fields. Cyborg symbol reworked by Corey Alexander Grayson.

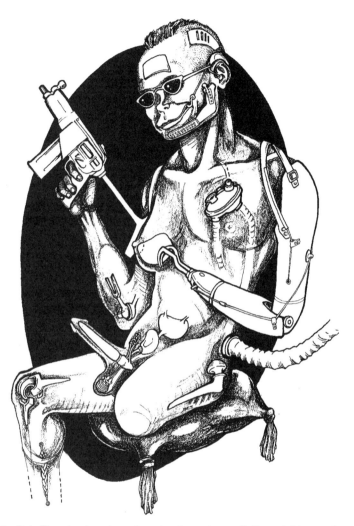

FIGURE 5. Bob Thawley has here imagined a science-fiction nightmare based on the real cyborgian research in medicine and the military that is driving much of the technoscience that lies behind our cyborg society. It is one thing to consider these changes in the abstract; it is quite another to see them, even in artistic representations. Phallic gun and prosthetic penis, programmable organs and programmed grimace—the marriage of war and technology breeds nightmares.

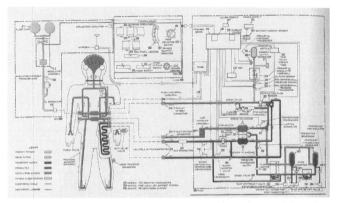

FIGURE 6. Without technology humans could not exist in space. It is one of the major sites for practical cyborg engineering and so it is fitting that the very word cyborg was created to help us think about how humans might be modified to make space our natural environment. Humans don't go into space, organic-machinic systems do, as this foldout diagram from an Apollo astronaut's handbook makes clear. One wonders how useful this information would be to a cyborg astronaut in trouble out in space, but fortunately most such crises are managed by the whole team of humans and machines, from ground control on up, a perfect example of a meta-cyborg system.

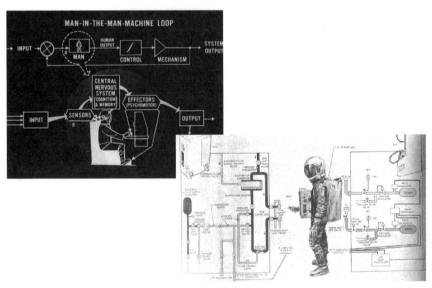

FIGURE 6B/C. Here are several more NASA diagrams showing the relationship of life-support system to the living astronaut. Notice how the human is often portrayed as a sort of black box, an icon represented by a little picture or diagram. The real interfaces of the human system with the machinic one are actually much more complicated, and intimate, but are seldom shown in public or even engineering documents. The intimacy of the interface is something NASA doesn't like to talk about, just as it has always been shy about embracing such concepts as the cyborg.

FIGURE 7. While it really has not been commented upon, in the deep sea as in outer space the human needs technology to survive. For free diving that technology must be replete with effective interfaces especially as human performance often degrades precipitously at the outer edges of the free diver's range. The equipment worn here by Terence Tycell includes computer's monitoring of the gas mixing that allow deep free diving, which does not destroy the human part of the system with the "rapture of the deep." A different rapture calls to many humans who evoke images of mother ocean to explain their desire to live in the seas. One of the first genetically engineered posthumans could well be mer-creatures who will live machine-augmented lives permanently in the four-fifths of the Earth's surface that is water.

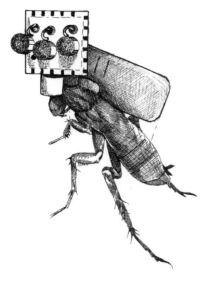

FIGURE 8. All cyborgs aren't necessarily part human. Biocomputers, artificial life programs, and genetically manipulated mice are all cyborgs in different ways. This is "roboroach," drawn by Joshua Gray. Roboroach was engineered at Tokyo University so he could be remotely controlled through electrical shocks, a dream many a city dweller has no doubt had. The big backpack with electronic receiver, microprocessor, and connections to electrodes implanted in roboroach's brain makes it possible for a human operator to direct the creature at will. On another level this makes a system of human-machine-roach where the roach-machine interface is hardwired implant, the human-machine external controls, and the human-roach the machine.

FIGURE 9. In academic discourse, gender and sex have been carefully delineated as fundamentally different. Sex is the anatomical markers of genitalia, secondary sexual characteristics, hormones, and DNA. Gender is the socially constructed system of male-female behavior and signs and the recognized variations such as lesbian, gay man, tomboy, and transvestite. These differences between the categories of sex and gender are beginning to collapse under the combined weight of medical advances and direct cultural attack. Thanks to the hormones and knives of doctors, transsexuals are proliferating and more enlightened medical practices have opened a space for intersexuals. Meanwhile, transgender activists are claiming the right to construct their own gendered space inhabited by transgirls, transboys, androgynies, and bidykes and all the possible in-betweens, free of any biological determinants at all. John Kopp's image evokes the combination of freedom and desire that empowers these changes.

the hopeful monsters of genetic engineering

THE RHETORIC OF LIFE:
DNA AND DR. FRANKENSTEIN'S DREAMS

Is it possible? Who knows? Is it natural? So what. Is it good science? You bet.
— A scientist (Danny Devito)
on adapting a male (Arnold Schwarzenegger)
to carry a child in the movie *Junior*

Whenever there is an advance in a cyborg technoscience such as genetics, you can count on a gaggle of public commentators with nice hair to mention Frankenstein. Hardly ever do they differentiate between Dr. Frankenstein and the unnamed monster he created. Why is it so hard to remember that it is Frankenstein's *monster* who horrifies us? The conflation signifies that the doctor is monstrous in our minds. Equally revealing is that Mary Shelley never actually refers to Frankenstein as a doctor; only Victor or Baron Frankenstein. But it is the doctors we fear today, so we have made him a doctor, and a monster as well.

Women have always had the opportunity of creating new life through pregnancy. But that process was impossible to control, and it is still not available to men. Now, with the reproductive technologies discussed in the previous chapter and the promise of genetic engineering, we can seriously dream of fulfilling the most extreme creation desires, from superchildren to bizarre chimeras. Few realize just how sophisticated genetic engineering is today. There are machines that produce DNA sequences on demand. Others "slice and dice" DNA with precision, performing in minutes tasks that would take humans days.

Our ability to manipulate genes is rushing ahead of our understanding of what they do and how they do it. To help bridge this gap, the U.S. government launched the Human Genome Project. This multimillion-dollar initiative has cataloged all of the human genome with the goal of perfecting gene sequencing technology and the bioinformatic (computerization of biological information) apparatus. While the sequence of human DNA is inherently useful knowledge, the truly important information is knowing which part of the DNA does what, and that is beyond the scope of the project. Meanwhile many private companies have focused on understanding human DNA. They want to own it.

Andrew Kimbrell has written a frightening book called *The Human Body Shop: The Engineering and Marketing of Life*. He shows just how far this commodification of the human body has progressed through a long history that includes slavery. But even while slavery survives as indentured servitude and in the horrible ancient tradition of "trafficking" in women, the human body is being redefined as just another source of saleable commodities and, therefore, profits.

It began with blood, the first body product that developed a real market. When I was traveling through Greece in 1972, I stayed at a youth hostel in Thessolonika and had a firsthand experience with the blood market that shocked me. I had taken a train in from Yugoslavia and because I had been exploring the powers of apricot brandy that some Romany people were generously sharing with me, I do not really remember getting to the hostel. The next morning, a bit worse for wear, I staggered out into the Greek sunshine to be accosted by a crowd of men with big black mustaches who were yelling at me in broken English, trying to buy my blood.

Their interest waned when I showed them my passport with my blood type, the all-too-common O positive but they did tell me that I could sell my blood for good money down the street. It turned out that Greeks really do not like to give blood. The fathers of children who need transfusions, especially of rare types, had discovered that young travelers from Western Europe and North America were more than willing to sell their bodily fluids, and so every morning outside the youth hostel new potential donors were met as I was. Sometimes the owners of rare blood would spark bidding wars between desperate fathers whose children needed the same blood type. It was actually quite horrifying. Several young men and women I knew gave more blood than was safe in a desperate attempt to meet the demand and assuage the anguish in the eyes of the fathers they saw every morning. Others I knew sold their blood even knowing they had hepatitis.

One such knave was a young, charming, upper-class Englishman who was on his way home from several years in Katmandu after sending all his money up in hashish smoke. We went to the blood bank together because even for my boring blood they were paying the equivalent of $17 in drachmas. Good money for a poor traveler. However, I have a problem with blood. The thought of it makes me dizzy, and giving it made me almost faint. So they would not take it! They thought I was ill. Yet they gladly drained a pint from the yellow-tinted Brit without a qualm. Raw capitalism is prone to such simple allocation errors.

British economist Richard Titmuss proved this when he brilliantly analyzed how blood is collected: he found that blood banks received more and better-quality blood from volunteers than from those who were paid for their blood. Britain collects almost all blood voluntarily. In the United States, despite strong donation programs, much of the blood is bought from poor people. The blood stock in the United Kingdom far surpass those of the United States in both quantity and quality. Still, many people assume that a commodity has value only if it has a price. What if blood is worth money but the lives of the poor are not? Then they are bled to death.

Which is what happened in Nicaragua. The scandal of the Plasmaferesis blood clinic was revealed by the newspaper editor Pedro Joaquin Chamorro. Owned by the dictator Somoza, the clinic was taking so much plasma from the poor in Managua that many died. The blood was sold to the United States. After he had exposed the scandal, Chamorro was assassinated, and the resulting popular uprising started with chants of "Vampire Somoza!" at the burning of the Plasmaferesis clinic and ended, 18 months later, with the collapse of the Somoza regime. There were many other causes for the revolt, and it would have been impossible without the established Sandinista revolutionary movement, but the blood bank (what a great label for these institutions) of the dictator was an important catalyst.

In the United States there has been a long legal struggle over whether or not blood is a commodity. Early court cases found that it was not, and courts allowed the medical community to regulate blood and blood products, but over time, especially as blood has become worth more, it has become increasingly commodified. Kimbrell reports that by the middle of the 1980s the United States was the leading exporter of blood, then a $2 billion market; so dominant is the United States in the production of blood products (60 percent of the world's total) that it has been dubbed "the OPEC of blood." The United States processes its blood for the rare factors that are particularly valuable. The Red Cross also sells millions of liters of plasma that it collects for free, and over four hundred commercial blood centers buy and sell blood from the poor.

The market for rare blood factors led to another major step in the commodification of blood. Margaret Green has a rare type of AB negative blood. In her tax returns she claimed as business expenses her trips to Serologicals, Inc. to sell her plasma and the cost of her special diet and medications. Eventually the tax court agreed with her claim and granted her the status of a "container" so that she could claim a full deduction for her travel. However, the court denied her claim for the depletion of her minerals, ruling that her body was not a "geological mineral resource."

The relentless spread of this "body for sale" culture includes the commercialization of reproduction as well as the culture of transplants, as seen in earlier chapters. Genetics has taken this process the furthest with the actual patenting of natural processes.

Kimbrell traces this strange legal story carefully. In 1971 a microbiologist who worked for General Electric applied, with GE, for a U.S. patent on an oil-eating microbe. The Patent and Trademark Office (PTO) rejected the application, but the Court of Customs and Patent Appeals overruled the rejection, stating that it was "without legal significance" that the patented object was alive. In 1980 the U.S. Supreme Court upheld that ruling.

In 1988, the PTO granted Patent No. 4,736,866 to Harvard University on a living animal, a transgenic mouse that possessed genes from chickens and humans. The Harvard researchers had made the mouse susceptible to cancer so they named it Oncomouse. The rights to the patent were bought by DuPont, which had financed the research. Oncomouse was modified at the germ line level, which means that the modifications are reproduced when the mouse is mated or cloned (somatic alterations are genetic engineering interventions that are not passed on). The PTO mistakenly accepted a great deal of language that the Harvard and DuPont lawyers had included as wishful thinking. The patent actually grants Harvard and DuPont the rights to any "transgenic nonhuman mammal" whose cells have been altered to make it susceptible to cancer.

Four years later, in 1992, three more genetically engineered mice were patented, including a second one from Harvard that will suffer, through all its generations, from an enlarged prostate gland.

When the Supreme Court allowed the patenting of the oil-eating microbe, it specified that humans could not be patented because the Thirteenth Amendment of the Constitution outlaws slavery, but the court failed to mention "genetically engineered human tissues, cells, and genes." Kimbrell notes that an engineered kidney, arm, or other body part might legally be patentable. This certainly applies to genes, as the sad case of John Moore illustrates. His genes were patented by someone else.

A leukemia sufferer, Moore had his spleen removed in 1976 at UCLA. His doctor and a researcher, David Golde and Shirley Quan, used part of his spleen to breed Moore's white blood cells. Moore recovered, and it turned out that his white blood cells produced strong anticancer and antibacteria biochemicals. In 1981, Golde, Quan, and UCLA applied for a patent on the genetic information in Moore's cells. Over the next few years, they licensed Moore's genes to a number of corporations.

Moore found this out and, as a good American, he sued. The California Supreme Court found that while Moore did not own his own cell line and had no property rights to "the tissues of his own body," he was due some money since his signed consent form did not give UCLA or his doctors the right to profit from his genes. Several other such cases have confirmed that an individual cannot patent part of his or her body but an institution such as the University of California can. It gets worse.

Patent No. 5,061,620 means that the genetic information in your stem cells, the cells in your bone marrow that produce blood, belong to Systemix, Inc., of Palo Alto, California. The patent should have covered only the way Systemix extracts these cells, a very difficult process, but the PTO, for some inexplicable reason, granted a patent that "covers the stem cells themselves."

In 1991, an NIH researcher filed for a patent on 2,337 brain genes; the next year he started his own company with $70 million in venture capital. The European Patent Office has received applications from Baylor Medical School to patent genetically altered human mammary glands. Numerous other people have attempted to patent genes, but as of this writing none has been approved. Looking at the recent history, one cannot be optimistic about future attempts.

The patenting of your body is not the only political issue of genetic engineering. One of the most volatile is "Frankenstein foods"—genetically engineered grains, fruits, and vegetables. This has become a major public controversy in Europe, where the labeling of such foods has led to a massive drop in their sales, and in North America. Not only is it unknown whether or not there are any health risks for the consumers of such food, but there is a real danger that engineered genes might escape into other species or have unanticipated consequences. Already it has been discovered that corn engineered to resist pests also kills monarch butterflies. Other genetic engineering issues include whether multinational corporations should be allowed to patent agricultural biota in the Third World, or whether the human body is an object to be bought and sold in parts or as a working whole. Genetic therapies raise the standard political issues of cyborg medicine:

- Are the experiments truly based on informed consent?
- Will everyone have equal access to such therapies or just the rich and well insured?
- Will insurance companies use genetic knowledge to discriminate against those with "bad genes"?
- How does the quality of a patient's life balance against the quality of that patient's death?

More than other cyborg technosciences, genetics foregrounds the issue of human versus posthuman. Genetics offers the most likely, and certainly the most effective, way of using artificial evolution to produce intelligent nonhuman creatures. Who is monitoring the dangers of such eugenic engineering or other potential disasters?

Biowar research (as discussed in Chapter 4) or careless genetic engineering could produce a terrible biological accident. What if scientists accidentally created a form of deadly cancer as contagious as a typical cold? Unlikely as such a scenario might be, it is technically possible and therefore it is a risk worth preventing. In the United States, where the National Institutes of Health is in charge of both regulating and promoting genetic engineering, there have been cases in which scientists have helped judge "the propriety and scientific merit of gene experiments or procedures in which they may have a significant financial or personal interest."

In 1980 Dr. Martin Cline, a scientist from the University of California, tried to treat two women suffering from thalassemia (a genetic defect of the red blood cell repair system) using a genetically engineered cell. When the local review board disallowed the procedure, he performed it abroad without his patients' consent. It was a failure, and he was reprimanded by the NIH. The resulting scandal produced the President's Commission for the Study of Ethical Problems in Medicine and Biomedical and Behavioral Research. The commission looked into several issues but ultimately recommended banning only one line of research, that on human-animal hybrids.

This "mermaid" ban was greeted with some skepticism. Kimbrell quotes a *New York Times* editorial:

> The commission has boldly vetoed animal-human hybrids, which are on no one's agenda, but has tiptoed around more concrete issues. Let mermaids be free of bans, at least until someone has serious plans of creating them. The more tangible problem is whether to permit heritable changes to the human gene set.

Ironically, even the mermaid ban recommendation was ignored, and now research on such hybrids is thriving.

In 1986, the World Council of Churches called for a ban on all research "involving the genetic engineering of the human germline." Three years later the genetic engineering of humans began with an experiment that inserted genetic markers into immune cells from cancer patients. The reintroduced cells helped chart which cells still worked as patients died. The experiment went forward, but only after intense public protests by scientists and public critics like Jeremy Rifkin forced the NIH to revise its guidelines so that more review would be necessary for human genetic experiments, especially those that can affect future generations.

But in 1990 a more serious and controversial experiment was performed. Dr. French Anderson and his NIH team injected a girl suffering from "bubble boy syndrome" (a failure of the immune system) with a billion cells with a new gene in them. Yet it was impossible to determine if the experiment worked because the girl had been taking medication to treat the syndrome. Even fellow geneticists accused Anderson of using the treatment for publicity, and many scientists criticized the scientific basis for his experiment. Anderson, who had been a reviewer approving NIH funding for gene research for years, formed a company with a venture capitalist to exploit this research, Genetics Therapy, Inc. In 1990, they hired the former head of the NIH oversight committee: foxes starting chicken farms.

Despite the more immediate dangers of genetic engineering (genetic screening, the patenting of nature, Frankenstein foods, biological warfare, and horrible accidents) it is cloning that has captured the public's imagination. In 1997, Scottish researchers used a spark of electricity, just like Baron Frankenstein, to stimulate an adult cell to regress to a point where it could reproduce the whole organism. This set off another round in the ongoing public debate on the regulation of science and the future of the human. Yet it is doubtful that these debates will greatly affect technoscience itself.

CLONING: A MULTIPLICATION OF MES

According to Sen. Sam Brownback (R-Kan.), cloning people "for the purpose of bringing new life into the world is intrinsically evil and should be absolutely prohibited." Sen. Kit Bond's (R-Mo.) condemnation is just as sweeping: "Science has given us partial-birth abortions and Dr. Kevorkian's assisted suicide. We should say no to these scientific advances and no to the cloning of human embryos." David Baltimore, President of Cal Tech and a Nobel Prize–winning scientist believes that: "What looks to be revolutionary one day is common practice the next," and that the public may come to accept human cloning. Randolfe Wicker, of the Clone Rights United Front (CRUF), told a House committee that: "Every person's DNA is his or her personal property," a statement for the rights of cloners, not clones. As William Saletan pointed out in *Mother Jones,* this means that not only do you "own your own clone," but parents "collectively own" their children as well. According to the Cyborg Bill of Rights, sentient clones should own themselves, cloned body parts would belong to the DNA donor, and neither could be patented. A creature in between these two extremes, for instance a dog with a partially human brain, would have to pass the cyborg citizen test to qualify as a citizen, but even without citizenship it could receive other rights.

Saletan observes that most people approach the cloning debate with assumptions from the abortion wars or struggles around gay parenting. This can lead to some confusing conclusions:

> Some pro-choicers pretend that cloning is just a small step from gay parenthood and in vitro fertilization, but it's not. Cloning abolishes the genetic difference between parent and child. If gay parenthood means that Heather has two mommies, cloning doesn't just mean that Heather has one mommy: it means that, genetically, Heather *is* her mommy. So if Heather's mommy has a husband and daughter, then genetically, Heather is her sister's mommy and her daddy's wife.

Antiabortion forces generally oppose cloning, but since cloning does not involve conception, some "pro-lifers" believe clones are not even alive! Sen. Orrin Hatch (R-Ut.) reasons that since clones are just "asexually produced totipotent cells," he doubts they could be human.

The clone wars are just starting. In early 1998, heavy scientific lobbying defeated a bill that would have made cloning a human a felony. The bill was in response to the physicist G. Richard Seed's announcement that he would attempt such cloning. The debate over the bill revealed some surprising positions. Many scientists would rather have a federal agency dominated by geneticists and biotech companies control cloning, instead of laws and legislation that are hard to change.

Soon after President Clinton called for a ban on human cloning, the FDA asserted that it would block any cloning attempts, although it has never regulated *in vitro* clinics. The 750 biotech companies in the Biotechnology Industry Organization supported this move. As Lori Andrews explains, they hope the ban will prevent the outlawing of all cloning research by nervous legislators and that the "organization realizes that if the FDA can regulate human cloning, it is likely to permit cloning once the procedure becomes safer."

In Europe, 19 countries led by France signed a pact prohibiting "any intervention seeking to create a human being genetically identical to another human being whether living or dead." Britain refused to sign because it was too strict, and Germany considered it too liberal because it was less stringent than already existing German legislation against research with human embryos. President Chirac of France stressed that for a ban on human cloning to be successful, it must be international.

He could have added unanimous, for Dr. Seed has already promised that if U.S. authorities intervene in his attempt to clone a human, he will move to Tijuana, Mexico. "Dr. Seed will not do human cloning in this country," declared Donna Shalala, the Heath and Human Services Secretary. Seed promised to have a human clone by 1999, a date he has missed already, and professed encouragement at the number of infertile couples who had contacted him, but a few months later he announced that he was cloning himself, with his wife Gloria's help. Seed is 69 and Gloria is "postmenopausal." Secretary Shalala said Seed brings to mind a "mad scientist" and that he was no expert in genetics, fertility, or even biology, though he does have three Harvard degrees. While money may be one of Dr. Seed's main motivations, he is also inspired by the hubris that energizes many technophiles:

> God made man in his own image, therefore, he intended that man should become one with God. Man should have an indefinite life and have indefinite knowledge. And we're going to do it, and this is one step.

His defense of cloning becomes a call for immortality and then for infinite knowledge, a common theme among those advocating all forms of cyborgization, and one that apparently fits some theologies. A Swedish religious group, the Raelians, have offered Seed a laboratory and funding for his cloning.

At least one group of proscience celebrities has come out in favor of cloning higher animals. The International Academy of Humanists issued a statement to that effect signed by 30 of its members, including Francis Crick, Richard Dawkins, Edward O. Wilson, and Kurt Vonnegut, Jr. Several theologians and rabbis also argue that cloning humans would be moral. The general public seems more ambivalent.

Cloning became a public issue with the announcement of the creation of Dolly the cloned sheep, but several important issues have been obscured by all the jokes and protestations. First, scientists have been cloning creatures (insects, reptiles, and amphibians) for some time. That it is finally possible with larger mammals is no surprise to anyone who has followed genetics. Second, and more importantly, she was not cloned so that someday you might have a child-clone or a brain-dead double whose organs you might harvest, although these may well come to pass. Dolly is an investment with a much shorter time frame. She is a prototype factory.

Scientists want to clone large mammals to genetically engineer them, often with added human genes, to produce things humans want. This is called "pharming." Pharm products will eventually include human skin, cartilage, bone, bone marrow, retinal and nerve tissue, as well as hormones, vaccines, and therapeutic biologicals. Eventually pigs or other animals may be modified to produce organs suitable for human transplants. A human woman modified so that her breast milk would include antibiotics will be, of course, a "pharm-woman."

This industry has spent years creating trangenetic animals, or "beast machines," including Oncomouse, discussed above, superpigs and supermice with human genes that help them grow to twice the normal size, sheep with an insect-killing gene from tobacco, salmon with chicken and cattle growth hormones, "geeps" with the faces and horns of goats and the bodies of sheep, tobacco plants with firefly genes that make them glow in the dark, and various plants with freeze-resistant properties from flounder genes.

Scientists have already created production animals, such as the three Genes. Gene, Gene 1, and Gene 2 are bulls who were cloned for semen production in late 1997 by ABS Global (with $65 million in annual sales of bull semen and services to 70 countries). One observer described Gene as "a little factory and it is very cheap to maintain." In early 1998 Advanced Cell Technology in Texas produced two clone calves, George and Charlie, who are prototype living pharmaceutical factories. The next step is to engineer cows who will produce albumin, a blood protein, in their milk. Dolly herself was the forerunner to Molly and Polly, who have been modified with the human gene that produces the blood-clotting protein factor IX.

A few days before George's and Charlie's debut, scientists at the University of Wisconsin-Madison announced the successful cloning of five different species (sheep, pigs, rats, rhesus monkeys, and cattle) using the adult cells of the respective species and the unfertilized eggs of cows. While none of the pregnancies went to term, the scientists are confident they will overcome this last barrier to transspecies clones. The Wisconsin scientists stressed that this might be a way to revive extinct species, and other experts say it could also produce human clones more quickly than other methods. Related techniques could make it possible for pig testes to produce human sperm.

In 1997 Arthur Caplan, director of the Center for Bioethics at the University of Pennsylvania, predicted that there will be a human clone by 2005. So far his prediction looks accurate. In July of 1998, scientists at the University of Hawaii cloned over 50 mice from adult cells, including the first ever clones of clones. This opens up cloning to all sorts of actual applications, from research to pharming to seeking immortality for one's pet.

In August of 1998 Texas A&M University announced that an anonymous couple had donated $2.3 million so that the university would clone their dog, Missy. The university points out that the project, named Missyplicity (after Michael Keaton's cloning film *Multiplicity*) will further advance cloning in many ways, since dogs have complicated reproductive processes and have yet to be cloned successfully.

Research will continue despite public doubts and bizarre possibilities. In 1974, when the first gene was cloned, there was a tremendous uproar as there was for the first *in vitro* fertilizations. Again, in 1993, when the first human embryos were cloned and then destroyed, there was even a *Time* cover story. Now we have Dolly and Molly and Polly, and the discoveries are coming quicker than ever. Eventually these technologies will be accepted because there are cures and money to be made. There is no threshold in sight.

Lee Silver's *Remaking Eden* shows how inevitable human cloning is. Upset about breeding humans to donate biological material to the living? It already happened in 1988 when the parents of a Los Angeles high schooler, Anissa Ayala, had a baby who saved her life (see Chapter 6). Worried about someone stealing a cell and using it to clone a copy? Silver calls this the "Michael Jordon scenario" and points out that it is already technologically possible. Finally, while Aldous Huxley and Jeremy Rifkin obsess about the government's desire to breed docile soldier-workers, it is the parents of the world who will be the strongest advocates for cloning, just as they have pushed for surrogacy and *in vitro* fertilization despite government refusals to fund such research.

There are over 280 *in vitro* fertilization clinics in the United States alone and half of them have the equipment for cloning. While human eggs cost $2,000 each, cloning technologies that use cow eggs, for example, will be cheaper than current approaches. Cloning success rates are up to 5 to 10 percent, close to the 13 percent success rate of frozen human embryos and better than the 7 percent rate for fertilizations of women over 39. Cloning processes will make it much easier to eliminate genetic diseases such as Tay-Sachs', since multiple embryos will make successful gene modifications a matter of persistence instead of luck.

Potential parents might not be the only people pushing for cloning. News in 1997 that scientists at Bath University had created headless frog embryos by turning off certain genes was welcomed by those worried about the shortage of transplant organs. This development is an important step toward the creation of partial human embryos with key organs and a circulatory system but no brain or real body. Some academics argue that harvesting organs from such semicreatures will not violate anyone's rights and would allow everyone to have perfectly compatible organs for transplants. But Oxford ethicist Professor Andrew Linzey disagrees: "It is scientific fascism because we would be creating other beings whose very existence would be to serve the dominant group.... It is morally regressive to create a mutant form of life." This debate opens up the issue of eugenics, which lurks behind all genetic research.

BRAVE NEW WORLD ... ORDER?

Brave New World was greeted more as a metaphor, a compelling parody of the modern condition than as a very real possibility.... Today, Huxley's vision is fast becoming commonplace. Engineering principles and mass production techniques are rushing headlong into the interior regions of the biological kingdom, invading the once sacred texts of life. The genetic code has been broken and scientists are rearranging the very blueprints of life. They are inserting, deleting, recombining, editing, and programming genetic sequences within and between species, laying the foundation for a second creation—an artificial evolution designed with market forces and commercial objectives in mind.

—Jeremy Rifkin

The brave new society consists of biologically engineered classes: alphas, betas, gammas, epsilons, and deltas. Programmed contentment ("I wouldn't want to be an alpha, they work so hard"), the proliferation of legal psychotropic drugs (soma), and government-encouraged promiscuous sex keep most of the consumers (they are hardly citizens) in the brave new world quite content.

Will this be our future? Probably not. If we do reach the point of breeding subintelligent workers, our democracy will be over. Besides, government is not as totally in control in the new world order as it is in *Brave New World*. Instead of genetic engineering by a central authority, semifree markets and dispersed authority will lead to the profligate promulgation of possibilities. The pressure of commodification combined with the argument that we are just meat machines or instruments for passing on genetic information makes for an incredible dehumanization. Robert Lewontin, an insightful observer of the genetic engineering industry, is right when he remarks:

> It is not Dr. Wilmut and Dolly who are a threat to our sense of uniqueness and autonomy, but popularizers like Richard Dawkins who describes us as "gigantic lumbering robots" under the control of our genes that have "created us body and mind."

If we become nothing but our genes, we will have bled most initiative and choice out of the world. And inequalities such as racism and sexism, which people have struggled against for centuries, will become enshrined for all time by science, even if things seem "nice" on the surface. This is the future painted in the science-fiction film *Gattaca*. *Gattaca* is a world designed by positive eugenics, breeding and engineering for improved humans. Negative eugenics, which tries to destroy "inferior" gene lines, was the central idea of Nazism. Many people seem to think that the exterminism of the Nazis is inconceivable now, but today there are many active groups with the same hateful (and scientifically stupid) message.

More frightening is the way nonextremists uncritically accept negative eugenics in various cultures. For instance, of 8,000 abortions of nondefective embryos in Bombay during one four-year period, 7,999 were of females. This led to legislation in some Indian states making it a crime to report the gender of a fetus. Similarly, surveys of doctors in the United States and Europe pose scenarios ("a couple has four daughters and wants a son") in which the majority of doctors admit they would facilitate a sex-selective abortion.

As doctors analyze the genetic code of fetuses with greater accuracy, the pressure to eliminate defective embryos will increase incredibly—a smooth, slippery slope to the abortion of fetuses with below-average intelligence, height, on even looks. Kimbrell sums it up nicely:

> We no longer have political or racial eugenics as practiced earlier in this century, most notably in Nazi Germany, but instead have begun a "commercial" eugenics being peddled by clinics, researches and biotechnology companies for profit. We no longer are preventing the marriage of "undesirables," sterilizing the "unfit," or exterminating races viewed as inferior. But we are creating a new market in genetic trait selection of children; a business peddling the prevention of birth for those that do not meet the expectations of parents; an industry that would destroy the unborn if they do not fit into "the perfect baby" mold, be they female, predisposed to obesity, or potential victims of disease decades into their lives.

I would, however, disagree with Kimbrell that these "commercial" eugenics are not "political." There is nothing apolitical about aborting females because of a preference for males, or about the elimination of those whose DNA has not passed some scientific standard that in the end is based on societal prejudices, such as labeling shortness a disease.

So just how much will genetic engineering be able to do? Michael Gruber, a writer for *Wired*, analyzed several trends at the second Annual "After the Genome" conference in 1997. First, the biotech industry, as measured by employees and capitalization and by the number of genes analyzed, is growing geometrically. Second, the number of well-funded Ph.D's working on seemingly incredible projects, such as linking DNA strands to computer chips for superfast biological testing or building machines to make proteins on demand, comprises a surprisingly large sector of the field. Third:

> The hype that afflicts the software industry is nothing, compared with biotech's bombast. Everything conceivable in the biologic realm has been discussed, worried over, science fictionalized half to death. Of course, we'll cure all disease, live forever, change our shapes, have feathers, grow gills and dwell beneath the sea—ho hum, tell me something I don't know.

One genetic engineer admits that it is hard to tell what might actually happen because when someone announces they are going to attempt a daring new project, "everyone assumes it is already accomplished." Still, one expert told Gruber off the record that by 2010, altering the inherited traits of mammals will be routine and will become a major political issue. In 2020, humans will be altering their germ line regularly for nonmedical reasons, and around 2030 the first generation "of children altered for intelligence, longevity, and appearance" will be growing up, and then things will really get interesting.

Gruber casts about for an analogy to describe how the biotech revolution might impact human society. He rejects the frontier metaphor; rather, he says, we are entering a great Age of Exploration. He reminds us that the European colonization of the Americas and Australia was also a biological experiment, "a monster gene-mix party" that eliminated 90 percent of the New World's indigenous population. He reaches back to those times to resurrect an Italian word that expresses the "ambiguous feelings roused by mighty forces beyond the normal human scale: *la terribilita*.... How horrible, we say, how marvelous!"

cyborg society

prosthetic territories

cybercolonializations

There are places only cyborgs can go. The most obvious are cyberspace, aquaspace (living and working in the deep sea), and outer space, but there are smaller places that also exclude pure humans: the lips of live volcanoes, inside shattered nuclear reactors, and the tiny spaces between and within molecules and atoms. This chapter looks closely at the three first spaces, but the political questions that apply to them are also relevant to other cyborg spaces. Who defines such territories? Who are the border guards? Who owns them? How do they construct the cyborgs that explore and use them?

These are all colonizations of seemingly empty spaces, but in actuality cyberspace is only there when it has content, the deep sea teems with life, and even outer space is far from a perfect vacuum. Still, we think of them as empty, but we shall see how quickly they can be filled by military paradigms, cyborgs, and our dreams. In the long run such new spaces will shape the colonizers. Right now cyberspace, the most visited of these places, is not "there" at all.

CYBERSPACE: DISEMBODIED OR DECONSTRUCTED?

Although I have been around computers for years, my first real experience with cyberspace was organizing an academic meeting there—on cyborgs, ironically enough. It was a strange disembodied experience. Of course, there are those who would say describing an academic meeting as disembodied is a tautology in any case. But rhetoric is one thing, actually meeting in real time without your bodies is reality now, and it is certainly different from being there in person, maybe even better. At your typical academic meeting, the body grows lethargic as it drags from one panel discussion to another, until finally even massive transfusions of espresso are incapable of raising its heart rate. The only surefire stimulant in such meetings, and probably for academics in general, is talking. Take a comatose, nearly dead professor and give him or her the floor, and a Lazarus-like resurrection takes place.

Maybe this explains the exhilaration of virtual meetings. First, you can "talk" a great deal, although the "talk" is actually typing messages onto a computer screen. In what truly must seem a miracle (the immaculate conversation?), everyone can talk at once, because your text eventually comes up, with everyone else's, on the screen. As you sit there with your mind racing and your fingers dancing, the most your body can do is squirm. After several hours of this, you want to stand up, wave your arms, and scream.

This is certainly not advisable if you are in a monster computer lab surrounded by a hundred undergrads who are already looking at you askance because of your forty-something appearance and the fact that you are chuckling maniacally at the clever things you are writing while exclaiming "hello" out loud when a friend logs on from Puerto Rico and then gasping when someone you just met licks your face! Virtually licks your face, I should clarify...but it is very upsetting just the same.

Five or six hours of being cyborged on-line had incredible effects on my body. When I walked outside into the rain, I felt lighter, not all there. And it was not because my consciousness was still back in that virtual elsewhere in cyberspace where it had just been bumping clumsily (textually) into the other attendees' projections. While talking at once to the simulations from Australia, England, Germany, Puerto Rico, New York, Boston, Seattle, and San Francisco, it became impossible to think of the world as anything other than hanging in space showing one face after another to the sun. Morning in Australia was afternoon in Oregon and late evening in London. It reminded me of the reaction all astronauts get once they soar above the atmosphere. "Hey!" they always exclaim, even if they have promised themselves they would not go gooey about it as all the other space-traveling cyborgs do: "It's one world. It's just...hanging there in space." Strangely enough, cyberspace and outer space impose the same perception, although in other respects they are so different. Disembodiment in cyberspace is hyperembodiment in outer space, but both places are dependent on machines and therefore both places are inhabited only by machines—and cyborgs, of course.

Millions now visit cyberspace, prompting a new field of research on cyberculture itself and on how it affects our lived reality. Sherry Turkle, a professor in MIT program on Science, Technology, and Society and a leading researcher in this area, observes in *The Second Self* that computers, and particularly the Internet, are evocative technologies, bringing out latent habits of mind and body. According to Turkle, people relate to computers in two major patterns: mastery and cooperation. Mastery is seeing the computer as a microworld that one can control in all its aspects. Cooperation is conceiving of the computer as an ally in creating, communicating, and doing other tasks. Males tend to try to master the machine, while females tend to cooperate with it, but these approaches do not map perfectly onto gender. Turkle also explores how computers mediate communication between people in surprising ways, such as the tendency to confide in a non-judgmental machine rather than another person.

In *Life on the Screen*, Turkle argues that the Internet gives rise to a post-modern personality that is supplanting the modernist persona that has dominated technological culture for the last few centuries. While the modernest personality is unitary, at least on the surface, the postmodern personality is more flexible and playful. Contradictory aspects can coexist comfortably in a single bricollage and not be seen as incipient insanity, because such complexity reflects a postmodern understanding of reality and our limited ability to map it.

While Turkle does not focus on politics, others have speculated on the political implications of cyberspace at great length. Some analysts look just at one central issue, such as Jerry Everard's *Virtual States*, which argues that while the Internet undermines traditional nation-states in some ways, it will not lead to their disappearance but rather to their redefinition. There are also collections (Marc Smith's and Peter Kollock's *Communities in Cyberspace* is a good example) and single-author works along the lines of Tim Jordon's *Cyberpower: The Culture and Politics of Cyberspace and the Internet*. All of these offer their own positions on the key political issue cyberspace raises: Who will control cyberspace, and how will that power impact the physical world? Related to this are specific problems of power, privacy, virtual social action, intellectual property rights, consumerism, and inequality (and not just gender-, race-, and class-based, but technopeasants versus the digerati as well). Even though the real point is that cyberspace is just another site for real politics, some enthusiasts forget that they have not really left their real bodies and the physical world behind when they log on. Sandy Stone warns:

Cyberspace developers foresee a time when they will be able to forget about the body. But it is important to remember that virtual community originates in, and must return to, the physical. No refigured virtual body, no matter how beautiful, will slow the death of a cyberpunk with AIDS. Even in the age of the technosocial subject, life is lived through bodies.

While cyberspace is part of the rest of reality, it does open ways of relating and being that are entirely new. For instance, race and gender distinctions are hard to enforce if you cannot tell with whom you are interacting. As the famous cartoon points out: "No one knows you're a dog in cyberspace." Another traditional political issue cyberspace reconfigures is, strangely enough, property rights, particularly intellectual property. The ownership of computer codes and databases, the use of trade names, the limits of fair-use quotations, and the collection of personal data are all areas of intense disagreement. Efforts to forge agreements between publishers, Web users, libraries, and other interested parties on access to published material have collapsed, for example.

The material control of virtual "space" is the most important political struggle there. Since the Internet grew out of a U.S. military network, the U.S. government originally had a great deal of control. But the first inhabitants of cyberspace were actually computer geeks, not soldiers, and they made it a self-governing anarchy. Realizing they could not control the Net, the Department of Defense passed nominal supervision to the National Science Foundation and delegated power to establish "domains" and other chores to various private groups, some of which reap large profits from their monopolies.

Meanwhile, the voluntary associations that establish Net standards and interest groups such as the Internet Society and CPSR have joined with many European countries in calling for more democracy in governing the Net. They fear that either the U.S. government or for-profit proxies will assert control over what many have called "the greatest working anarchy ever."

In a sense, the Net is more of a frontier than a highway, but what it really is can only be described as . . . the Net. It is its own best metaphor. Unlike a physical frontier, the Net is truly infinite. The more it is inhabited, the wilder it becomes, not the more "civilized." Its fundamentally cyborg character makes it a new kind of space, just as cyborgization allows for new types of bodies.

On the Internet, attention replaces media and mobility replaces space as the primary values and organizing metaphors. It is not important how often you speak or how widely you broadcast it, but how many people listen. Space can be bought at the local computer store, but what counts is how easy it is to access your space. Sometimes this depends on skill with software and access to the best hardware. Technology can therefore produce power, as in the real world, but power has other sources as well.

Charisma and knowledge are power in the real world and perhaps even more so in the virtual. On the Net your identity is changeable, produced rhetorically and sustained or deconstructed by manipulating knowledge. This is particularly true of sexual practices on the Net. "Tiny Sex," some call it, but it is not tiny in its political implications.

TINY SEX

Aficionados are at pains to point out that sex on the Net is real, not simulated, although it is impossible to tell which orgasms ("OHHHHHHHH!!!!") are real. At its best, it is like two people watching each other masturbate while reading Anaïs Nin. But few computerists, if any, write as well as Anaïs Nin, nor are you watching a person or even an image of a person, unless you are just pleasuring yourself looking at sex sites. Truly interactive sex basically consists of words, which brings up another common complaint: few people can type fast enough, especially one-handed, for really good Netsex. But, like phone sex, Netsex involves real people, real bodies, and if you are lucky, real orgasms. One caveat: your partner may not be a real man, or a real woman.

David Jacobson, a professor of anthropology at Brandeis University, has been researching the plasticity of gender in cyberspace and has discovered some surprising attitudes toward gender on the Net. Jacobson and a female graduate student visited various political and sexual chat rooms. First, one of them would openly visit the site while pretending to be of the opposite gender. After participating for awhile, that researcher would leave and the other, who had been silently lurking on the site, would question the people in the chat room about any doubts or conclusions they may have had about the first researcher. Then they would reveal the true gender of the first researcher and the scientists would record the reactions. Jacobson predicted that there would be a fair amount of anxiety, even anger, at being tricked, particularly in the sex sites. Instead, they found that their virtual sex partners were almost indifferent to the actual sex or claimed gender of the investigators. Deception seems almost expected in sexual encounters. It was the political discussion groups that were distressed at the experiment. People feel very betrayed when they discover that the "man" or "woman" with whom they have been discussing politics is really a "woman" or "man."

But if sexual deception is part of a real relationship, the anger can be very intense indeed, as demonstrated by the case of the male psychiatrist who pretended to be a disabled bisexual woman. Dr. Sanford Lewin says it happened quite by accident. In the early 1980s he joined CompuServe using the handle "Shrink, Inc." During one of his early visits to a chat room, he ended up in a private conversation with a woman who clearly thought he also was a woman. Dr. Lewin noticed that the conversation was unlike any he had ever had; the gender confusion allowed him to experience how women talk together.

One thought led to another, and he soon opened a second account under the name Joan Greene. While the good doctor was a shy, conservative, heterosexual, Jewish male, Ms. Greene was an outgoing, liberal, severely disabled, bisexual atheist. Soon she was a major presence in CompuServe's niche of cyberspace. She helped start the first woman's discussion group there, she counseled and advised many different women friends, she seduced some of them into having tiny sex with her, and she even started a vigilante group to ferret out and expose gender-pretenders.

Dr. Lewin had second thoughts and tried to virtually kill Joan Greene, but the first stages of her terminal decline evoked so much pain from her many friends that he was forced to abandon this plan. Eventually the deception collapsed, and Dr. Lewin lost not only most of his and Joan Greene's friends and lovers but also, he laments, a large part of himself. The victims of this masquerade did not usually complain about the sexual posturing, which was targeted at heterosexual women who often joined in on-line masturbation sessions with Joan purely out of sympathy for her disability; they were outraged by the emotional transgression. Even though they admitted that Joan's advice and support helped many of them change their lives for the better (returning to college, for example), they could not forgive Lewin's successful trespass into women's mental space. The sex, after all, was one removed from reality; the friendships were as real as could be. While Net encounters are virtual, they can be a significant part of real relationships.

Other aspects of sexual culture, like harassment and even assault, can be both virtual and significant, such as a famous incident of "cyberrape" in 1993. A member of the LambdaMoo virtual community named Mr. Bungles used a computer trick called "Voodoo Dolls" to simulate two other players, Legba and Starsinger, making it seem as if they were committing unpleasant virtual sexual acts such as sodomy with kitchen knives, eating their own pubic hair, and intercourse with other players. Cyberrape is pretty common, especially of characters identified as female. Someone named Scumbag comes up to you and says (types): "I rip off your clothes and . . ." You can quickly type "@gag scumbag" and Scumbag's verbal attack becomes invisible to you, but other players in the room will read the attack, unless they type the "@gag" command as well. But the Voodoo Doll approach makes this technofix impossible, and the hijacking of one's character seems worse to many cyberspace regulars than the verbal assaults that are so common.

A wizard (one of the controlling programmers) named Zippy finally captured Mr. Bungles and his dolls with a special command. Members of LambdaMoo, the oldest and perhaps biggest of the multi-user domains (computer sites where many interact), began an intense debate about what this assault meant for their society, where democracy had just been imposed by Pavel Curtis, the creator-wizard. The details of this debate, and the different technopolitical theories of wizardists ("All power to the wizards!"), liberals, technolibertarians (invent a new technology to fix the problem), and anarchists are discussed at length in *Tinylife* by Julian Dibbel, which includes the best account of the "Voodo Doll" rape.

In the end new technologies (such as a command to control Voodoo Dolls) were created, but before this happened a lesser wizard unilaterally eliminated the Mr. Bungles character. Some people called this murder, others, execution, and still others, exile. The technical term is "toading," from the Dungeons and Dragons games, where wizards were apt to make some character they did not like into a slimy toad. But toading now includes the virtual death penalty that was enacted on Mr. Bungles, who, it now turns out, may have been a group of male students living in a New York University dorm.

Mr. Bungles's real-life persona(s) was not hurt physically, of course, nor were Legba's or Starsinger's. But for serious participants in virtual communities, the possession/rape or execution of one's avatar (their created Net personas) is a very serious matter. LambdaMoo continued the experiment in democracy, while Curtis and some of his more loyal wizards created their own hierarchical, invitation-only, virtual world where they could experiment with multi-user domain technology without the distracting brouhahas of the virtual masses.

The political questions this affair raises are striking. Where is the line between free speech and physical assault in a textual world? What is the difference between mind and body in virtual space? Can one be a good citizen in real life and a sociopath in virtual reality at the same time? Are there any limits on the technoeuphoria of true believers in virtuality?

Consider the hubris of the computerists: "Reality is 80 million polygons per second," Alvy Ray Smith declared. Michael Benedikt of the University of Texas is even more outspoken. He argues that resentment of our bodies is the fundamental impetus for cyberspace. He singles out their "cloddishness, limitations and final treachery, their mortality." For Benedikt, reality "is death." Yet we *will* die, and cyberspace cannot free us from that grim necessity until the improbable "uploading" of organic intelligence into machines takes place. Benedikt desperately counts on cyberspace to end the reality of death and give us a pseudo reality predicated on high-speed computing:

> If only we could, we would wander the Earth and never leave home; we would enjoy triumphs without risks, eat of the Tree and not be punished, consort daily with angels, enter heaven now and not die.

But triumphs will be only pretend without real risks, and knowledge only simulated without a price to pay, and the virtual angels will inhabit a virtual heaven, with no real grace or redemption.

If we are interested in real knowledge, true grace, and the possibility of technoredemption in the realm of imposed binary gender and vanilla sexuality, then we must look to those cyborgs who take real risks and make real sacrifices to real knives with their very bodies: transsexuals (discussed in Chapter 11). For reality, we can also look at those physical places where only cyborgs go that definitely involve taking risks. The two most important are exemplary of prosthetic territories: aquaspace and outer space.

OUTER SPACE AND AQUASPACE

> Space is an unnatural environment, and it takes an unnatural effort from unnatural people to prosper there.
> —Afriel, a Shapist

Space is an unnatural environment for humans. Unlike cyberspace, which was constructed for and by people so that they could instantiate various fantasies, from pure communication to fluidless sex, space has always been there and it is not hospitable. So it is not surprising to realize that the term cyborg was first articulated to describe altering humans so we could go into space. But what is surprising is the politics around space exploration and the raging debates about the role of human-cyborgs in space exploration.

There are two major political debates NASA has never been able to escape. First, how militarized should the U.S. space program be? There has been constant pressure for militarization from the beginnings of NASA, which were in the military's own space programs. But there has also been pretty effective resistance to it within NASA. The second major debate has been over the role of humans in space ("man-in-a-can" as some wags termed it). Why launch people into space when machines can function as well and more cheaply? But this question is wrong on two counts. First, people do not go into space; cyborgs do. Astronauts are humans embedded in complex systems. And second, for many jobs these cyborgs are much better than machines. Of course, this was not always the case. The first cyborgs in space were just test subjects, but then, they were not human.

Before the word "cyborg" was even coined, astronautics in the late 1950s had produced the first fully realized cyborg: Ham the chimp astronaut. As Donna Haraway explains, with his pressure suit, his telemetric devices, his special electronic-lined couch, all enclosed in the capsule,

> Ham is a cyborg, the perfect child of space.... There could be no more iconic cyborg than a telemetrically implanted chimpanzee, understudy for "man," launched from earth in a space program....

But where Ham went first, human cyborgs have followed. They pave the way for human (or posthuman) space colonization. NASA is fond of saying that space is just another place to work. That is an exaggeration. Outer space and aquaspace are particularly unforgiving environments where you must be a cyborg—and very careful—to survive, but there is some truth in the jest, especially as more private companies set their sights on the stars. Besides, most corporate leaders would now argue that you must integrate workers and machines into complex computerized systems to work effectively anywhere, especially in capitalist space.

Despite Tom Wolfe's claim in *The Right Stuff* that NASA only wanted astronauts for publicity, it was always understood, even before NASA, that humans were needed to explore space. However, it was also understood that humans would work in concert with machines. This reality of "the human-as-a-system-component" was worked out in a number of different sites: life support systems (spacecraft and space suits, biotelemetry, teleoperators), communications, and mission design. All were predicated on excellent human-machine communication and on treating the humans as just another component that needs good maintenance, careful preparation, and constant monitoring, just like any other key node. As one NASA analyst, D. R. Hitchcock, noted:

> During an actual space flight, the capacity of the astronaut to continue the mission and to perform the tasks required of him must be continuously assessed.

Even space flights without humans on board are often cyborgs, since they involve equipment controlled remotely from the ground. Various terms are used for these systems: teleoperator, telepuppet, telechirics, telefactors, cybernetic anthromorphic mechanisms (CAMs), master-slave machines, and waldos. Edwin Johnsen, a NASA scientist, concluded:

> The human being is the most successful machine on earth. However, engineers, psychologists and physiologists know that man, as an operator, is far from being an optimum system. From the neck up, he's great. From the neck down, other machines can out-perform man by a country mile. It appears that a system that combines the best features of man with the best features of other machines will add to the success of man as a machine.

Effective as such systems are, the time delay and poor sensor data of remote-controls render on site cyborgs necessary. Someday, perhaps, posthuman cyborgs will be able to survive space directly but for now human-cyborgs need flying space suits and wearable spacecraft, or some combination of these in order to get there and work there. Some day we might terraform planets or even leave the solar system altogether, but for the near future, if not forever, we will be living below the speed of light. If we do colonize beyond the earth's atmosphere, many of the same issues that bedevil humans on Earth will haunt cyborgs in space, including war, corruption, government, and even tension between different posthumans, modified for their different habitats—Moonies versus Martians, perhaps.

Because it is infinite and off the planet, space is very different from the deep sea in many respects. But in one key aspect they are the same. Humans can survive in the deep only as cyborgs, and where cyborg-humans go, so goes politics.

I never really thought about the cyborgian implications of deep-sea diving until I met a remarkable man, Terrance Tysell, a former Navy Seal and one of the most accomplished divers in the world. He explores underwater caves and shipwrecks and holds a number of records for free (without a pressure suit) diving, which include experimenting with breathing-gas mixtures and inventing computers to keep track of them.

Humans have a long history of exploring the deep: swimmers, sailors, submariners, and divers. Talking with Terrance at length, I began to understand just how different the sea is from land. Everything you do when you are on it, and especially in it, depends on your equipment and how you use it. Terrance described for me an incident that occurred when he and another diver were exploring an underwater cave:

Frantically the man clutches at his throat, tearing at the thin drysuit neck seal that holds back the cold black water. Before I am able to reach him the watertight integrity of the suit is destroyed, and in a huge burst of air, the thermal protection and buoyancy characteristics of the suit vanish, and he falls struggling into the darkness below me.

Eventually Terrance rescued his companion by reinflating the broken suit and then restraining the other diver from hastily surfacing so that the disorientation the pressure caused them both, the onset of the bends, due to nitrogen poisoning, did not become a fatal case of "rapture of the deep."

Terrance's work on deep free diving shows how machine-dependent serious divers are. That is part of the attraction. Harnessing the power of the technology to make the deep sea part of his "turf" is a crucial part of the psyche of free divers. For them it is totally different to be in a pressure suit or a submersible rather than in a dry suit with tanks and computers and other equipment. It is the difference between flying in a plane and skydiving, or even more apropos, between walking and driving on land.

We inhabit the land because we walk it, and we do not really inhabit the air because we are just flying through. Someday many humans will inhabit the sea, as a few already do in undersea labs. First it will be with equipment such as Terrance is developing, but eventually, with proper genetic engineering, post humans should be able to breath water as well as any fish.

Already, maritime law has become a matter of intense international concern because of declining fish stocks and the realization that the seabeds and the sea itself contain a great deal of organic and mineral wealth. What will happen to these controversies when it becomes easy for cyborged humans to live in the sea? The same issues will come up as people adapt themselves to living on the polar ice caps and on alpine peaks. Cyborg technosciences will open every inch of the globe to human colonization, with profound political implications dealing with the environment, national boundaries, and self-determination. In the long run these new spaces will produce new types of citizenship, just as is happening in cyberspace.

With a little reflection this should not be a surprise; after all, these are cyborg territories. But cyborgization can also transform other aspects of society that at first might seem quite remote from the pressures of posthumanism and the technosciences that make it possible. Even the family, that defining human institution, is being cyborged, which is the subject of the next chapter.

cyborg families

THE TECHNOLOGICALLY MEDIATED FAMILY

"The family" is one of the major political issues of our time, in large part because of the incredible changes technology fosters in this ancient institution. What is a family? Who may have one? What exactly constitutes a healthy family? Social scientists define families around shared meanings, relationships, gender, and kinship. Legal definitions include relationship, emotional and financial commitment, everyday life, and mutual reliance. Average people have definitions that are broader than any of these, or much stricter. What this boils down to is that what "family" means is socially determined and currently very contested. This contestation about the family has been particularly obvious in the lamentations over the last few centuries about its decline.

The causes of this purported disaster have been debated at length. The main evidence of family breakdown is the post–World War II increase in the divorce rate and the related rise in the number of single-parent families. Yet families are not breaking down at all; they are changing dramatically. Family structures have always evolved, but now they are changing faster than ever before as a result of the interactions between science, technology, and medical practices. Families are becoming cyborgian; their very forms are mediated or determined by technoscience. Just as different types of cyborgs are now proliferating, so are cyborg families.

By the 1950s, technological advances had caused extreme changes in the structure of European and American families. Medical advances produced basic demographic shifts that reconfigured families in several ways. For example, a greater understanding of hygiene radically reduced instances of infant and maternal mortality. The development of antibiotics, advances in surgical techniques, and breakthroughs in the diagnosis and treatment of diseases drastically lowered death rates for all family members. The result is that people are living longer and more active lives.

Stephanie Coontz, in *The Way We Never Were,* notes that increased longevity created the potential for marriages to last longer and therefore for more marriages to end in divorces. In the nineteenth century the average length of a marriage was 10 years, mainly due to the high mortality rate. Today divorce rates compensate for life expectancies that produce, on the average, 40-year marriages. In essence, divorce has replaced death in terminating many unions. Coontz also demonstrates that the image of the stable nuclear family is not supported by historical evidence. In the early nineteenth century, the "golden age" of the family, the frequent deaths of parents and children and the severe economic conditions of the poor and working classes led to many extended families, blended families, single-parent families, extensive child labor, and extraordinary rates of institutionalized children (10 percent in 1940).

Today reproductive technologies have blurred the traditional emphasis on the conjugal (sex) and consanguine (blood) relationships that have traditionally defined families. But it is not just reproductive technologies or cyborg medicine that are restructuring today's families. Most of today's technoscientific creations have some impact on family structure, whether it be computers, toys and games, or communication technologies. As Coontz argues:

> We will not solve any of the problems associated with the new family terrain by fantasizing that we can return to some "land before time" where these demographic, cultural, and technological configurations do not exist. Much of the new family topography is permanent. It is the result of a major realignment of subterranean forces, much like plate tectonics and continental drift. Women will never again spend the bulk of their lives at home. Sex and reproduction are no longer part of the same land mass, and no amount of pushing and shoving can force them into a single continent again.

The family is a moving target and an evolving, ever-changing institution. In the case of surrogate families, developments in reproductive medical technoscience have produced families that were literally impossible a few years ago.

SURROGATE FAMILIES

Parenthood can now be achieved through numerous different strategies, which involve the melding of reproductive technologies and the bodies (and/or parts) of the parents and other people. In other words, the production of children can be accomplished by a range of interactions, from two naked people exchanging bodily fluids on a bed of flowers to a complex clinical procedure involving various technologies and dozens of participants in a multimillion-dollar laboratory.

Today a couple or individual with enough money may hire a surrogate mother whose own egg may be fertilized, or the fertilized egg of the parents may be implanted in a surrogate mother, or a sperm donor may inseminate the mother. Traditional benchmarks of family, such as biological ties, are often eliminated. Kathleen Biddick observes that:

> Several females may now contribute to the material process of procreation. It is possible now for one female to provide an egg for procreation, another female to provide her uterus for nourishing a fetus and birthing, yet other females (and even males), including child-care workers, may act as social mothers to the growing infant. The acts of conception, pregnancy, and birthing, which had once unified the dominant cultural notion of the maternal and connected it as a "natural" sequence to social mothering, are distributed across different procedures in reproductive technology.

The variety and profusion of custody litigations is one site at which society tries to sort out the changes that have blurred the biological and marital criteria that legally define the family. The legal system cannot keep pace with the technological advances that are drastically redefining the family.

Other achievements in reproductive technology that have bedeviled the legal system are the ability to extract eggs from aborted fetuses and the use of eggs or sperm from people who are already dead. There have been cases in which one or both of the parents are dead at the time of conception, leading to numerous legal battles over custody and rights. Judith Hart, for example, was initially denied survivor benefits by the Social Security Administration because the State of Louisiana declared her fatherless. Heart did have a father who had been married to her mother, but she was conceived from his sperm after his death. When the baby was born, Nancy Hart felt as if she had "cheated" death. Apparently, the government felt another kind of cyborgian cheating was taking place, but after legal challenges the state relented, and Judith was proclaimed a true daughter of her father and was awarded social security benefits.

The idea of the parent has also drastically changed. Now fathers and mothers need not be directly involved to reproduce. Although historically it has been common for others to nurse and raise one's progeny, surrogacy, a new cyborg reproductive option, takes this to new levels. It does not always go smoothly.

The first well-publicized case of a surrogate mother who changed her mind about giving up the child was Baby M's birth mother, Mary Beth Whitehead. Now such cases are common, though there are many happily executed surrogate contracts as well. Two cases show the range of experiences possible in surrogate arrangements as well as how these arrangements can affect family politics in subtle and unsubtle ways.

In 1995, soap-opera actress Dierdre Hall told on TV her story of a 20-year "battle" with infertility that spanned two marriages. She underwent six *in vitro* fertilization attempts, all of which were unsuccessful. Hall and her second husband, Steve Somer, then decided to hire a surrogate mother. Soon after the couple began their relationship with their surrogate, Robin B., herself a single mother of three, they became very close, particularly Dierdre and Robin. Hall was very involved in the decisions of pregnancy, including diet, doctors, and other medical choices. Robin describes the relationship as "intense" and "almost like a marriage." By the end of the pregnancy, Robin was living with Hall and Somer. At the birth Hall lifted the baby out of Robin.

Robin described her feelings about continuing the relationship beyond the fulfillment of the first contract: "At the end you can choose to go your separate ways or you can stick together and make it through life." A high level of adaptability, flexible boundaries, and healthy communication helped the three adults develop a close relationship. This gave them the ability temporarily to blend the two families. The arrangement worked so well that they signed a second contract a few years later. Before the second pregnancy, however, Robin had begun dating a man, and her surrogate family became a source of discomfort for the couple. He was embarrassed in public because people automatically attributed her pregnancy to him.

The introduction of another primary relationship into Robin's life necessarily changed the boundaries between the two blended families, and they became much more autonomous. Still, their high level of adaptability helped them comfortably adjust to the new dynamic and to remain friendly after they disengaged. Robin describes her feeling of accomplishment at the end of the year after the first son was born: "There's a family here that wasn't here before." Steve Somer describes it as the "perpetuation and fulfillment of the family."

Many surrogate relationships end happily, but all is not sweetness and light. For one thing, not all parents are loving. Another problem is that the surrogate contract often exploits the birth mother by underpaying her and turning her into a baby-producing machine. Finally, most of the medical technologies are costly, which makes them available primarily to the wealthy.

In contrast to Hall's family experience, there are tragedies like the case of James Austin's son. In 1995, Austin used a $30,000 inheritance from his mother to contract for a surrogate child. He received his 10-pound son at one day of age. Five weeks later the boy was dead. Austin admitted beating his son to death with his fists and a plastic coat hanger. Perhaps he felt that since he had bought the child, he could do with him as he pleased. This family was a tightly closed loop, unadaptable, with monolithic cohesion. Communication was violence. Family images, themes, boundaries, and social issues were reduced to patriarchal murder. Of course, many biological parents murder their children, which is a good argument against "traditional family values" but in no way validates Austin buying/breeding his murder victim. We do not own children, bred or brought; we foster them.

Another danger of surrogacy and artificial insemination is bringing to life a child without intimacy or physical contact between the biological parents, or indeed anyone. It is hard to differentiate baby Austin from an owned slave. In many respects it was like cloning, which could produce similar dynamics in kinship ties, although parent-child self-identity would be even more absolute.

In instances of surrogacy or artificial insemination, technology replaces physical and/or emotional intimacy to some degree, but perhaps new ties of intimacy can replace these. The outcomes of these relationships are probably no more predictable or unsuccessful than old-fashioned sexual relationships. Inevitably, the potential for positive outcomes such as Hall's are linked to the increased possibility of tragedies such as Austin's. Technology is never neutral. Some technologies are obviously detrimental (weapons of mass destruction, torture, and mind-control machines) and others are beneficial (a cure for the common cold, pollution-free energy). But most technologies, including most cyborgian ones, are ambiguous. They may reify horrible dynamics (children as property) or allow loving parents to have children, but they are not neutral.

CYBORG FAMILY VALUES

Over the last few years, we've heard a lot about something called family values. And like many of you, I've struggled to figure out what that means. But since my accident, I've found a definition that seems to make sense. I think it means that we're all family, that we all have value.
—Christopher Reeve at the Democratic National Convention

We probably have no cause to fear (or hope) that The Family will dissolve. What we can begin to ask is what we want our families to do. Then, distinguishing our hopes from what we have, we can begin to analyze the social forces that enhance or undermine the realization of the kinds of human bonds we need.
—Jane Collier, Michelle Rosaldo, and Sylvia Yanagisako

The 'borging of the contemporary family is only going to get stranger. In 1995 Jared Diamond wrote an article in *Discover* called "Father's Milk." It described in loving detail how and why human fathers can be easily modified with a few hormone shots and some manual nipple stimulation so that they can nurse their young. "Experience may tell you that producing milk and nursing youngsters is a job for the female mammal, not the male. But your experience is probably limited, and the potential of biology—and medical technology—is vast." Slightly more difficult, but just as likely, is the modification of men to carry a baby, as in the Arnold Schwarzenegger movie *Junior*. As genetic engineering improves, creating a baby that has the genes of three, four, or 100 parents will be possible. Can the family adapt? Considering what it has already been through, the answer is an unequivocal yes, although it will not necessarily look like your family.

Already, today's family systems are often cyborg systems where a significant aspect of family image, sense of well-being, growth, and even the family's very existence are intimately connected to technological interventions, but this is not the only important factor. Judith Stacey, in *Brave New Families*, gives several case studies of contemporary families that make it very clear that many other forces besides technology are crucial in the construction of new families. Particularly important in her examples are the roles of economics and of ideologies such as feminism. Still, economics and ideologies are, in turn, always coevolving with technological developments. It is not a coincidence that feminists make crucial contributions to both family studies and cyborg theory. Technology, which Stacey somewhat neglects, as do most scholars of the family, is central to contemporary culture.

Families can now be charted only when their relations to cyborg technologies are as well understood as economic, blood, and emotional ties. This has important implications for political relationships. There are many cyborg family issues that are directly political—not just well-known debates around abortion and the right to die, but also the politics of less publicized decisions such as cutting off public money for artificial insemination. These debates often turn around the question: What is a family anyway?

The government has the power to define a legitimate family by what it legislates and funds. In 1995, a legislator unsuccessfully introduced a bill to make it illegal in Oregon for an unmarried woman to be artificially inseminated. It also would have prohibited surrogate-mother contracts for money. Debates around same-sex partners and their legal and financial rights raise similar issues. This is why the Cyborg Bill of Rights includes protections against these arbitrary acts of government intervention.

Ultimately, even without the blessings of the government and other authorities, many people will go ahead and construct the families they want. After all, the technology for artificial insemination is less complicated than what is needed for cooking Thanksgiving dinner. Even more difficult procedures, prenatal sex selection for example, have become widely available. And if you have the resources, there is *in vitro* fertilization or surrogacy.

The key issue is political: Who decides? Society certainly has a stake in these debates, as Ellen Goodman argues in many of her newspaper columns, because of the natural limits on medical resources. As Goodman has pointed out, the decisions are often made out of greed and hubris. Whenever possible, it seems the people most directly involved should have the ultimate say. They will have to live or die with the consequences.

The best decisions will not be based on simplistic categories such as cyborg equals good or cyborg equals bad. Cyborg transformations and technologies can be either good or bad; the details are what matters, for every interface of family and cyborg technoscience is a "situated knowledge," in Donna Haraway's phrase, and must be examined specifically. The issues should also be evaluated by other criteria, such as fairness, effectiveness, and happiness. Tolstoy claimed that all unhappy families are unique; Judith Stacey adds that today all happy families are unique as well. Every cyborged family is particularly special and must be understood in its particularities.

In many cases technology responds to the impact of earlier innovations in a mutilation-prosthesis cycle that is profoundly cyborgian. This can be as subtle as giving women the power to bear children much later in life, an option predicated on increased health and longevity, or as direct as interventions that allow women to overcome childbearing difficulties caused by medical practices on the previous generation.

In other cases cyborg interventions break new ground, such as with the impregnation of lesbian mothers or even such elegant and ornate family constructions as the gay brother of a lesbian donating sperm to her partner with the joyful approval of an extended family of grandparents, aunts, uncles, and cousins. As Valerie Hartouni reminds us, the technologies that make headlines such as "Dead Mother Gives Birth" also give us the chance to "invent ourselves consciously and deliberately."

Anne Hill's article in *Cyborg Babies* gives a beautiful account of how such technical choices can be embedded in sophisticated and nurturing political and spiritual practices that in no way deny our love of (indeed oneness with) nature while accepting the pleasures and powers of technology. She uses a neopagan analytic, but it validates the same principles—complexity, life, choice, tolerance, and empowerment—as Donna Haraway's atheist-materialist manifesto and of many humanistic thinkers from Judaism, Christianity, Islam, and Buddhism. We need these values because choices will always have unintended consequences. For instance, the ideology of family makes reproductive technology available to heterosexual families. Capitalist ideology makes it something anyone with the money or insurance can buy. Now lesbians are having babies.

Certainly, as Stephanie Coontz says, we cannot return to "that land before time" where these changes do not exist. We can only go forward. But in truly becoming cyborgs who are responsible and unnaïve, we must question the powers and the motives that drive these technologies. We must make ethical choices between the good and the bad. And at times we must be able to say, as Ellen Goodman reminds us, that "enough is enough."

sex machines, human beings, in-betweens

DILDONICS

Now it was my turn to take the ride. Truthfully, I was a little apprehensive, despite all the endorsements. I thought it might be too much like having a pneumatic drill inside you. My husband held me and Dave turned the juice on, very slowly. At first, I felt hardly anything. Big deal, I thought, like the first time I had sex. What's all the fuss about? Then he turned up the power, and the sensations hit me. I was on a roller coaster, going up slowly, coming down at dizzying speed. I passed the point of no return. Orgasms were bursting forth crashing against each other. I lost track of time, space, the people in the room. There were just lips, hands and that unstoppable human thing inside me relentlessly pushing me further and further.

— Jessica West

In five years the penis will be obsolete.

—A body-morph salesman in John Varley's novel *Steel Beach*

The "unstoppable...thing" inside Jessica West was not "human" at all. It was a realistic rubber penis mounted on a vinyl seat, part of a sex machine called Sybian. The name comes from the ancient Greek city of Sybaris, famous for its pleasure-loving citizens. The machine is complex, two $\frac{1}{50}$ horsepower motors with separate controls for vibration and rotation, retailing at $1,395. According to the inventor, a former dance instructor named Dave Lampert, it took 14 years to design. He rejects the label "sex toy" for what is actually a robotic penis with capabilities far beyond any natural member. "It is a breakthrough in artificial intercourse!" he proclaims. True enough, but it is not the first nor the last.

Most visions of cybernetic sex are virtual, focusing on the technologies of phone and modem and the future promise of teledildonics with feelie-suits and datagloves, but the important sex development happening right now is the proliferation and growing sophistication of human-machine sex.

Sex tools have a long history. Penile prosthesis of metal, horn, and wood are described in the *Kama Sutra*. The ancient Greeks and Romans used leather dildos (olisbos in Greek) for both heterosexual and homosexual penetration. The women in Aristophanes' *Lysistrata*, who are staging a sex strike to force their men to end war, complain that: "Since the day the Milesians left us in the lurch, not an olisbos have I set eyes on, eight inches long, that might give us its leather aid...." Even thousands of years ago, sex toys were also political tools.

Many cultures have invented dildos, including the Bisayan of the Philippines, the Hausa of Africa, and the Japanese. They can be made of any metal from gold to lead, of ivory or buffalo horn, or of wood, as long as it is smooth and clean. Various braces, or a full tube held by a belt, can be used prosthetically to strengthen and enlarge the penis (lingam) as well. The *Kama Sutra* goes so far as to recommend that they can be designed to fit specific vaginas and, if one is caught "unprepared," it notes reassuringly that an *apradravya* can be rustled up out of materials at hand, such as a reed, a gourd, or an apple branch. Ritual phalli are even more common, and many of them were used for sexual acts, both sacred and profane. It is only a small step from modeling the penis with a dildo or strengthening it with a prosthesis to modifying it through direct surgery and implants. In erotic and anthropological literature, penile prosthesis, dildos for sex acts, and penile mutilations and inserts are almost always described together.

Mutilations and augmentations of the male member range from punching simple holes to a complicated process of beating it with the hairs of "certain insects which live in trees," rubbing it with oil, and suspending it through a hole in a swing over the course of ten days to make it swell permanently. Both of these indelicate processes are mentioned in the *Kama Sutra*. Tattooing, scarring, and the insertion of crystals, bones, and metal of various types and shapes were also widespread in many cultures and are now making quite a comeback in the industrial world. Today one can find piercing salons in most of the large cities of the world and in many smaller North American and European towns—even Great Falls, Montana.

It is dildos that have undergone the most spectacular changes over time. The once-inert fake phallus has been empowered, so to speak, starting with steam and water more than a hundred years ago. The original steam-

and-water-powered vibrators were invented to mechanize the standard treatment for female hysteria: physician-assisted orgasms. Masturbating the clitoris and/or vulva of female patients as a cure for hysteria and other female disorders is a treatment that goes back to classical times at least. The goal was to produce a "hysterical paroxysm" to relieve pent-up energy. It was very common in the eighteenth and nineteenth centuries as well, and it was such an onerous task for some physicians that they welcomed steam-powered vibrators such as the Manipulator, invented in the 1860s, and various water-jet pelvic douches as hydrotherapy. Since these treatments did not involve vaginal penetration, they were not generally seen as sexual, although a minority of doctors apparently understood it was indeed a sexual act, not a treatment, and therefore opposed it. Many others warned that it was a procedure that only doctors of the highest morals should perform.

The 1890s saw the development of the electrical vibrator, which was much cheaper than the water-and-steam machines. Because hysteria was generally accepted as a real condition, and because the dildo was just one of a number of electrotherapeutic machines, their sexual aspects remained "camouflaged" for quite some time, until the sale of dildos to the general public and the collapse of the hysteria diagnosis undermined this pretense. By 1913, advertisements in such women's magazines as *Modern Priscilla* were touting vibrators that give "30,000 thrilling, invigorating, penetrating, revitalizing vibrations per minute. . . . you will have an [i]rresistible desire to own it, once you feel the living pulsing touch of its rhythmic vibratory motion." Vibrators were still sold as "Swedish massagers" and as quasi-medical aids until the sexual revolution of the 1960s (dependent on effective technologies of contraception) made it possible to proclaim openly their sexual function. This transition from sex therapy to sex toys marks a change in the way pleasure has been conceived in Western society. It has gone from a medical problem to a matter of consumer choice.

In ancient China, some adventurous soul invented ben-wa balls, spheres of a certain size, composition, and weight that would move inside a woman to the rhythm of her body, producing pleasure. These have been modified today to include remote-controlled sex eggs, the first example of sex machinery without an organic analog. Most sexual toys are bionic, meaning they are based on naturally occurring organs capable of sexual response. Lately, thanks to improvements in plastic casting, there has been a proliferation of artificial yet lifelike vaginas, penises, and other organs copied from porn stars and including full-sized dolls such as the Milk Maid, with breasts that spurt as well as two vibrating holes with "deep suction." There is also Ms. Perfection, a "perfect replica of a real woman," with vaginal rotating action for only $93.95. Ms. Perfection, it turns out, is just a vagina and anus. It's frightening to think that this might be someone's version of feminine perfection or of a real woman.

Sexual toys can be marital aids, they can comfort loneliness, they are even related to the penile prosthesis discussed in Chapter 7, but their greatest use is simply as a helpful interface for mutually consenting humans seeking communion. A more drastic intervention is possible for those who seek harmony between their physical and psychological genders. It is called sex reassignment surgery.

TRANSSEXUALITY

> Perhaps it is appropriate not to characterize the intersex movement as another species of identity politics but rather as a liberatory technology project seeking more and better choices for the consumer in the body-morphing marketplace.
>
> —Stephanie Turner

A professor at the University of Texas at Austin, Allucquere Rosanne "Sandy" Stone demonstrates in her academic presentations the implications of moving the clitoris to the palm of the hand. Imagine how startling it is to observe this handsome and dynamic transsexual cyborgologist seduce a crowd of resistant professors and more willing graduate students with various jokes and insights (what would it mean to shake hands?) into a rhythmic supportive chant as she rubs her palm to a dramatic orgasm. One of Stone's (many) points is to get her audience to confront the reality of what cyborg transitions like sex reassignment surgery mean for our future, sexual and otherwise. Her insistence is all the more powerful because of her own transition from man to woman.

One of her main focuses is the relationship between virtual personalities and the construction of subjectivity that transsexual surgery enables. She argues that cyberspace allows people to manipulate their gender identity just as sex reassignment surgery does, and both combine to challenge those key assumptions of Western culture—that "biology is destiny," and that destiny is binary: either boy or girl.

Careful attention to biological realities have already severely undermined this binary worldview. Anne Fausto-Sterling, a leading analyst of sexual categories, has argued for years that there are at least five sexes: male, female, and three types of hermaphrodites, herms (true), merms (male pseudo), and ferms (female pseudo). She admits that even these are somewhat arbitrary and that "sex is a vast, infinitely malleable continuum that defies the constraints of even five categories." When one considers that any of these biological arrangements might belong to people whose desire is homosexual, bisexual, or heterosexual, and that any of these biological arrays also might belong to people whose gender does not fit their biology. Well, simple math gives you five times three times two, which is 30. And then you have committed celibates, those who do not like these categories, those who do not fit them, and so on. Then there is cyborg science, ready to change genders or even create new ones.

A variety of influences have challenged our culture's belief in the immutability of gender and sex, including the feminist rejection of sex roles, aided and abetted by the "new" men who change diapers and have feelings; the spread of cyberspace, where people can choose their own gender; the gay rights movement, most threatening of all to those who are threatened by their own desires; the transsexual movement; and the revolt of the intersexed.

The intersexed are hermaphrodites, people born with ambiguous genitalia and/or chromosonal or hormonal anomalies. Estimates of just how common this is generally start at 4 percent, and rise from there. It is an inexact category. Doctors perform sex assignment surgery on baby boys whose penises are too small (.06 centimeters), and on girls whose clitorises are too big or who otherwise have confusing genitalia. In general, however, if a girl seems capable of reproduction, she is left alone. Parents of children who are deemed good surgical candidates are pressured to have this surgery performed as soon as possible—ostensibly "for the sake of the child," but societal confusion seems just as important a factor.

The medical establishment gave much weight to the theory that since gender is socially constructed, a child could be socialized to accept whatever gender the surgeons choose. But consider the famous case of a young boy, a twin, whose penis was amputated after an infection resulting from his circumcision. The uninjured twin was raised as a boy. His mutilated brother was subjected to transsexual surgery (the removal of the rest of his male genitalia, construction of a vagina), treated with female hormones, and raised as a girl; it seemed to "take." But nobody bothered to check up on the little "girl" after the first few years, until Dr. Milton Diamond and Keith Sigmondson tracked "her" down as an adult. It turned out that she had always felt like a boy, grew up and demanded her medical records, sought sexual reassignment through hormones, married a woman, and became a step-father. So much for imposing gender on someone with a sharp knife. This revelation came in the midst of a growing revolt by children who found out they had been born "intersexed" and had been assigned one gender or another, the parents of intersex children, and intersex people whose parents had resisted the medical model of sex assignment.

In 1996 the Intersex Society of North America staged a protest at the meeting of the American Academy of Pediatrics against imposed sex assignments, proclaiming themselves "Hermaphrodites with Attitude." They have found ready allies among some medical professionals, a number of academics who study gender, and many feminists, especially a group of transgender activists who have organized around the rights of transsexuals to control their medical destinies and their self-definitions.

If you spend enough time with transsexuals, bisexuals, "baby" lesbians experimenting out of feminist ideals, celibates, transgender activists, and so on, you begin to think outside of binary terms. You do not assume someone's mate is of the "opposite sex." You do not try to fix friends up with "single men" unless you know that is what they want. You do not even try to guess people's sexual orientation (except perhaps as a game) because the performance of gender and politics is just too complicated.

Anne Balsamo, in *Technologies of the Gendered Body,* claims that the proliferation of potential genders actually reinforces the old male/female dichotomy and the patriarchal system it supports:

> in hardware, software, and wetware it becomes clear that the liberation of the few is bought at the expense of the many. These technological stages are in fact deeply conservative.

Yet very few technologies are purely reactionary or liberatory, for technologies are no more pure than the humans and cyborgs who construct them. In other words, they are not pure at all. Balsamo's view is unsubtle and one-sided. In some cases, at some times, cyborg technologies reify social relations, conserving gender, class, and racial hierarchies. But just as often they do not, as the work (and life) of Sandy Stone proves. Pat Califia makes an extended argument in *Sex Changes: The Politics of Transgenderism* that also refutes the claims of Balsamo. She argues that transsexuality is profoundly political, not in terms of an "oppressed" group achieving liberation, but

rather of individuals finding the liberatory potential in new ways of thinking about their sexual identity. The technology is a mental prosthesis. Simply the possibility of sexual reassignment surgery serves as a psychosexual
tool for people rethinking their gender identity, so many do not require the
actual surgery.

This is only the beginning. Once the transition from male to female is
routine, people will move smoothly back and forth. John Varley has explored
a possible future with easy transsexual surgery in his novels and short stories, especially *Steel Beach* and "Options." "Options" traces two lovers as they
change their sex for both positive and negative reasons, experiencing alienation, fulfillment, and the complexity of gender. It is not horrible but rather
enticing. If this seems strange, compare it to the exotic possible futures of sex.

FUTURE SEX

Humans over time have collectively constructed the values that shape the
bodies we have today. Even though rituals and rules have varied widely,
between many different cultures, the bodies they produced were identical
and the genders they constructed were quite similar. Today, the construction
of gender is more than cultural, because the production of bodies is
cyborged. In the future, many different sexes are likely to be produced, driven by desire (to create and live) and fear (of death and sterility).

If engineering and invention are valued above all else, it is because they
are seen as true procreation; if death is so feared, it is due to the death of
faith; and if war is assumed to be inevitable, it is because masculinity is still
defined around it. This shift in emphasis from gender production to sexual
reassignment and innovation has led to a new variant of the American
body complex with its own "double logic of prostheses . . . panic and exhilaration." Among men, especially, panic and exhilaration describe many sexual experiences, although more mundane emotions probably predominate.
But if prostheses accelerate us into the future, there will indeed be an
inevitable blurring of the body, and new genders, new sexes, will be constructed out of the new bodies.

How can this be? Is anatomy up for grabs? Certainly it is. As Thomas
Laqueur points out in his seminal history, *Making Sex: Body and Gender from
the Greeks to Freud,* anatomy is not destiny; it is ambiguity and aporia. In his
research, he discovered "the fundamental incoherence of stable, fixed cate-

gories of sexual dimorphism, of male and/or female." For much of Western history there was only one sex (male), of which the female was but a variation. The metarule of two sexes and the idea that "genitals... matter as the marks of sexual opposition" were introduced to the "millennial traditions of western medicine... only last week."

Laqueur shows that at different times various sexual codings have been enforced, whether a "biology of hierarchy" with one sex, a "biology of incommensurability" with two sexes, or, as in some feminist arguments, "the claim that there is no publicly relevant sexual difference at all, or no sex." Today, the erotics of cyborgs promises the actual bionic construction of many sexualities and sexes. With transsexual surgery, complicated mechanical sexual aids, and the virtual magic of teledildonics, sexual identity is more plastic than it has ever been. As anatomies are modified, so are genders, because "anatomy is an epistemology," as Lisa Moore and Monica Clark point out. The cyborg epistemology is "thesis, antithesis, synthesis, prosthesis"; gender binaries are overthrown through cyborg anatomies. One-sex and two-sexes models were defined through maleness. Both no-sex and many-sexes models argue for a new set of power relationships around the erotic body, with possibilities for incredible displacements and pleasures. With the rise of the cyborg body, the signification of the body is open again for contestation.

Anna Tsing, the anthropologist, issued a call for "Responsible Fetishes" at the 1998 American Anthropology Conference. We may be slaves to our passions but that does not mean we should not pursue them responsibly with honesty, tolerance, humor, and humility. Mark Dery gives a good cyborgian example of responsible fetishism when he writes of the underground fan movement to remake/reveal Star Trek's Borg as gay. They are the Slash Borg and their slogan is: "Resistance is Fertile!" Their motto, "Infinite diversity in infinite combination," could well be a call for tolerant and fluid genders instead of a war of the sexes. Men may be from Mars and women from Venus, but there is the rest of the universe to think of. Cyborgs are from all the other planets. No matter the preference or fetish, we must act responsibly to have a bearable future.

If contemporary technoscience stays on its cyborg course, we can comfortably predict the many paths that will be taken. Judging by the dreams of writers and scientists and the plans of bureaucrats and officers, we can expect war and space cyborgs to fulfill those fantasies of "steel men" forged on the battlefields of modern war. We can also predict that medicine will gift us with repaired and enhanced cyborg males and females, including both more "manly" men and supermom females as well as a much easier bodily transition between the two sexes and, perhaps, back again. Finally, cyborgism could well be a bridge to different types of posthumans, some with male bodies, others clearly female, others yet who are hermaphrodites, and still more people who will be quite genderless. And there will be new sexes.

There has been a great evolutionary advantage for creatures who enjoy sexual dimorphism, which produces so many new and evolutionary useful combinations. Now that humans are well into participatory evolution, there are some who would say that we no longer need male and female bodies. We should be leery of such hubris. Most humans cannot even plan, predict, or control their own future, let alone the evolutionary trajectory of a planet's dominant species. For all their problems, male and female bodies do remain key human sites for procreation, recreation, and all new sexes as well. Male/female may be just one coding, but it constitutes part of our pleasures and our future. We can add to it, but let us not discard it before its time.

The incredible technoeuphoric fantasies about future sex contrast with the spread of what Arthur and Marilouise Kroker call "cynical" or "panic" sex under the sign of AIDS. One way the Krokers communicate such conflicting emotions as euphoria and cynicism is through their rhetorical pyrotechnics. Do not worry if it is hard to decipher at first reading; it should be, if it has any rich relationship to our complicated reality:

> The result is a production of a *cynical* sex, of sex itself as an ideological site of disaccumulation, loss, and the sacrifice as the perfect sign of a nihilistic culture where the body promises only its own negation; where the previously reflexive connection between sexuality and desire is blasted away by the seductive vision of sex *without organs*—a hyperreal, surrogate, and telematic sex like that promised by the computerized, phone sex of the Minitel system in France—as the ultimate out-of-body experience for the end of the world; and where the terror of the ruined surfaces of the body translates immediately into its opposite: *the ecstasy of catastrophe and the welcoming of a sex without secretions as an ironic sign of our liberation.*

But it is not really so much "an ironic sign of our liberation" as a sign of an ironic liberation. Future sex will no doubt include the panic of catastrophe and juiceless sex, but it also might offer much more.

So what is the ultimate cyborg fantasy? Polymorphous perversity? Bypassing the body? For many it is simply retrieving what was lost, as the Viagra mania of 1998 revealed with slogans such as "Let the dance begin" and "Be able to respond naturally once again."

That actually sounds more appealing than the author Anton Wilson's off-stated dream of sex with a virtual Marilyn Monroe or even the ultimate cybermergings that were so graphically represented in the movie *Lawn-mower Man*. But to each their own. After all, there is a virtual space called FuzzyMoo where all the avatars are cute, cuddly, little animals with sexual fetishes, like foxes who lust for hamsters, and the like. If the present is confusing, the future will be more so.

The Extropian leader Natasha Vita More speculates on this:

> In society today there are bisexuals, transsexuals, homosexuals, asexuals, and intersexuals. Soon there will be negasexuals, solosexuals, technosexuals, postsexuals, multisexuals, VRsexuals or even just plain ol' sexuals who remain nostalgic for the 20th Century.... The possibility is that we might have as many genders as colors in the rainbow or as many types of genitalia as patterns of flowers.

Maybe sexuality will simply "phase out," she muses. But, she concludes, the penis may not become obsolete after all, at least for the next few decades. Freud's term, "polymorphous perversity," seems to apply more to the future of adult sex than it ever did to childhood sexuality.

Perhaps there will be a puritanical reaction to the proliferation of sexual choice. Few things scare some people as much as sexual pleasure. The studies that have shown that the most rabid male homophobes are repressing their own homoerotic desires are a case in point. Imagine what these men think when the scientists hook up little erection-measuring devices to their penis and then, *on its own*, it insists on rising to the pictures of naked males. If this is how a little self-understanding affects some people, the backlash against the promises and destabilizations of cyborgian sex may be extreme. After all, Wilhelm Reich and others argued that repressed sexual energy fuels fascism. Let us hope the angry and unsatisfied find other outlets, such as the inequities of cyborgian work, which is the topic of the next chapter.

taylored lives

microserfs and superheroes
in the age of semiintelligent machines

The morality thing is a little confusing to me.

—Bill Gates

LONE EAGLES OR SITTING DUCKS?

The rise of industrial capitalism has witnessed the first "scientific" attempts to convert workers into just another element of production. One of the driving metaphors for this was "the human motor," as the historian of technology, Anson Rabinbach, explains in his book of the same name. He traces the history of the disciplining of the worker-body from early Christian appeals against idleness, through punitive control, to today's focus on internal discipline:

> Consequently, the ideal of a worker guided by either spiritual authority or direct control and surveillance gave way to the image of a body directed by its own internal mechanisms, a human "motor."

At the beginning of the industrial revolution, former peasants and freeholders, accustomed to the cyclical work patterns of agriculture, resisted the relentless production of industrialism in what their employers considered a moral failing. But physicians and engineers reconceptualized it as "fatigue" to focus on possible "treatments" that would produce higher productivity. Rabinbach shows the underlying force behind this "invention" of the problem was "the daydream of the late nineteenth-century middle classes—a body without fatigue."

Starting in the mid-1800s, intellectuals in Europe and North America began scientifically analyzing the working body specifically and work in general. Etienne-Jules Marey, a French physician, focused on medical measurement as well as hydraulics and time-motion photography, and was one of the first "engineer(s) of life." These engineers tried to make real the claims of René Descartes (the most famous proponent of the body-equals-machine metaphor) and Julien Offray de La Mettrie (who wrote *L'Homme machine* in 1748)—that we are simply *La Machine animale*, as one of Marey's works is called.

Studies such as Marey's and those of other physicians, such as Paul Bert, who analyzed the diet of prisoners at the same time in *La Machine humaine*, gave substance to the old Cartesian metaphor. In Europe a widespread movement developed to study the "science of work," within which different currents argued for either more supervision of the workers or, influenced by Marxism, their empowerment. Other leftist currents, such as anarchists and Christian socialists, rejected the very metaphor of man-machines.

The next step for the scientists, Marxist or capitalist, was to analyze this "human machine" as it worked, with a focus on its "scientific management." This simplification was the great contribution of the American efficiency expert Frederick Taylor and his many disciples.

Resistance to the European and Taylorist forms of work rationalization based on vitalist, romantic, and individualistic points of view was fragmented on the left by Marxism's scientific claims—it is no accident that Lenin ferverently embraced Taylorism when the Bolshiviks came to power. But the deciding factor in the struggle over the conception of work was war. As far back as Marey, the Prussians' defeat of the French was a major issue. In the United States, the strong labor resistance to Taylorism was brushed aside with the U.S. entry into World War I and the militarization of the economy.

The history of industrialism is indistinguishable from the rise and perfection of modern war. Industrialized destruction needs industrial production. The development of managed bureaucracies is as important to large standing armies and navies as it is to industries benefiting from economies of scale. From the use of interchangeable parts to the perfection of the assembly line, military thinking and its hunger for material goods were behind the creation of what has been called the American system of manufacture.

After the triumph of the idea of the "human motor" came its fall. Workers did not behave as machines, which should have been predicted when soldiers at the end of World War I failed to kill and die with machinelike precision, and instead mutinied. So the metaphors and programs aimed at mechanizing—or at least rationalizing—work shifted. In some cases they took on a decidedly fascist cast, as with the German approach called psychotechnicism, which attempted to bring "the tempo of the machine . . . into harmony with the rhythm of the blood." Other industrialists started dreaming of wholly replacing workers with machines.

It was during this period that two Czech brothers, the Capeks, coined the term "robot" from the Czech and Polish word for indentured worker, *robotnik*. Karel Capek's play, *R.U.R.*, about the invention and triumph of Rossum's Universal Robots, swept the world in the 1920s. The play's success marks the popular understanding of industrialism's long attempt to make the worker a producing machine. While production processes and the integrating system have shifted over time, the basic desire has never wavered.

Today, industry attempts to integrate seamlessly workers and their work through computerization by improving the technical and economic interfaces. Even though technical interfaces are continually being revolutionized, the new postmodern political-economic interfacing of capitalism with its workers is the most innovative new relationship of all.

This has led to the proliferation of contract workers, who are usually described with bird metaphors. A few are lone eagles living in the Rocky Mountains, from where they telecommute to the contracts they choose. The rest are sitting ducks, scrambling for low-paying jobs without benefits—the new last-hired-first-fired cohort.

Because people depend on their jobs for the benefits, companies can maximize both control and productivity through rather schizophrenic practices. Workers are given more control over their own work through mechanisms such as quality circles since that does result in higher efficiency, but they are given less control over their own lives. Interventions into workers' lives include drug testing, psychological profiling, and computer and phone monitoring. But large companies go further to make their regular employees (as opposed to their sitting ducks) completely dependent on them through such means as stock options (so overtime is volunteered religiously), sports and recreation activities right on site (no straying off "campus" to get into trouble), free financial and marriage counseling (early warning for the managers of workers with problems), and subsidized education (quit and you will never get that degree). But when all is said and done, it is a stifling corporate culture whose only sign of independence are the ubiquitous Dilbert cartoons. Quality circles in panopticon's gaze. It is a life of well-upholstered indentured servitude, robotniks with La-Z-Boy recliners at home, or in the argot of the computer industry: microserfs.

REVOLT OF THE MICROSERFS AGAINST THE SOCIOTECHS

I feel like my body is a station wagon in which I drive my brain around, like a suburban mother taking the kids to hockey practice.
—danielu@microsoft.com, in *Microserfs*

We design business spread-sheets, paint programs, and word processing equipment. So that tells you where we're at as a species. What is the search for the next great compelling application but a search for the human identity?
—danielu@microsoft.com

Just how much have "factories" changed in the knowledge economy? After mechanization, the next attempt to rationalize the workplace was automation. Leaders in industry hoped automation would break the power of unions, and military theorists thought it was necessary to outproduce the communists; they also liked the idea of deskilling and disempowering the workers—all potential communists. But complicated machines need smart workers, and automation reached its limits early because of a lack of information-processing power, as with the air force's numerically controlled metal-working machines of the 1950s. So while production did increase, it did not become perfect, and the workers retained much of their power.

Now the panacea of automation has been supplanted by computerization. While the myth of the paperless office has drowned in mounds of computer printouts, computerization has changed work to an incredible degree. It has not done away with the proletariat, but it has led to the rise of the knowledge worker, and those companies that can effectively keep track of their informational resources can use them to "informate," to use a term coined by Shoshana Zuboff, a leading sociologist of work. "Informating" means using computerization to leverage all aspects of a firm's data. Zuboff emphasizes better understanding of one's market, improving quality control, and maximizing working efficiency. But informating also offers great opportunities for analyzing workers' productivity and micromanaging their time and integration into the production process. This integration has many names. In the United States, it is the conscious creation of a corporate culture, such as "the H-P way." In Japan, where cyborgization is more openly sought after, they speak of "sociotechs" and "humanitechs," evincing the intimate integration of the worker and the industrial system that is the postmodern corporation's goal.

Industry rather than academia has often led the way in modifying other creatures to be cyborgs, whether it is roaches who explore pipes, mice for genetic research, cloned sheep for pharming, or workers intimately linked to their machines. Still, in most areas of cyborg research governments have been ahead even of industry, driven as they are by the continual revolution in military technology and their fear of "technological surprise." The cyborgian innovations of business are supported by governments, who see economic competition as "war by other means," and companies are urged on by the unforgiving, invisible whip of competition.

Microsoft certainly practices economic competition as war, using every coercive power at its disposal to gain market share and eliminate or absorb its competitors. It has become more effective at this even as the quality of its once superlative products has declined, showing that it is better to be big than good, at least in the short run. Recently, a combination of Bill Gates's hubris, his cluelessness, and Microsoft's competitors has pressured the government into trying to reign in Microsoft's wilder practices, but the company still remains dominant in computer software. Microsoft is more than the IBM of the millennium; Microsoft is part of the Zeitgeist, as is demonstrated by *Microserfs*, a serious novel written in computer-entry prose by Douglas Coupland.

The narrator works for Microsoft and he hates it. Most people I know who work there do. So, fulfilling the typical geek-slacker fantasy, he and his friends are off to Silicon Valley to get rich by founding a start-up company. The book is full of insights about Microsoft in particular and the computer industry in general, but what was particularly striking was how the story's epiphanies were linked to cyborgization.

Early on the narrator describes a recurring dream he has about his desire to be a machine. Once, after a mild sunstroke, he was hospitalized and while he was being tested for blood clots and other causes of the paralysis he had suffered, he realized he was literally a "body/machine system" injected with isotopes and inserted into the body scanner. He said to himself, "So *this* is the feeling of being a machine." Instead of fearing death, he was curious; perhaps because there is no death for machines. Finally he concludes: "I felt glad to be no longer human for a few brief minutes." On the surface it seems a typical nerd fantasy—how wonderful to be a machine. But instead the character decides he has to pay more attention to his real body, not just as a machine but as a living system with erogenous zones and all sorts of cool features.

The second cyborg epiphany is at the end of the book. The narrator's mother has a stroke and seems comatose. But one of the other programmers helps her access a computer and it turns out she is conscious after all. It is a sappy ending with everyone crying and experiencing feelings they had repressed throughout the book:

> Karla lost it and started to cry, and then, well, *I* started to cry. And then Dad, and then, well, everybody, and at the center of it all was Mom, part woman/part machine, emanating blue Macintosh light.

So the son finds his humanity by rejecting the identification of his body with machinery and the mom finds her humanity by becoming a cyborg that is part machine. Cyborgization offers no simple answers to the new knowledge workers, *Microserfs* suggests, but it cannot be ignored.

Besides their cyborgization, another crucial aspect of the new workers is that they must keep learning the new software, interminable upgrades, and whole disciplines and sciences that never existed before. To meet the need for lifelong learning to keep up with this deluge of computerized information that must be absorbed and utilized requires new types of education, dependent on computers—prosthetic solutions for our ignorance.

HUMAN-MACHINE LEARNING SYSTEMS

Computer-mediated education has become a major political issue. As with cyborgs themselves, it is not a simple equation of good or evil. Distance learning can be very effective, or it can be a joke. Computer programs can teach some important things, or they can bore you to tears.

Recently the number of computer-mediated distance-learning programs has exploded. Students work hard and learn a great deal in these programs without a doubt—those who finish, that is. For it takes a great deal of self-discipline to learn pretty much on your own, even if you have a committed faculty member urging you along at a distance. Unsurprisingly, it is the older students who do better with distance education—people who know what they want from school and know how to organize their lives to make room for classes along with jobs, kids, and other distractions. Younger people, even if they have nothing else but school to worry about, do not do as well. The crucial factor is how good the teachers are and how often they communicate with the students. The technology can aid in this but it does not do the teaching. Only people teach.

Despite this, there is a technomania in contemporary education that at first glance does not make sense. A closer analysis reveals that its roots are political, both historically and in terms of what is happening today. Historically, the military pushed for high-tech education because of its need for more effective training and indoctrination. The same desire powers the politically motivated drive by conservatives and businesses to undermine education that aims to foster citizens, instead turning it into a profit-making enterprise that will produce useful workers.

Douglas Noble has written extensively about the historical roots of education in military priorities. A whole range of teaching technologies have come from the military, including overhead projectors, language labs, instructional films, TV, teaching machines, and all sorts of computer teaching systems. But the very theories behind these technologies also come from the military. In its desperate attempt to solve the paradoxes of postmodern war, the military has had to develop smarter weapons and then smarter soldiers to operate the smarter weapons. Along with failed attempts to make autonomous systems, the military attempted the "amplification of human intelligence within man/machine systems," the aim of so-called cognitive science.

Noble quotes one cognitive scientist who says that his work is "prescriptive . . . to design . . . the information processor of interest, either a computer or a human being." The goal is the cyborg—as with the cyborg soldier, so with the cyborg student. The very first technical use of the idea of human-computer symbiosis comes from J. C. R. Licklider's famous article "Man-Computer Symbiosis." Licklider, a leading computer educator to this day, is also a former director of the U.S. Department of Defence's Advanced Project Agency's Information Processing Techniques Office.

Most of the new high-tech educational initiatives pay lip service to "critical thinking" and "improving the student's ability to reason," but the programs focus on automated instruction, well-defined problems, and quantitative measurements. Is it any surprise that:

the new appreciation of intellect represents the desiccation of human intellectual potential at the very moment it appears to be celebrating it. This is because cognitive processes of learning and thinking, needed as components in the complex information system of the military and industry, are cultivated only with such needs in mind. The new "higher order" education consists in the training of cognitive procedures derived not from a deep appreciation of human ingenuity but instead from computer models of machine learning and artificial intelligence.

Many conservatives in politics and industry see distance education as a chance to kill a number of birds with one computer.

The Western Governor's University (WGU), also called Virtual U. by its critics, is the prime example of this. One almost-virtual institution hopes to earn profits, undermine liberal universities, and produce trained workers. In 1995 a majority of U. S. governors from the West founded WGU. Originally set to go into operation in 1996, it opened in 1998. WGU is a conscious effort to use the combined political power of the governors to bring about several fundamental reforms in higher education in the United States. To this end, WGU does not offer courses of its own but packages already existing distance-education offerings of a number of accredited colleges and universities, professional certification schools, and industrial training programs. The governors hope to obliterate the distinction between education and training while replacing traditional criteria of accomplishment, such as grades and class hours, with testing and other formal evaluation methodologies.

Traditional academics and their students have been the strongest opponents of the university. In an editorial in the *Daily Utah Chronicle* at the University of Utah, Kristen Riedelback wrote:

> Virtual U. is a real joke.... (It's) real purpose is to decrease enrollment in state colleges so the state will not have to fund the construction of new buildings and classrooms.

Riedelback is no doubt right that keeping taxes down is one major motivation for Virtual U. but she does not give the governors and their corporate allies enough credit. Their goal is the fundamental dismantling of higher education, using technology as the lever. They want to reconstruct it as a market- and technology-driven component of industrialization to serve the needs of business and the state, and to integrate students into human-machine systems that produce not citizens but workers and consumers.

But not every case of worker cyborgization is driven from above. One group of very elite workers is intent on their self-cyborgization: professional athletes.

'BORGING THE PROFESSIONAL ATHLETE

There may be some sportsmen who can win gold medals without taking drugs, but there are very few. If you are especially gifted, you may win once, but from my experience you can't continue to win without drugs. The field is just too filled with drug users.

—Michel Karsten, sports physician

More and more, high-level athletes have to be treated like normal workers.
—Prince Alexandre de Merode of Belgium,
head of the International Olympic Committee's
medical commission

Kids love their superhero action figures, and there are hundreds of them for sale these days. A few are traditional human heroes—Zoro, or knights who fight dragons. But the vast majority of action figures are actually cyborgs—not just the Ninja Turtles and the X-Men, obvious genetic mutations, or fun guys like Inspector Gadget with his pop-up head, or the alien from *Independence Day* that has a motion sensor that makes it open up its space suit and growl at our dog every time she walks past (boy, she hates that); even most of the toy soldiers have been 'borged with implants or complex computer gear (which is only an accurate reflection of what is going on in the real military). And, while the sports-hero action figures look normal enough, every fan knows that a high percentage of the real ones have been modified with performance-enhancing drugs.

This is just part of the cyborgization of professional athletics. The inventor of the artificial kidney, Willem Kolff, once predicted that athletes with artificial organs would be banned from competition because of the unfair advantage. Artificial organs have not made that much progress yet, but perhaps someday the marks in the Special Olympics events, where many competitors use prosthetics, will surpass those of the Olympics. In 1992 a Little League catcher used his plastic leg as an advantage by blocking runners trying to storm home ("It doesn't hurt me"), and a young Oregon man competed successfully as a bodybuilder despite the fact that his plastic foot was built by someone else. In 1998, a 49-year-old climbed Mount Everest with a prosthetic leg. Already the record for the longest drive of a golf ball belongs to a cyborg, the astronaut Alan Shepard who took his famous swing on the moon. Someday Dr. Kolff's prediction will be true for less esoteric records.

But for now the controversial modifications in sports are more subtle; they are in the high-tech training systems, the state-of-the-art equipment, and the undetectable drugs coursing through the bloodstreams of many of the world's top performers. When top athletes train, they are filmed and analyzed by computers. They are weighed and measured, and every key metabolic function is digitalized and manipulated with various foods, supplements, and training regimes to maximize performance. The equipment they use, the shoes, the pole vault staffs, the bobsleds, and the bicycles are constructed using the latest scientific equipment and the most effective metals and plastics, often developed for military applications. It is a weird sort of inverted Taylorism because the machines are used to perfect the human—the athlete is the product.

Consider Olympic bike racing. Before the 1984 Olympics, a team of scientists and engineers were recruited to improve the aerodynamics of U.S. racing bikes. They introduced the streamlined "funny" bikes with solid disc wheels and teardrop helmets for the riders that everyone now uses, and the United States won nine medals. After poor performances in 1988 and 1992, the U.S. Olympic cycling team introduced Project '96, which sought to bring the same level of technoscientific expertise to all aspects of bike racing: "[W]e not only look at the technology—the bikes, wheels, and components— but... we also look at the athlete and we address the training, preparation, and psychology of athletes as intensely as the equipment." The team modified helmets, bikes, clothing, training patterns, and even the food and drink the athletes consumed. As the coordinator of Project '96 pointed out: "We can't just rely on the athletes anymore to help us win medals. It takes technology, training, and a team of people behind them."

Anyone who has seen *Chariots of Fire*, the movie about the 1928 Olympics, knows that this is not a new development. Coaching and training have been improving in all sports for at least a hundred years and the continual improvement of performance measures results from this refinement. Yet the balance between an athlete's will and genetic ability and his or her support system of coaches, technologists, and dietary supplements seems to have shifted decisively away from the athlete. Great athletes cannot win alone now. They must have infrastructure.

The most important and most controversial modifications in sports are to the athletes themselves. The hunger that world-class athletes have for first-place gold may be the single greatest factor behind illegal doping. An article by Michael Bamberger and Don Yaeger in *Sports Illustrated* cited a shocking 1995 poll of almost 200 Olympic-level U.S. athletes on the use of performance-enhancing substances. When asked if they would use a substance that both guaranteed winning and could not be detected, over 95 percent said yes. When another question added the proviso that in five years the athlete would die from this drug, over 50 percent still said they would use the deadly, illegal, undetectable, and effective substance.

According to the International Olympic Committee (IOC), doping is defined as the "unfair and unethical" use of "any physiological substance taken in abnormal quantity for the purpose of enhancing athletic performance." But there are several problems with this definition. One is that testosterone, human growth hormone, erythropoietin (EPO, a hormone that stimulates the production of red blood cells), androstenedione (used by the body to make testosterone), and creatine monohydrate are all normal in the human body and so detection is meaningless. Secondly, when I was a high school jock I consumed incredibly abnormal quantities (at least according to my mother) of all sorts of substances, mainly pork chops, ice cream, and pasta. What makes such consumption "unfair and unethical"?

Creatine, which has been used since 1992 to build athletes' muscle mass, is one thing that makes athletes crave meat. It is an amino acid found in fish and red meat that people burn at the rate of about two grams a day. Some individuals can experience startling muscle gain when ingesting extra amounts; others show no effect. Long-term negative impacts are not known since, as a natural substance, it can be marketed without tests. In gyms across the globe, coaches and athletes sing its praises or warn about its hidden dangers.

Some athletes will even inject or implant fetal tissue to increase hormone production. This so-called "baby power" fix relies on the special qualities of fetal tissue, which can be differentiated into testosterone-producing cells but lacks the ability to trigger an immune response. As the sports commentators Gerard Thorne and Phil Embleton observe: "When you're dealing with multimillion-dollar salaries, morals go out the window."

Another problem is that the technology of drug detection always lags behind the technology of drugging itself. Besides taking natural substances, athletes can also take drugs that are not tested for, or take yet other drugs that mask the illegal, detectable drugs. Despite constant testing, the highest technology, such as steroids manufactured to fit perfectly the athlete's own natural steroids, insures that a smart athlete will never be detected. As one expert put it: "Athletes are a walking lab, and the Olympics have become a proving ground for chemists." The head of the Netherlands drug testing center for athletes, Emil Vrijman, said that to get caught, an athlete has to be "incredibly sloppy, incredibly stupid, or both."

In the summer of 1998, the Tour de France, one of the top marquee athletic events in the world, was shattered with revelations of illegal drug use. A member of the top-ranked Festina team was caught at the French border with enough EPO for the entire team and they were disqualified and their director and doctor were arrested. Despite a sit-down protest by the remaining riders, who were "angered by the attention given the scandal," investigations continued. At least five other riders admitted to using EPO, and another top team, EVO, came under suspicion.

During the same period, several top track athletes were suspended for failing random drug tests, including the 1996 Olympic Gold Medal winner in the shot put, Randy Barnes. Irish swimmer Michelle Smith, winner of three gold medals in the 1996 Olympics, was banned from competition for four years because a urine sample she had submitted for a random test was useless since it was contaminated with a "lethal concentration of alcohol." Whisky was the likely culprit.

These suspensions are part of a steady stream of such cases since the 1980s; what was new was that Juan Antonio Samaranch, the president of the IOC was quoted as suggesting that "some performance-enhancing drugs be stricken from the list of banned substances." He went so far as to say that unless the substance hurt the athlete, it should be legal. The next day the IOC came down on him with full force, and he retracted his statements. The IOC has since embarked on a campaign for a permanent drug testing consortium for all Olympians.

A month later the press revealed that Mark McGwire, on his way to breaking the U.S. baseball home run record, regularly used androstenedione. McGwire argued: "Everything I've done is natural. Everybody uses the same stuff. It's legal." He's right. The drug can be found in baseball, hockey, and basketball, and in the local health food store. In the weeks after McGwire's use was publicized, sales of androstene skyrocketed 300 percent. Said one company CEO: "This has gone from a $5 million-a-year industry to maybe a $100 million industry." McGwire has since stopped using the drug. Dr. A. Scott Connelley, the chairman and founder of MET-RX Engineered Nutrition, which manufactures the drug, argues since the consumer turns androstenedione into testosterone at a healthy rate, it should be allowed in sports. On the other hand, the Association of Professional Team Physicians called for removing it from drugstore shelves and banning its use by athletes.

High-level sports have no consensus on what should be banned. The IOC has the strictest standards. The National Basketball Association bans only cocaine and heroin, ignoring a raft of other illegal and performance-enhancing substances. The National Hockey League and Major League Baseball ban only illegal drugs, while other groups fall somewhere in between.

The issue of drug use in athletics cannot be separated from the larger context of the drug war. If taking dangerous drugs is okay for our sports heroes, why is it not okay for the average citizen who needs a little edge? Between the antidrug hysteria, the lure of superior performance, and the continual improvements in biochemistry, the issue will remain at an impasse, despite the 1998 scandals, until a high level of hypocritical tolerance is breached. While new drugs are developed faster than they can be banned, arguments continue around substances proscribed in the past.

One bioethicist, Dr. Norman Fost, argued in 1983 in a *New York Times* opinion piece for the legalization of steroids:

> The objection that steroids provide an "unnatural" assist to performance is inchoate. Many of the means and ends which athletes use and seek are unnatural. From Nautilus machines to...Gatorade, their lives are filled with drugs and devices whose aim is to maximize performance.

But if all enhancements are legalized, then what happens to the nature of sports competition? Will the victory be awarded simply to the athlete with the best drugs and other cyborgizations? Perhaps sports will separate out into a whole range of competitive levels, from the disabled, through the normal, to the heavily cyborged, just as there are age competitions now. Or perhaps our fascination and love for athletics will focus even more on the average participant and less and less on the genetically unusual and heavily modified performers who now dominate professional spectator sports.

The transformations in mass participatory sports have more political ramifications than the cyborging of elite athletes. Improvements in everything from general nutrition to ski bindings to knee surgery has meant that more people in high-tech societies can play sports and they can play them later in life. High school athletes and weekend warriors often take performance-enhancing supplements and drugs, and anabolic steroids and human growth hormones (hGH) are endemic among high schoolers. A 1992 poll found that 5 percent of tenth-grade boys used hGH. Many experts believe such use can contribute directly to cancer, so there is the potential for a horrible epidemic in the future.

173

Illegal sales to athletes are a limited market, so pharmaceutical companies began strongly marketing hGH as a treatment for a new disease: shortness. They advocated that any child in the lowest 3 percent for height of their sex/age group should be diagnosed as needing treatment. Of course there will always be a bottom 3 percent, so there will always be a "diseased" population. Dr. John Lantos, an ethicist at the University of Chicago notes that shortness is being labeled a disease:

> only because a manipulation has become available and because doctors and insurance companies, in order to rationalize their actions, have had to perceive it as one. What we're seeing is two things—the commodization of drugs that are well-being enhancers and the creeping definition of what it means to be healthy.

While the disease is spurious, its effects are real. Not only is height a distinct advantage in many sports, but it helps procure jobs and attractive mates. Heightism is as persistent as racism and sexism, and it is not illegal. Yet hGH does not help short children grow taller. Only children already deficient in hGH grow taller with injections of hormone. But eventually the combination of drugs and genetic engineering will allow normal children to grow taller; then shortness will become a treatable disease.

The public health aspects of the cyborgization of sports are wide-reaching, but not all of the implications are negative. There has also been an incredible upsurge in the participation of girls and women in sports. This has inevitably led to a merging of gender roles, since "jock" used to be solely a masculine identity. Now girls are proud to be athletes. This explosion of women's athletics has been studied by participant-anthropologists such as the bodybuilder Anne Bolin, who notes how the gender blurring of intense sports overlaps with impacts of other cyborgian technologies like transsexual conversions to create new possibilities for identity. In work and in play, cyborg technologies have both good and bad effects. The worst responses are to try to merely stem their utilization without any consistent reason, or to embrace them for short-term profits or victories. Our cyborgian choices should strengthen the values we are proud of, not those that debase us. To do this we have to understand the forces we are dealing with.

This is the job of cyborgology, the latest of the cybernetic sciences. This term covers everything from the philosophy of information to systems analysis, and it is the topic, appropriately enough, of the next chapter.

cyborgology

sciences of the
third millennium

Now, facing muscle atrophy, loss of bone density, osteoporosis, and all the other side effects of a spinal cord injury... I have to rely on self-discipline and faith, although my faith is based on science rather than religion.

— Christopher Reeve

THE GAZE OF SCIENCE

Science is our religion. While many people profess to believe in this god or that goddess, when they are ill, when they need weapons to kill those who believe differently, when they broadcast their truth to the world, they invariable turn to science. What happened between the birth of science and today is not central for this story so much as the fact that many things did happen, particularly in terms of the tension between seeing the world and the human body as natural and seeing them as machinic. Today they are conceived as both, and this is why instead of natural bodies wielding machine tools, we have systems that incorporate both—cyborgs. As Donna Haraway notes:

> Broadly within late twentieth-century scientific discourse, the natural body is conventionally a biotechnological cyborg—an engineered communications device, an information generating and processing system, a technology for recognizing self and non-self (paradigmatically through the immune system), and a strategic assemblage of heterogeneous biotic components held together in a reproductive politics of genetic investment.

The metaphor of information processing and the idea that information is the key element of scientific knowledge dominate many fields. Ironically, attempts to make information its own scientific discipline, cybernetics, failed because the central conceit that information is the decisive way of looking at the natural world had instead colonized all the rest of science. But information theory itself is still in its infancy.

THE HUMAN USE OF HUMAN BEINGS: CYBERNETICS

Render unto man the things which are man's and unto the computer the things which are the computer's.

—Norbert Wiener

The cybernetics of men, as you, Socrates, often call politics. . . .

— Plato's *Clitophon*

We can think of reality as being made up of three basic elements: energy, matter, and information. We happen to know a tremendous amount about matter and energy. Albert Einstein proved that energy and matter can be translated into each other, a discovery that has had its practical drawbacks in the form of mushroom-shaped clouds. But information is still very much a mystery. When engineers talk about information theory, they usually mean the mathematics that calculate how much redundancy a signal needs to make sure it is communicated, not what information the signal carries or what knowledge is.

In the 1950s computer scientists attempted to create artificial intelligence. They were sure it would not be difficult and they made many confident predictions. Now their predictions are in ruins and their greatest accomplishment has been to show just how complicated the process of knowing information really is.

Still, some progress has been made in the last 3,000 years, roughly the time humans have been keeping track of ourselves. Our biggest step was probably our first: language. If Noam Chomsky is right, language is hardwired into our brains, language is the net we use to hold information and the main tool we use to work it. Logic is the formal relationship of hunks of information to each other. Mathematics, a strange protolanguage, stems from language, logic, and the fact that much of reality comes in discrete chunks with formal arithmetic relations to each other.

All three of these fascinating and overlapping forms of information have been improved over time, but we have also come to understand their limits.

The ambiguities and lapses of language are well known to any speaker, and the paradoxes of logic have been paraded for the amusement of the general populace by smart-ass philosophers since ancient times. But it was not until Kurt Gödel mathematized an old philosophical paradox (what if a liar tells you he always lies?) that it was provable that mathematics is not the language of God; instead it is a formal system that has to be flawed by either being incomplete or having at least one paradox. It could well be incomplete and replete with paradoxes.

This is one of the key insights of the fledgling field of cybernetics: all formal systems are limited. Alonzo Church and Alan Turing showed that Gödel's incompleteness theorem also applies to infinite computers. So even before it was well under way, thoughtful technoscientists knew that computerization had its limits. Gregory Bateson was one of a number of cyberneticists who discerned another limit: a system cannot fully understand itself. Only partial understanding is possible, for understanding is a map and the map is not the territory. Two insights from physics also help delineate the negative boundaries of postmodern information theory: 1. that the observer affects (becomes part of) the system he or she observes; and 2. that to know one thing (like the position of an electron) often precludes knowing something else.

Cybernetics has other important concepts as well, starting with Norbert Wiener's main fascination, feedback. He chose the term cybernetics because it was based on the ancient Greek word for steersman. Feedback is what keeps a steersman on course by taking in the information from the wind, sea, and boat and using it to turn the rudder this way and that. Feedback can be positive (carrot) or negative (stick), but in most complex systems it is both. Wiener noticed that feedback and other system dynamics were the same in both artificial and natural systems. This is what makes the cyborg possible—communication across the divide between the living and the inanimate.

Complexity theory, often misnamed chaos theory, has shown that many complex systems that seem chaotic instead follow complex or counterintuitive patterns. Some systems are so unstable at certain points that a very small input can radically change them. This is known as the butterfly effect, after the example that a butterfly in Brazil could change the weather in Montana. But only in very unique, singular cases can such a small effect have such large impacts, because systems tend to stabilize. Most Brazilian butterflies live lives that never impact most of Brazil, let alone Montana. Sometimes system stability takes the form of entropy, such as the much-feared heat-death of the universe, but sometimes it is the stability of a higher complexity. Some systems reorganize themselves when overloaded with new energy, matter, or information. They are called dissipative systems, and the chemist Ilya Prigogine won a Nobel prize for describing them mathematically. Prigogine's math works best on simple chemical phase changes such as the transition of a supersaturated saline solution into a giant salt crystal with the addition of just one grain of salt, but he has also argued that intelligence and even life itself are also dissipative systems. What his work shows is that there is much more to information than we now know.

Gregory Bateson maintains that it is the "pattern of patterns that connect," as is the case with fractals, systems whose patterns repeat themselves on different scales such as snowflakes and landscapes. These patterns or system rules necessarily apply to cyborgs. Bateson also said:

> We might regard patterning or predicability as the very essence and raison d'être of communication...communication is the creation of redundancy or patterning.

One of the best investigators of the relations between pattern and communication is the English professor, N. Katherine Hayles. She has shown how discourse itself is a cybernetic system, which we can modify by talking or writing about it. She discusses another information paradox that Bateson raised. If redundancy is information, so too is randomness (known as "noise" to engineers) although the first is old information and the second is new:

> Identifying information with both pattern and randomness proved to be a powerful paradox, leading to the realization that in some instances, an infusion of noise into a system can cause it to reorganize at a higher level of complexity. Within such a system, pattern and randomness are bound together in a complex dialectic that makes them not so much opposites as complements or supplements to each other.

This returns us to Wiener's argument that artificial and natural systems are basically the same. Kevin Kelly describes dozens of different systems in a book called *Out of Control* that links them together along with the naïve Libertarian political agenda that is championed by *Wired*, which Kelly happens to edit. "Out of control" does not mean running amok; it means outside of external control: These systems run on their own dynamic; they cannot be directed. By looking at contemporary systems research on everything from living coral reefs, new management theory, and the building/evolving of little mechanical creatures that are "fast, cheap, and out of control," Kelly has come up with some new system rules, which he calls "The Nine Laws of God." They are: 1. distribute being; 2. control from the bottom up; 3. cultivate increasing returns; 4. grow by chunking; 5. maximize the fringes; 6. honor your errors; 7. pursue no optima—have multiple goals; 8. seek persistent disequilibrium; and 9. change changes itself.

One can argue with this list, but there is something important in these rules and in the other insights of systems thinking I have just dashed madly through. These are the baby steps toward a real information theory, and their similarity to postmodern clichés and to the dynamics of cyborgs is more than suggestive. The information revolution profoundly affects many areas of research, including what might be the most important new field of research in the twenty-first century: nanotechnology.

SMALL IS POWERFUL: THE NANO REVOLUTION

Living bodies are even in the smallest of their parts machines *ad infinitum.*
—Gottfried Wilhelm von Leibniz

As was explained back in Chapter 4, when the military implications of nanotechnology were discussed, nano means very small. Nanotechnology is the technoscience of very small things, including micromachines incorporating both computers and motors made of only a few molecules. Such tiny machines will someday live throughout our bodies, colonize other planets, and perhaps replicate themselves. Nano is overdetermined, which means that there are multiple historical and cultural causes for its existence. The same is true of cyborgs. For cyborgs, overdetermination is a sign that human tool use and human machine creation have reached a new stage: cyborgization. The same force that drives progressive cyborgization—technoscience—is behind nano, and nanotech is an integral part of current and future cyborgizations. A major cultural impetus behind nanotechnoscience is the human urge to explore, which can be a wonderful and aesthetic desire (small *is* beautiful), but successful exploration inevitably leads to other, less fine emotions. Once researchers realized that "small" was a place, the nanoworld became a destination. Exploration is often followed by conquest (the will to power), and then colonization and exploitation, driven by that fundamental human desire to prosper and more-than-prosper (greed).

Therefore nanotechnology is not just a little corner of contemporary science/engineering/business; it is the expression of our postmodern age, replete with the postmodern characteristics: bricollage (different types of nanotechnology at whole different levels and with different strategies), the centrality of speed (milli- and microseconds are now important in many processes), and information.

In many ways info is nano. What is smaller than a bit? Conceptually, it is almost nothingness. Physically, instantiated in a computer, it is very small indeed, and optical and quantum computing are literally nanocomputing.

Nanotechnology partially defines the other two great sciences of the postmodern era: physics and biology. Physics gains its power from understanding the smallest possible elements and forces in terms of both science and engineering. Biology leverages its explorations of the subcellular (genetics and biochemistry) for its growing power. Nano is indeed pomo, which means that there is bad news with the good. The dark side of nano includes its possibly horrible impact on war (see Chapter 4), crime, and, perhaps even more threatening, the danger of overeffective government and other institutions using nanotechnology to eliminate the last vestiges of privacy in our society in their zealous "wars" on crime and drugs.

Nanotechnology may someday result in:

- Tiny spies everywhere, even in the form of mists or clouds.
- Drug and DNA analysis performed on people without their knowledge as they simply pass by.
- Tiny machines measuring bioresponses to detect lies.
- Nano methods of doing drugs, committing murder, or other crimes that remain ahead of the police's ability to detect them.
- New ways to harm the environment by extracting valuable elements from the land, the sea, and even the air.

At a minimum, traditional surveillance will increase drastically; prisoners and parolees will be monitored continuously; homes will be turned into effective prisons; mind-and-emotion reading will improve tremendously; new drugs will lead to either legalization or massive repression; and assassination will become undetectable. The "escape" of nanotechs into their own life cycle poses a further environmental danger, because many scientists have presented proposals for making nanos that can reproduce: nanocyborgs. Just how much nano will change the world we cannot say, but the indications are that it will be almost beyond the scope of our imagination.

Nanotechnology is just one of many sciences based on cybernetic/bionic metaphors and the deep, thick understanding of the smallest processes of the natural world. They are all "sciences of the artificial," to use Herbert Simon's phrase, and that includes their own self-understanding and its implications.

THE SCIENCES OF THE ARTIFICIAL
AND THE REFLEXIVE TURN

Everything said is said by an observer.
—Humberto Maturana and Francisco Varela

Nazism is applied biology.

—Rudolph Hess

Manfred Clynes, one of the researchers who coined the term "cyborg," is a deeply cultured man. His work—physiologically analyzing emotions, computationally producing classical music, and speculating on the modification of humans through various stages of cyborgization—represents a great love for the Enlightenment principles defined by humanism—all the more ironic because what he does often undermines the human.

Cyborgization transcends the human, dissolving old distinctions between nature and culture or organic and machinic. Herbert Simon's "sciences of the artificial" are also being elided because everything can now be viewed as both artificial or natural. Consider one small part of cyborg research, biocomputing, and the range of hybrid systems is staggering.

Researchers have noticed that animal bodies perform very complex biochemical calculations that digital computers cannot manage, and this observation has led to attempts to turn beasts into calculating machines: neurobotics. As Michael Gruber explains:

> They would take a rat, wire it for blood-pressure and heart-rate tracking, and insert recording and stimulating electrodes at various sites of interest in the baroreflex system. Ultimately, they could play the system like a video game.

Scientists are also exploring biocomputers based on viruses, algae, nucleotides, and even DNA itself. One of the leading researchers on DNA computers, Leonard Adleman notes:

At one extreme, you can view everything in the world as a computation. The universe and its interactions might be thought of as some huge cellular automaton involved in its own peculiar form of computation.

The line between artificial and natural and between life and machine has never seemed so nebulous. How can we understand this philosophically? We need an approach that can deal with these changes as well as look at itself within the same framework.

In science studies several scholars have raised the question of reflexivity. Any system of knowledge with pretensions to completeness should be able to use its own tools and paradigms to analyze itself. Science, for example, should be capable of scientifically studying itself. But in fact this is very difficult to do. Science effectively explores certain phenomena, especially that which can be quantified and isolated for repeated experiments, but many things do not lend themselves to that treatment, and one of them is science itself, which involves a great deal of interpretation, cultural baggage, and complicated arguments. How would one experiment on science?

Some areas in science studies can analyze themselves using their own methodology, since science studies usually relies on a combination of quantitative and qualitative approaches linked by a guiding analytic such as discourse analysis. Cultural systems can be understood as discourses with artifacts, actions, and texts all representing arguments. Discourses contain rules, metarules, and the possibility of changing them through discourse itself, which applies to science studies.

Cyborgology, if it is based on the cyborg epistemology of *thesis, antithesis, synthesis, prosthesis, and again,* has the potential to be reflexive as well because it is consistent throughout the metaphor, and what is learned of the dynamics of cyborgs can also be applied to cyborgology itself. Where conceptual worlds collide, there are often fireworks. And since the stakes in science and science studies (of which cyborgology is a part) are profoundly political and concrete, it should be no surprise that their supposed disagreements have generated controversy—the so-called Science Wars.

"Science Wars" has replaced C. P. Snow's idea of "Two Cultures" as a metaphor for discussing the tense relations between science and the rest of Western culture. It is ironic that scientists' main target in these "wars" is the discipline of science studies, which has tried the hardest to bridge this gap. In part it is another case of blaming the messenger, but there are other dynamics at work as well that have more to do with political and epistemological divisions within science and science studies than the purported battle between scientists and the academics who study them. The Science Wars draw their fury from tensions between math and physics, successful and unsuccessful academics, wild and conservative physics, traditional history and philosophy of science and science studies, and old "New" Leftists with a Marxist outlook and pomo Leftists who are post-Marxist or even anarchist.

The Alan Sokal controversy serves as a lens through which to view these disagreements. This academic brouhaha resulted from an article Sokal wrote as a satire but which was published as a serious contribution by the journal *Social Text*. In it, Sokal argues that there are important similarities between the postmodern theory of a number of noted science studies scholars and theories from the "new age" edge of physics. This is actually a legitimate perspective, held by established physicists and philosophers both, but this article was neither well argued nor carefully written.

What are the hidden agendas of the Science Wars? Sokal's spoof essay focuses its attack on other mathematicians and scientists, not science studies scholars. It singles out mathematicians such as Ralph Abraham of UCSC and many of the wilder physics theoreticians for satiric pillorying. Observers have speculated that Sokal's animus is derived from his failure to get tenure as a mathematician and his relegation to a below-average physics department, but that does not explain the behavior of other participants in the debate. In discussions about the Science Wars, "rationalist" scientists often forget their science studies targets and instead lash out at their fellow scientists, especially Fritjof Capra and Ilya Prigogine. The Sokal article was mildly convincing because it cited so many scientists who do look at the world in a postmodern way (vague and general as that term is). This internal war within science, of the rationalists against the "new" physics, is a key part of the Science Wars that is usually ignored by commentators.

Even less noticed is the internal war within science studies. Most of the key players in this drama are feminists and Leftists, including Sokal, many of his scientist allies, and perhaps most of the science studies protagonists, although there are those from both camps who are on the right, such as the apolitical aristocratic Bruno Latour and many of the rationalist apologists and their funders—the Olin Foundation, the Bradley Foundation, and the National Association of Scholars.

The main point is that the Science Wars are about policing science by scientists on the one hand and about Leftist doctrine among science studies people on the other; they are not about scientists and those who study them. The way this war is waged is by simplifying what everyone says about science.

While the critics of science studies claim that it argues that reality is "made up" it is very hard to find people who are pure social construction-ists, and most of them are in literary studies, not science studies. There has been an incredible misreading of science studies texts by people such as Gross and Levitt (especially in their book *Higher Superstition*) and Sokal. On the other hand there is a problem with some cultural critics of science in that they do not love, or like, or even know science. But that is not true of most science studies scholars. If we did not find science beautiful and fascinating (and very important), we would study something else. Anyone who closely reads Donna Haraway's work, for example, will note that not only is she a trained scientist (Ph.D., biology, Yale) but she also loves science for its beauty and its power. It is simply not an uncritical love. Most science stud-ies scholars have a rich understanding and appreciation of science, but what seems to rankle the handful of scientists and their "defenders" who have declared war is that we do not make science into a religion, something Marxists are as apt to do as some practicing scientists. It is true, however, that science studies people can say stupid things.

On the science studies side, Steve Fuller claims that "Science critics generally believe that the idea of scientific progress is little more than a well-ingrained myth...." This is very uncarefully stated. Certainly, the idea that all scientific discoveries are good and that they lead us closer to some absolute truth is one that few would ascribe to. But many of us can see that science does grow better and better at manipulating the physical world.

Science clearly progresses, understanding that love and cancer both progress. Fuller compounds this problem by admitting that he is a believer in a grand narrative of science after all, ignoring all of the epistemological work from Nietzsche, Gödel, Heisenberg, Church-Turing, and the post-modernists. Unfortunately, he is mimicking that famous postmodernist, Jean-François Lyotard, who also secretly harbors an uncritical admiration for science. The one thing the best science studies people and the best scientists agree upon is the limits of human knowledge. Let us not lose that. Science and science studies are intertwined discourses that, when they are at their best, can interrogate and modify themselves and each other, leading to new understandings and modifications of lived reality.

Which brings us full circle. Human knowledge is limited but it is improvable; besides, it is all we have got. What do we now know about the politics of cyborgs that can help us shape our future and the possibilities of the posthuman?

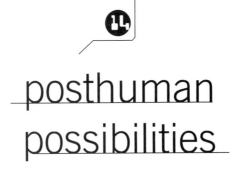

posthuman
possibilities

Man is an invention of recent date. And one perhaps nearing its end.
—Michel Foucault

We have modified our environment so radically that we must now modify ourselves.
—Norbert Wiener

CYBORG EPISTEMOLOGIES, ETHICS, AND EPIPHANIES

Norbert Wiener's comment encapsulates the mutilation-prosthesis dynamic. Does every technoscientific intervention/mutilation require a new intervention/prosthesis to repair it? And as the prosthesis is no doubt a mutilation as well, is the cycle endless? In a sense, yes. Human culture does not stand still, nor do ecosystems, nor do species, nor does evolution. Is it a dynamic we can control? Within certain technologically determined limits, we can socially construct the future we choose. The process of choosing, however, is profoundly political and therefore it is anything but straightforward. Not only are politics always by definition contested, but for good or ill modern political schemas do not map well onto the future. There is no simple left-center-right of cyborg politics, so most of our old guideposts are useless.

Donna Haraway's famous manifesto was an argument for socialist feminism. The Extropians are strong Libertarians. Left anarchists are a major presence on the Net and among both cyberpunks and postmodern theorists, and many of them are feminist-anarchists. Feminists of all stripes are also very well represented in the debates over transsexuality and medical technologies and on both sides of debates over censoring the Internet for sexual and other content. On the one hand, government and multinationals push cyborg technologies forward, and on the other, individuals are drilling holes in their heads to wire themselves to their computers.

Left and right political stances just do not predict attitudes toward cyborgization. Primitivists, neo-Luddites, and ecologists tend to be anarchists and feminists of the far left, but those tendencies are almost as well represented on the other end of the cyborgization scale by many an anarchist-feminist cyberrgirrrl with piercings and a kick-ass computer. Libertarians dominate on the extreme protechnology side.

Some corporations lobby for absolute freedom on the Net and few restrictions on informational property rights, while others take the exact opposite view. On the Net, race and gender distinctions dissolve, but access to the Net is clearly a class (and therefore a race and national) issue, and right-wing groups have proliferated there almost as fast as left-wing ones. Both lag behind e-businesses. Klaus Theweleit and others have shown that there is a fascist cyborg identity going back at least to World War I. It is alive and well in the military, in dark corners of the Net, and in toy departments around the world. The earth as one system appeals to ecologists and one-world-government authoritarians alike. Liberals and moderates are generally open to cyborgizations, while conservatives fear them, but some conservatives love cyberculture, while many liberals loathe it, and very few people would want to die if they could live on as a cyborg, so what is a cyborgologist to do?

We start by being specific. Politics become extreme during "interesting" times; cyborg politics are no exception. While liberals, moderates, and conservatives have positions on most cyborg issues, they do not set the agenda nearly as much as the more radical political and religious groups. However, totalitarianism of either the left or the right has nothing to offer the cyborg citizen. Totalitarianism, whether fascist or communist, is a threat to any kind of participatory evolution or politics. The illusions of blood (fascism) and of a science of politics (communism) are only made worse by command economies, unrestrained state power, and new class systems based on false ideologies. Every other political view has something to offer a cyborg society, even conservatism, whose pleas to slow it all down do have merit; totalitarianism promises only nightmares.

Our cyborg society is not the reinvention of everything from politics to poetics; it is the transcription of old forms on to new problems. New political principles arise from shifts in our understanding of epistemology. Many people assume they know what they know because of some authority: the Bible, the president, their mommy. This is not a useful position philosophically or pragmatically. The mainstream understanding of epistemology is we know what we know through our senses. But, as many philosophers have demonstrated, sense data alone is meaningless; it must mentally be organized or "constructed" to be useful. Does this sense data construct our view of reality? Is this reality hardwired into our brain, as Noam Chomsky argues language is? Is it culturally constructed? If so, on what basis? Stories? And which stories? To these questions the cyborg epistemologist answers: Yes! Yes! Yes! It is all true, and it is not.

Along with the realization that no totalizing theory explains everything is the corollary that a number of different perspectives together are capable of creating a better model of reality than any one point of view. Similar actions may have wildly different explanations. Context is crucial, as a key cyborgian phenomena illustrates beautifully: body modifications.

The popular body-piercing craze fits right into our cyborg society. What could make more sense in the face of expanding cyborgization than taking control of the process and modifying your own body for beauty and pleasure? Many people do not find pierced tongues pleasing, but that repulsion forms part of the beauty of piercing for others. Piercing is often motivated by love for the body, not hatred as some psychoanalysts have claimed. A piercer from San Francisco says: "Bodies are beautiful and deserve to be decorated and celebrated. I choose to ornament my body as an act of caring."

Of course it is more complex than that. The contemporary reclaiming of ancient body-modification philosophies has both uncovered some of their more subtle goals as well as drifted into expropriation at times. Yet most practitioners carefully respect the so-called "primitive" traditions that have inspired them and the many meanings their practices hold, such as the belief that the body should be subordinate to the will, even as their unity is celebrated. There are important arguments about reinterpreting the messages of the body, of pain and discomfort—as pleasure, surely, but also as more spiritual information about the nature of existence. Driving it all is the assumption that the body belongs to the soul (not the state, society, or God) and that humans have the freedom to make of their body what they wish.

Contrast this to the psychological disorders that involve self-mutilation and to implant mania. Implants figure centrally among UFO devotees and right-wing militiamen. While the body-piercing movement seeks to turn its fears of cyborgization into empowerment and pleasure through taking control of the process and making of it art, the victims of the UFOs and the One World Government have succumbed to their dislike of their own bodies and their anxiety about technoscientific changes, turning to a politics of paranoia and, inevitably, defeat.

The majority of people who are cyborged are modified for medical reasons. Some are in denial, but many more have chosen to take power over the process. This can be working for new cyborg technologies, as Christopher Reeve does, or accepting a dependency on machines as a way of gaining cyborgian independence, as the surviving polio victims did. We can see how our very subjectivity can be constructed in large part by the choices we make about our own cyborgization.

SUBJECTIVITIES OF POSTHUMANITY

I'M...TRAPPED IN THIS WORTHLESS LUMP OF MATTER CALLED
FLESH! I WANT TO BE FREE TO CRUISE THE WIRES AND MOLEST
PEOPLE'S APPLIANCES...LONG LIVE THE NEW FLESH! FUCK THE
OLD FLESH!
—MODERNBODYMODERNBODYMODERNBODY

In 1995 I taught a semester at Masaryk University in Brno, the second biggest city in the Czech Republic. My undergraduate and graduate courses were in the Informatics Department and they included many discussions of computers and society in general and cyborgization specifically. When I teach such courses, I always ask my students questions about their own cyborgian desires. For example, would they download their consciousness into a computer or a robot for an extended life, if it were possible? In general 50 to 80 percent of my North American students are enthusiastic about such a transformation, depending on their major, their sex, and their age. Female feminist philosophy students are much less excited about being a "brain-in-a-box" than the male high school computer geeks I once took to MIT's Media Lab. Still, North Americans are usually quite open to being cyborgs.

The majority of my Czech students, on the other hand, did not want to be "enhanced" in any way, although they did support restorative interventions such as pacemakers and prosthetic limbs and organs. These were all male computer students, and yet only a quarter of them were interested in being downloaded. On questioning them, I discovered that half of them did not even like computers! They worked on them because it was important work, for their future and their country's, but that did not mean they had to love them as the vast majority of North American computer students seem to.

This difference is not because the Czechs have a culture and Canada and the United States do not. The cultures are different. The United States has been called "technology's nation"; we evince great love for tools, machines, and, inevitably, cyborgian technologies. Though we are not the only nation with such a passion—the Japanese even call their country "The Robot Kingdom"—the United States leads the way in the creation of cyberspace and in other areas of cyborgization. Mark Seltzer explains:

> [N]othing typifies the American sense of identity more than the love of nature (nature's nation) except perhaps its love of technology (made in America). It is this double discourse of the natural and the technological that...makes up the American "Body-Machine" complex.

At the center of this complex "is the notion *that bodies and persons are things that can be made.*" Today Americans labor at remaking themselves in incredible variety, from grim yuppies imbibing wheat germ soaked in vegetable juice, to jocks using dead iron and complex machines to resculpt their bodies, to technopunks piercing themselves for sexual display and pleasure; and almost all of us diet, it seems.

Things have progressed beyond such crude interventions. Bodies can now be remade technologically, not just morally or willfully through the self-discipline of abstinence and exercise. The discipline of tools and machines, long a part of human culture, is no longer just inscribed on the body. Today, metaphorically and physically, the discipline of technoscience is incorporated into the body as information, and it is surgically added, prosthetically.

Our sense of ourselves, our subjectivity, is shaped just as our bodies are, and that explains why in this cyborg age there is a proliferation in pop culture of posthuman creatures such as vampires who live on the borders between the human and other. Sandy Stone comments on Anne Rice's vampire, Lestat, who inhabits a series of Rice's books:

> Lestat is a liminal creature and—though not to belabor the obvious—a cyborg. Cyborgs are boundary creatures, not only human/machine but creatures of cultural interstice as well; and Lestat inhabits the boundaries between death and life, temporality and eternity, French and English, gay and straight, man and woman, good and evil. He nicely exemplifies a

style of cyborg existence, capturing the pain and complexity of attempting to adapt to a society, a lifestyle, a language, a culture, an epistemology, even in Lestat's case a species, that is not one's own. Lestat is a vampire for our seasons, struggling with the swiftly changing meanings of what it is to be human or, for that matter, unhuman.

It is not just vampires who inhabit this terrain in popular culture, there has been a proliferation of aliens, immortals, posthumans, and, of course, hundreds of cyborg characters.

A number of political theorists have mobilized the idea of the cyborg, along with the Native American god Coyote and the reality of mixed races, to argue that living in more than one world confers leverage and therefore power. Chela Sandoval ("oppositional consciousness"), Joseba Gabilondo ("postcolonial cyborgs"), and others theorize that the cyborg opens a place in politics for disempowering master narratives and reinscribing the political margins into the center.

This is happening demographically in most of the world. Politically one can celebrate complexity and transgressing borders, as the best of multicultural theory does, or you can make a fetish of ethnic purity and move on to "cleansings" and other insane attempts to make pure something that never has been. Race is not even good science, let alone good politics, and so inevitably categories such as Asian, white, black, and Latino collapse under scrutiny just as, today, the category of human is collapsing under cyborgization. Still, for every border trespass there are new mobilizations that futilely attempt to keep identities unsullied and unified.

During my stay in the Czech Republic, I made it a special project to track down information and representations of the golem, that strange protocyborg mud creature vitalized by a hunk of code from sacred Jewish texts and created to defend the ghetto against pogroms. After all, the most famous telling of the golem story is set in Prague during its Golden Age under the occult-obsessed Prince Rudolfo.

Prague is famous for its puppets, and the little shops in the Old Town sell thousands of different ones, from Czech peasant goddesses to Prince Rudolfo himself, so I thought there would be little problem finding a golem puppet. But in shop after shop I was told, "No, we have no golem. The golem wasn't Czech!" Accustomed as I was to the relentless melting-pot appropriations of American culture, this comment surprised me. Then, hearing that there were some shops selling Jewish puppets near the Old Synagogue, I went there. On approaching the line of stalls I was encouraged, for there were clearly puppets of the famous Rabbi Low, the creator of the golem in the better-known tales. But there were no golem puppets. "Why?" I asked one merchant with the help of an English-speaking Czech friend. "The golem was not Jewish," she replied.

Startled at first, I realized that technically she was correct. He was certainly created by a Jew but uncircumcised, indeed inhuman; he was hardly Jewish. It brought home to me just how potentially alienating cyborg existence might be, especially once modifications become extreme. There are already cyborgs based on human bodies that are no longer human, such as neomorts, but someday soon there will also be living, thinking cyborgs based on humans that are no longer human. Will they identify with their antecedents, personal or national, or will they see themselves as new politically and in almost every other sense of the word?

The golem remained loyal to the Jewish community that fostered him, and some say he still lies in the attic of the Old Synagogue ready to come to life on command to defend it. But cyborgs as simple and as loyal as the golem will probably not be the rule. Cyborg identity is definitely more complicated than the golem's literal view of the world, and it will only get more so.

CARNIVAL CYBORG

We rather need more complexity, multiplicity, simultaneity and we need to rethink gender, class and race in the pursuit of these multiple, complex differences. I also think we need gentleness, compassion and humor to pull through the ruptures and raptures of our times.

—Rosi Braidotti

Humans have always aspired to be cyborgs and we have always feared that aspiration. Cyborging ourselves is costuming ourselves from the inside out, a disturbing technocarnival with permanent consequences, delightful, disturbing imaginings of beautiful and grotesque technoscience. Some dreams and some nightmares seem fated to come to pass. Overdetermined, as I mentioned above, is the academic mystification of this process. Overdetermined: multiple and oversufficient causes? The causes we can catalog, but beyond causes, overdetermination implies metacauses. They are probably unnameable yet may still be mappable in the intersections, mutations, and creations of images, objects, logics, myths, and reflections—intersections where thesis and antithesis cross; mutations that are always synthesis; amalgamation and creation in the invention of prosthesis.

We are a cyborg society of tools, machines, and organisms but we deny it. We deny our connection to the organic, the world in which we are embedded, and we deny responsibility for the technosciences we make.

To fail to come to terms with our cyborgian situation as part of both organic (the "natural") and machinic (industrial civilization) realms would be fatal. Crashing either of these systems will end humanity, and yet the two systems often seem to be on a collusion course. Perhaps this is how the repressed is returning in cyborg—as imperfection, self-contradiction, and unresolvable paradox. A good Gödelian (incomplete and paradoxical) model it is—sweet cyborgs, hermaphrodites, killers, and saviors, the crippled and the augmented as one system.

So it is with today's cyborg body politic, the text of humans and technology in the context of nature, ever more subjugated, ever more intertwined with civilization. Humans and our cultures have lived within nature for tens of thousands of years, but now, with the extinctions, the explosion of human population, the modification of every ecological niche to serve us, humans have become one cyborg system.

Cyborging is also something we do to ourselves as well as the world. We can use it to explore the limits of what control we can have. This seems to be the message of the militant cyborg artist Stelarc, whose body is his canvas.

What does Stelarc, or all the other cyborgs for that matter, tell us about the aspirations that have led to cyborg? It is only just becoming clear. Certainly, the body is the ground; it cannot be ignored philosophically any more than it can be ignored in real life, no matter how much one aspires to be virtual. Bodies inhabit space, whether it is outer (the "high ground" to the military), micro (now being colonized by nanotechnology), cyber (the simulated universe of virtual technologies), or symbolic (not cyberspace, as some virtual reality technicians claim, but the "high ground" of Platonic philosophers, the human imagination, origin of cyborg). Space is modified by speed (action), mass (presence), and by simulation (thought).

At the core of this web are the cyborg technosciences, which are extremely evocative technologies—evocative not just in terms of what they provoke from us as individuals, but especially in what possible futures they might evoke for our culture as a whole. Dreaming of possible constructions of the impossible leads to real transformations, new types of life, changes in the very way we think of space, time, erotics, art, artificiality, perfection, and life, ourselves. Technoscience is constantly deconstructing the idea of the impossible. The only set impossibility is making nostalgia real. The past is gone. We cannot go back to the future, except in the movies; we must go forward. The future is, after all, a new environment. The future is what cyborgs are for. We have evolved to ride out future shock. In the long run it may not be a good survival strategy, but we are committed. Our rush to the future can be a blissful or a nightmare carnival ride. Most likely it will be both.

> Thus one of the great future problems which we must face is that of the relation between man and the machine, of the functions which should properly be assigned to these two agencies.
> —Norbert Wiener

The daddy of cybernetics was certainly right about that. Here we are dozens of millennia after the invention of tools, thousands of years since the first machines were constructed by humans, hundreds of years into the Machine Age, and one of our greatest problems is our relationship to the very machines that we create. What is behind this irony?

The term cyborg was coined to describe the possibilities of intimate and liberating technologies.

> The purpose of the Cyborg...is to provide an organizational system in which such robot-like problems are taken care of automatically and unconsciously, leaving man free to explore, to create, to think, and to feel.
> —Manfred Clynes and Nathan Kline

But as the old tales of the golem show, and as Mary Shelly demonstrated in *Frankenstein*, liberation is not inevitable.

Cyborgs are invented as new technosciences. Like culture, they are constructed out of past and possibilities. They—we—are as much works of art as our identities. The proliferation of cyborgs is the promise of monsters, the promise of possibilities. Horror is possible, perhaps inevitable. But resistance, even joy, should be just as possible. Cyborg epistemology shows that there is no inevitable dialectical lockstep; prosthetic additions are always possible—on the body and on culture, and therefore on the future.

Monica Casper's image of the cyborg carnival is an apt one. Cyborgs are often grotesque, illegitimate, disordered amalgamations that transgress not just good taste but good sense. They are dangerous. They are exciting, transcendent, exuberant, even liberating. They dwell on the border between cultures, between living and dead, between organic and inorganic, between natural and artificial, between now and the future, and in doing so they obscure, and reify, these very boundaries. We must carefully choose the borders we inhabit and transgress. We must carefully choose our stimulations, the music we dance to, the costumes we wear, or the future cannot be ours and we will not even have a good time. We are, after all, our rituals. It is our life, our carnival. As individuals we can cry if we want to, we can dance, we can love and hate, we can leave early, we can pretend it is not happening. But we cannot stop the cyborg carnival; it is already well under way. We just do not know how it is going to turn out.

THE FUTURE IS NOT YET WRITTEN

... There are changes afoot in our embodied dispositions, changes that will surely take importantly different forms among different people and groups. We are experiencing not so much the end of the body as the ending of one organizational scheme for bodies and persons and the beginning of another.

—Emily Martin

Christopher Reeve, chairman of the American Paralysis Association, has called for a "mission" to conquer "*inner* space, the brain and central nervous system." Can this be balanced with the appeal of the antitechnology writer, Andrew Kimbrell, for "an empathetic future vision"? Kimbrell advocates radical limitations on genetic and other research, including limiting gene therapy to life-threatening diseases, a ban on germ line genetic therapy, a moratorium on cloning animals including transgenetic creatures, a moratorium on using fetuses in research, a ban on human cloning, no experimentation on embryos, a ban on neomorts and heart-beating cadavers, no expanded definitions of death, no prenatal screening for sex, weight, or height, no genetic screening of workers or insurance applicants, and no "eugenic use of 'superior' sperm or eggs."

This not only would stop genetic research dead in its tracks, but would severely curtail the "assisted" reproductive industry, organ transplants (meaning thousands of people would die who otherwise would live), and the development of the therapies that Christopher Reeve hopes will restore his broken spinal cord. Just how many deaths are "empathy" and a sacred view of the body worth? It is hard to believe that many people will politically choose, based on abstractions, to limit concrete technical advances that save and improve lives. Even among the members of the Christian groups that produce most of the opponents of cyborgization, such as the Catholic

Church, when a helpful technology meets a dogma, as with birth control, it is usually the dogma that gives way in practice. The Catholic Church might still oppose birth control but a majority of its members use it. Our techno-culture is deeply optimistic, maybe not about the last technology but certainly about the next one.

The central theme of the great cyborg movies such as *Terminator II* is: "The Future is not yet written!" In *Star Wars*, Luke Skywalker, maimed like his father and sporting a similar prosthesis, chooses a different side of the force from Darth Vader. In *Total Recall*, the hero, unsure which of his personalities is real, chooses the role of revolutionary over that of secret policeman, against the wishes of his original, "true" self. The *Robocop* corpus is about Murphy's stubborn humanity in the face of his cyborgization. Perhaps this validation of human spirit and life force is just an illusion we wish to foster in the face of the relentless mechanization of human culture, but I think not. It is more complicated than that.

Machines *can* serve the spirit. During the Yugoslavian civil war, a computer network was set up connecting people in all the battling nations. It was called ZaMir Net, "peace net" in Serbo-Croation. With donated equipment, contributed money, and great ingenuity, the wired citizens of the Balkans used the advantages of a low-grade network, including sending signals in batches whenever the phones were working, to perform all sorts of political acts of communication, from coordinating peace protests to feeding independent journalists noncensored news. But one of the most moving messages was not obviously political at all. A group of girls from the war-shattered town of Pakrac in Croatia sent a message using ZaMir Net to Krist Novoselic, the bassist of Nirvana, after Kurt Cobain's suicide, urging him not to follow his lead singer's example. Nirvana's music, the girls wrote, had been crucial in their own "struggle to survive." Novoselic, of Slovenian descent, wrote back and promised not to kill himself, and he sent $60,000 to the Pakrac Reconstruction Project.

What is the value of this in the grand scheme of things? I am not sure, but I do know that it is good and it matters that teenage girls can send a message of encouragement from a war zone to a superstar and get back hope and real money. It is things like this that help us all survive. Sandy Stone sums it up better than I can:

> It is a moment which simultaneously holds immense threat and immense promise. I don't want to lose sight of either, because we need to guide ourselves—remember, *cyber* means steer—in all our assembled forms and

multiple selves right between the two towers of promise and danger, of desire and technology. In the space between them lies the path to our adventure at the dawn of the virtual age, the adventure which belongs to our time and which is ours alone.

What have we learned so far in our adventure? First, we know that *technologies are political*. Richard Sclove has written a powerful book called *Democracy and Technology* that not only demonstrates this point at length, but shows how the prospects for democracy are determined by the technologies we choose. He concludes:

> It is possible to evolve societies in which people live in greater freedom, exert greater influence on their circumstances, and experience greater dignity, self-esteem, purpose, and well-being. The route to such a society must include struggles toward democratic institutions for evolving a more democratic technological order. Is it realistic to envision a democratic politics of technology? Isn't it unrealistic not to?

A "more democratic technological order" must be based on a number of principles, especially participatory citizenship.

Cyborgization and politics is about bodies. Joe Dumit and Robbie Davis-Floyd use the work of Nancy Scheper-Hughes and Margaret Lock to convincingly argue that the body is always three: the individual lived body, the social/symbolic body, and the body politic. The shift from modern to postmodern entails a parallel shift from direct control of individuals, meanings, and society itself to the power to transform these paradigms. While some postmodernists may claim that individuality is a recent invention, the individual human body and the consciousness it carries around are not. As Elaine Scarry and Hakim Bey each demonstrate, the body is the first source of power and wealth.

Cyborg politics are about power, as all politics are. Who has the power to develop and deploy cyborg technosciences? Is it the citizen or the government? Is it the patient or the doctor? Is it the scientist or the experimental subject? Power is both coercive and constructive. Coercive power can be incredibly augmented by cyborg technologies to our peril, so we need specific protections for the cyborg citizen. Constructive power, for cyborgs, arises from having information and controlling our technologies.

Knowledge is power. To be empowered, the cyborg citizen has to have the specific information that govern our technical and political situation, and we need to understand information theory, which lays out the limits of knowledge (Gödel, Church-Turing, Heisenberg, Bateson), its formative rules (cyborg epistemology, feedback), and its promises (complexity, dissipative structures, Kelly's Laws of God). Knowledge as power moves from the specific to the general and back again.

By looking closely at actual technopolitical issues, we can discover the principles that are important to the cyborg citizen. From examining the cyborg soldier, we learn that cyborgization cannot redeem a powerful discourse such as war; the cyborg soldier has not freed postmodern war from its contradictions. From the world of medicine and science, we get the principle of informed consent and the realization that some types of cyborgs (neomorts, beating-heart cadavers) can be created to give life to others. That trade-off has to be recognized, and it cannot be mediated through the market. The inability of the market to solve the contradictions of cyborgizations is a continual theme in this book. Whether it is the gift of life or the allocation of resources, there is nothing intrinsically fair or efficient about the market. To assume otherwise out of a misunderstanding of information theory and for the sake of ideology will prove politically disastrous. Cyborg families lead to cyborg family values: high adaptability, flexible boundaries, healthy communication, technological sophistication. Cyberspace may open up new possibilities for cyberdemocracy, but it does not mandate them. Finally, the proliferation of cyborg sexualities shows that technosciences can have incredible impacts on a human discourse that is even more ancient than war: the gender system. Love and lust will survive in at least some posthumans.

We must develop microknowledges of specific technologies, as the polio patients had to learn their wheelchairs and Christopher Reeve has to understand his cyborged body. This may involve renouncing our ideas of the human body's limits in order to achieve more freedom *as a cyborg*. Or cyborgization can lead to a loss of freedom.

Knowledge is situated. Specific types of cyborgization have their own histories and their own implications. *Meanings are constructed,* which means they can be chosen. Cyborgization does not have to mean giving up on romance, for example. Even a baby produced by the most high-tech cyborgian means is still a cute little creature who will bliss out at the sight and feel of a redwood and who still needs dirty diapers changed. We are involved in participatory evolution, and that means the responsibility to participate is ours.

If humans are going to accelerate our own evolution, we have to make political changes that keep pace, not changes after the fact. Along with new technologies we need new political institutions. We must also look ahead. We have to listen not just to the rational predictions of scientists, engineers, and futurists, but also to artists, especially those whose art is themselves.

Stelarc, a man who has pierced himself and put machines in his gut and wired his body to the Internet so people around the globe can manipulate it, is militant about the individual's right to claim his or her own evolutionary path:

> In this age of information overload, what is significant is no longer freedom of ideas but rather freedom of form—freedom to modify, freedom to mutate your body. The question is not whether a society will allow freedom to express yourself, but whether the human species will allow you to break the bonds of your genetic parameters—the fundamental freedom to determine your own DNA destiny.

Sympathetic as I am to Stelarc's cry, it is somewhat more complicated. First, the freedom of form comes out of freedom of ideas, and in most places, even the freedom of ideas is threatened. People must organize to protect all their freedoms, actual and potential. That ultimately involves working together.

Second, there are ways to work together that maximize freedom. They involve understanding how order comes out of what seems like chaos and how complexity can produce harmony. Many decentralized volunteer groups with few resources organize long-standing, elaborate, and effective campaigns against the biggest bureaucracies imaginable, such as the U.S. government. Their success depends on good communication, letting those who do the work make the decisions, and personal responsibility. Centralized control is fundamentally weak, because it is only one story about our very complicated reality. The wonderful anarchist writer, Colin Ward, contrasts centralized control with decentralized coherency from below:

> How crude the governmental model seems by comparison, whether in social administration, industry, education or economic planning. No wonder it is so unresponsive to actual needs. No wonder, as it attempts to solve its problems by fusion, amalgamation, rationalisation and co-ordination, they only become worse because of the clogging of the lines of communication. The anarchist alternative is that of fragmentation, fission rather than fusion, diversity rather than unity, a mass of societies rather than a mass society.

Cyborg technoscience renders mass society a thing of horror. Uniformity is technically possible as it has never been before, making totalitarianism a nightmare to be feared. The only alternative is to go in the other direction and allow for the blossoming of cyborg citizenship in many forms. Yes, it will have its horrifying moments, and the reaction of those who fear change will be more horrifying still. But reaching toward greater democracy, stronger citizenship, and a proliferation of human and posthuman possibilities is our only choice besides a turn to the past that, since it would be in the context of postmodern technoscience, would make the Holocaust and the Gulag look like rehearsals.

Cyborgization will not make us like gods, thank goodness, but we may be able to live better and longer than any human or protohuman has before. We may be able not only to live long and prosper, but to push the species into new, enlightening adventures in inner and outer spaces. Systems achieve equilibriums but they do not survive in stasis. It is thrive or die.

notes

INTRODUCTION

...a colossal cauldron of life Quoted in the display area of the Diego Rivera exhibition, San Francisco Museum of Modern Art, Summer 1996.

CHAPTER 1

The Possibilities of Posthumanism
We're going to be as gods... Brand 1994, p. 1.
...we'll be machines, or gods. Sterling 1990, p. 15.
..."Cyborg Anthropology"... Downey, et al. 1995.
...vital machine... Channell 1991.
..."Fourth Discontinuity"... Mazlish 1993.
...Gaia is a cyborg world... Haraway 1995, p. xii.
...metamen throughout the galaxy. Stock 1993.
..."Cyborgology"...to...thesis, antithesis, synthesis, prosthesis... Gray, Mentor, Figueroa-Sarriera, 1995.

Postmodern: The Times We Live In
...nervous laughter. Reid 1988, p. 32.
...postmodern condition is technoscientific... Rajchman 1985, p. 116.
...wholly adequate. Huyssen 1984, p. 181.
...more than style is at stake. Gitlin 1989.
...undermines the social structure... Bell 1976, p. 54.
...equivalent to the posthuman. Hayles 1987.
...The principle of simulation wins out... Baudrillard 1983, pp. 148-151.
...multinational capitalism...blood, torture, death and horror... Jameson 1984, pp. 54, 57.
...construction of our worldview. Griffin 1988, p. x.
...save the honor of the name. Lyotard 1985, pp. 81–82.
...powerful infidel heteroglossia... Haraway 1985, pp. 100–101.
...responsibility and tolerance. Hutcheon 1987, p. 193.
..."reality" will appear even more unstable... Flax 1987, p. 643.

The Importance of the Cyborg Idea
...melded into...cyborg... Clynes and Kline 1995 (1960).
There is an arrogance... and...we are told to vote in... Gray and Mentor 1995, pp. 463, 465.

CHAPTER 2

Acknowledgment
Parts of this chapter were published in my article "The Ethics and Politics of Cyborg Embodiment: Citizenship as a Hypervalue" in the journal *Cultural Values*, 1997.

[I]t is no longer enough... Gray and Mentor 1995, p. 459.

Who or What is a Citizen?
...weakening of the state... Pakulski 1997, p. 84.
..."the tree of liberty" and *..."the government that governs least"* Rawson and Miner 1986, p. 125.
Citizenship Studies... Turner 1997.
...the New Citizen... Isin 1997.
The Turing test... Turing 1950.

The Cyborg Bill of Rights
...Cyborg Manifesto... Haraway 1985.
...all manifestos are cyborg... Mentor 1996, p. 195.
...Bill of Gender Rights... S. Turner 1997.
...total theory... to *"perfect communication"* Haraway 1985.
...economy and satellites. Latour 1993, p. 144.
Lives are at stake... Haraway 1995, p. xix.

Cyborgian Justice
..."engineer" human responses. (p. 49) to *...questions of power.* (p. xii) to *...wave of deaths, deformations...* Restak 1973.
...Physical Control of the Mind... Delgado 1971.
...cyborg organs within... Haraway 1989, p. 109.
...AUM... Kaplan and Marshall 1996.
...electronic "leashes"... Associated Press 1983.
...Miller, who killed and mutilated... Associated Press 1998c.
I want to thank George Orwell... Associated Press 1998f, p. 5A.
...secrecy has always favored the mighty... David Brin quoted in Teitelbaum 1996.

CHAPTER 3

Acknowledgment
The discussion of Libertarianism in the last section is an updated version, in part, of some of my 1979 article "The New Libertarians" in *Black Rose*.

The Manufacturing of Consent
...he's a special effect. Bury 1994, back cover.
...Democracies Online... Cliff 1998.
...ability to influence... Guernsey 1996, p. A29.
...McWorld versus jihad... Barber 1996.

Technofixes
...communication, coordination, and information costs... Bonchek 1995, p. 1.
...electronic democracy... Miller 1996, p. 1.
...26% slower.... Taylor 2000, p. 47
...the basis of wealth... Bey 1998, p. 5.
Real communities are better... Etzioni and Etzioni 1997.
...Internet is incompatible with authoritarianism... Bennahum 1997, p. 172.
...if people are mature enough. Roy 1996.
...antithesis of democracy... and... *recede into darkness.* Roy 1996 quoting Arthur and Marilouise Kroker, italics in original.

Bioregions, Infospheres, Nets, Webs, Taz, and Community
...Net... Web... TAZ... Bey 1985/1996. Quote from 1996, p. 366.
...There is only one Net... Borenstein 1997, p. 1.
...absolute right... (p. 36) *...turfs my servant has cut...* (quoted on p. 33)
...the creator gets it... (p. 31) *Society is a collective concept...* (quoted on p. 39). Rothbard 1978.
...techno-resisters... Sale 1995, p. 275.
...digital citizen... Katz 1997.
...technorealism... Young 1998.

CHAPTER 4

Acknowledgment
The first two sections of this chapter are based in part on my 1997 book *Postmodern War*, but updated and revised. Part of the third section was published on the Web by *Technopolis*.

In these "post-modern" times... Levidow and Robins 1989, p. 7.

Postmodern War and Peace
...citizenship is... tied to war... Hanson 1989.
...destruction of Iranian Flight 655... Gray 1997a.

Human-Machine Weapon Systems
...wars make men. Ehrenreich 1987, p. 26.
...displaced into his body armor. to... *components explode in battle.* Theweleit 1989, pp. 155–199.
...virtual reality came out of this research. Gray and Driscoll 1992.

Future Conflicts
...TV news show 60 Minutes... March 1, 1998.
...epochs defined by power sources... Bunker 1994.
...a new informational age.... Toffler and Toffler 1993.

CHAPTER 5

Acknowledgment
Parts of this chapter are adapted and updated from my 1996 article "Medical Cyborgs: Artificial Organs and the Quest for the Posthuman."

The Digital Body
Convicted murderer... Wheeler 1996.
...a prosthetic disciplinary hand... Cartwright 1997, p. 130.
Viagra, the hit... to *...before Viagra.* Handy 1998.

The Medically Modified
...the "half man" Chicago Hope, Jan. 6, 1997.
...the prosthetic control system. (p. 3) *... "conventional body-powered prosthesis"* (pp. 1–2) *...man-machine interface"* (p. 3) McKenzie 1965.
...but the patient died... (p. 94) and *...hemodialysis was suspended...* (p. 93) Alwall 1986.
Motokazu Hori... artificial liver... Hori 1986, pp. 211–213.
...literal explosion of calves... Dr. Seth Foldy 1992, personal communication.

The Artificial Heart
The mechanical heart borders on science fiction... Quoted in Fox and Swazey 1974, p. 153.
...never been tested on a human being... Quoted in Fox and Swazey 1974, p. 205.
...dog survived for about 90 minutes. Dutton 1988, p. 92.
...eloquent science lobbyists. (p. 333) and *...both scientific and political.* Strauss 1984.
...most American of religions... Quoted in Fox and Swazey 1993, p. 162.
...services for the impoverished. Lubeck and Bunker 1982; Dutton 1988.
...paid off in spades. Quoted in Dutton 1988, p. 124.
...If ten's enough, we'll give you 100. Quoted in Dutton 1988, p. 123.
...none of which were successful. Dutton 1988, p. 125.
People do not want to die... Kolff 1979, p. 12.
...or benefit for the patient. Dutton 1988, p. 103.
...standing ovation from his peers... Fox and Swazey 1974, p. 176.
...mocked in public. Dutton 1988, pp. 114–115.
...others have violated FDA and other regulations. Dutton 1988, p. 115.
...instant immortality. Fox and Swazey 1974, p. 188.

Natural Transplants
...nonoral cannibalism... Youngner 1996, p. 49, original italics.
[W]e are intentionally... Fox and Swazey 1993, p. 210.
...courage to fail... Fox and Swazey 1974.
...all organs transplanted will... be rejected... Fox and Swazey 1993, p. 10.
...offer their organs... Fox and Swazey 1993, pp. 33–34.
...tyranny of the gift... Fox and Swazey 1993, pp. 55–56.
...chimeras... Fox 1996, p. 256
...animistic, magic-infused thinking... Fox and Swazey 1993, pp. 42–47.
...murdered for their kidneys. Youngner 1996, pp. 40–41, and Richardson 1996, p. 84.
...urban legends... Richardson 1996, pp. 85–86.

...corpse began to be bought... to *...worth more dead than alive.* Richardson 1996, pp. 70–74.

...favor white males... Fox and Swazey 1993, p. 75.

...donated organs are being exported... to *...the God Squad.* Fox and Swazey 1993, pp. 80–82.

...a profanation. Fox 1996, p. 262.

Perhaps the most famous xerotransplant... Altman 1992.

...especially disturbing. Fox and Swazey 1993, p. xv.

CHAPTER 6

I dedicate this chapter to Bailey and Sage, cyborg babies extrordinaire, and to my little guys, Corey and Zack, home birthed, unvaccinated, but cyborgs all the same.

Acknowledgment
Many of the issues in this chapter are dealt with in *Cyborg Babies*, Robbie Davies-Floyd and Joe Dumit, eds. The section titles: "Cyborg Conceptions" and "Postmodern Pregnancy" come from them as well.

Cyborg Conceptions
..."romance" of the sperm and egg... Martin 1991.

...addictive quality of our relationship... to *We are immersed in cyborgs...* (p. 1) ... to *...more technological options...* (p. 2) *...subversive potential of these technologies...* (p. 7)

...a wily subject... to *...four different perspectives deploy "cyborg"...* to *... "promise of monsters."* (pp. 8–13); Dumit and Davis-Floyd 1998, original italics.

....achieving and/or enhancing... Clarke 1995, p. 140, original italics

....semen as cyborg... Schmidt and Moore 1998, p. 34.

Postmodern Pregnancy
...plethora of fetal cyborgs... Casper 1995, p. 186*...incredible experience...* Hall 1995*...baroque cyborganic configurations.* (p. 191) and ... *"naturally" human.* (p. 195) Casper 1995.

...there is ample evidence... Mendelsohn 1984, p. 31.

...cheerful and affectionate little girl... Associated Press 1993.

...neglectful parents who rarely visited... Associated Press 1994.

...the "lost cause" that many doctors thought. O'Neill 1995.

Programming Cyberchildren
...as with the swine flue vaccine... Silverstein 1983; Neustadt and Fineberg 1978; Knox 1976.

...some whooping cough vaccines... Stewart 1979; Coulter and Fisher 1985.

...measles, rubella... Cherry 1980.

...and chicken pox... Mackenzie 1984.

...strong evidence of a relationship... Waisbren 1982; Miller, et al. 1967; Wilson 1967.

...eternal struggle... James 1988, p. 6.

...increase in the incidence of polio... James 1984, p. 28; Mendelssohn 1984, p. 231.
...only source of smallpox... and *These are fearful diseases...* Mendelssohn 1988, p. 232.
..."right not to vaccinate"... James 1988.
...limited liability... Journal of the American Medical Society 1984.

CHAPTER 7

Acknowledgment
The first two sections of this chapter are based, in part, on my article "Medical Cyborgs" published in *Technohistory* in 1996.

(Dis)Abled Cyborgs
...part of my body. (p. 105) *...invasion of my body...* (pp. 109–110) and
 ...a serious student of myself. (p. 114) Reeve 1998.
...Bruce Hilton... Hilton 1992.
...36 percent... Tzamaloukas, et al. 1990.
...8 percent... Van Nieuwkerk, et al. 1990.
...clicking of the pump... (p. 184) and *...cannot cope with life.* (p. 183) Kolff 1989.
Numerous studies... Gray 1996.
...into the life of the patient. Zimmermann 1989.
Several studies... Wolcott, et al. 1988; Gonsalves and Kotz 1987.
A study...of ten victims... ...given in to the disease (p. 872) *...the people in it.* (p. 875) and
 ...dependence upon technology. (p. 876, my italics) Kaufert and Locker 1990.
...growing disabled rights movement. Crewe and Zola 1983.
...through denial... (pp. 91, 115) *...somewhat more...* (p. 92) *...as natural looking as any*
 hand. (pp. 95–96) and *...wearing of artificial limbs.* (p. 99) Silber and Silverman 1958.

Penile Prosthetics
Scott's inflatable prosthesis... Renshaw 1979, pp. 2637–2638.
...no longer the old male cock. Kroker and Kroker 1987, pp. 95–96.
Studies of the recipients of penile implants... Tiefer, et al. 1988 and 1991.
It's just the way you make me feel. Tiefer, et al. 1991, p. 181.
In one study... Tiefer, et al. 1988.
...the "pump man." Tiefer, et al. 1991, p. 124.
...But wait (p. 50)*... to ...First, the implant man...* Manning 1987, pp. 106–107.
...Regneri De...Pearman's penis. Gee 1975.

Neomorts, Living Cadavers, and Immortals
...technology is death. Quoted in Dery 1996a, p. 225.
What will it even mean to be "dead"... Brin 1992, p. 664, italics in original.
...watching people die. Hogle 1995.
...felt she was alive... Youngner 1996, p. 46–48, italics in original.
...still technically alive. Fox, et al. 1996, p. 20.
...heart stops equals death... Youngner 1996, p. 42.
...death by protocol... Fox 1996, pp. 264–265.
...criminals to donate their organs... Youngner 1996, p. 41.
...never experience consciousness. Quoted in Youngner 1996, p. 50.

...metal of motors... Quoted in Dery 1996a, p. 190.
...instinctive fear of death... Lee and Morgan 1996, p. xiv.
A fear... Alldridge 1996, p. 11.
...death is not an evil... Quoted in Fox and Swazey 1993, p. 205.

CHAPTER 8

The Rhetoric of Life
...Frankenstein as a doctor... Fielder 1996, p. 63.
...Vampire Somoza!... (pp. 15–16) *...OPEC of blood...* (quoted on p. 21) *...the status of a container...* (pp. 22-23) *....that the object being patented was alive.* (p. 193)...*a transgenic mouse...* (p. 197) *...transgenic nonhuman mammal...* (p. 198) *...engineered human tissues...* (p. 199) *...tissues of his own body...* (p. 209) *...covers the stem cells...* (p. 211) and *...patent 2,337 brain genes...* (p. 189) *...significant financial or personal interest.* (pp. 163–164) *Let mermaids be free of bans...* (pp. 164–165) *...ban on all research...* (p. 166) *Dr. French Anderson...* (pp. 169-171); Kimbrell 1993.

Cloning
According to Sen. Brownback... to *...Sen. Orrin Hatch...doubts they are human.* Saletan 1998.
The clone wars are just starting... Kiernan 1998.
...permit cloning... Andrews 1998, p. B5.
In Europe 19 countries... to *...Tijuana, Mexico.* Basinger 1998.
...cloning himself... Associated Press 1998h.
...even biology. Associated Press 1998b.
God made man in his own image... Associated Press 1998a.
...offered Seed a laboratory... Andrews 1998, p. B4.
...cloning humans would be moral. Kiernan 1997.
...pharm-woman... (p. 191) and *...beast machines...* (pp. 177–178) Kimbrell 1993.
...very cheap to maintain. Associated Press 1997a.
George and Charlie... Fitzgerald 1998.
...transpecies clones... Los Angeles Times 1998.
...a human clone by 2005. Kruger 1997, p. 72.
...clones of clones... Gannett News Service 1998.
...Missyplicity... Associated Press 1998g.
...280 in vitro fertilization clinics... Andrews 1998.
...mutant form of life." Associated Press 1997b.

Brave New World...Order
Brave New World... Rifkin 1993, p.vi.
It is not Dr. Wilmut and Dolly... Lewontin 1997, p. 20.
...abortion of nondefective fetuses... to *..."commercial" eugenics...* Kimbrell 1993, pp. 122–123.
...biotech's bombast... (p. 194) *...children altered...* (p. 193) and *...monster gene-mix party...* (p. 198) Gruber 1997.

CHAPTER 9

Acknowledgment
I learned of David Jacobson's research in 1995 when I met him while teaching summer school at Brandeis University.

Cyberspace
... *Cyberspace developers* ... Stone 1991, p. 113.

Tiny Sex
... *women's mental space.* Van Gelder 1996.
Reality is 80 million ... and ... *enter heaven now and not die.* Quoted in Benedikt 1991, pp. 97.

Outer Space and Aquaspace
... *Afriel, a Shapist* Sterling 1990, p. 14.
... *iconic cyborg* ... Haraway 1989, p. 139.
... *must be continuously assessed.* Hitchcock 1965, p. 97.
... *man as a machine.* Johnsen 1968, p. 1.
Frantically the man clutches ... Tysell 1996, personal communication.

CHAPTER 10

Acknowledgment
Much of this chapter is based on an unpublished article I coauthored with Jane Lovett Wilson.

The Technologically Mediated Family
New York Supreme Court ... quoted in Stacey 1990, p. 279, n. 2.
... *rates of institutionalized children* ... (pp. 208–220) and ... *a single continent again.* (p. 204) Coontz 1992.

Surrogate Families
... *mothering* ... *distributed* ... Biddick 1993, p. 169.
... *she had "cheated" death.* Goodman 1995a, p. B6.
Deidre Hall ... *20/20,* April 21, 1995.
... *beating his son to death* ... *The Oregonian* 1995.

Cyborg Family Values
... *all have value.* Reeve 1998, p. 286.
... *human bonds we need.* Collier, et al. 1997, p. 80.
... *medical technology—is vast.* Diamond 1995, p. 83.
... *ideologies such as feminism.* Stacey 1990.
... *prohibited surrogate-mother contracts* ... O'Keefe 1995.
... *same-sex partners* ... Stacey 1990, pp. 3–7.
... *the families they want.* Agigian 1994.

...*Ellen Goodman argues*... Goodman 1994a, 1994b, 1995a, 1995b.
...*a "situated knowledge"*... Haraway 1988.
...*happy families are unique*... Stacey 1990, p. 17.
...*mutilation-prosthesis cycle*... Davis-Floyd 1998.
...*invent ourselves*... Hartouni 1991, p. 50.
... *"enough is enough."* Goodman 1994a, p. B3.

CHAPTER 11

Dildonics
...*inside me relentless pushing me further*... West, no date, no page.
...*give us its leather aid*... Forberg 1967, p. 66.
...*rhythmic vibratory motion.* Maines 1989, p. 8.

Transsexuality
...*body-morphing marketplace.* S. Turner 1997, p. 3.
...*sex is a vast, infinitely malleable*... Fausto-Sterling 1993, p. 21.
...*subjected to transsexual surgery*... Fausto-Sterling 1997, p. 248.
Hermaphrodites with Attitude. Turner 1997, p. 1.
...*in fact deeply conservative.* Balsamo 1996, p. 161.
...*Options*... Varley 1986, 1993.

Future Sex
...*double logic of prostheses...panic and exhilaration.* Dumit and Davis-Floyd 1998, quoting Levy, p. 142.
...*sexual dimorphism, of male and/or female.* ...*genitals...marks of sexual opposition...* ...*or no sex*. Laqueur 1990, pp. 22 and 23.
...*anatomy is an epistemology*... Moore and Clark, personal communication.
Resistance is Fertile! Dery 1996b.
...*secretions as an ironic sign*... Kroker and Kroker 1987, p. 15. Italics in the original.
...*respond naturally once again.* From an ad in the August 1998 issue of *Reader's Digest.*
...*genitalia as patterns of flowers.* More 1998, p. 3.

CHAPTER 12

Bill Gates, quoted in *Forbes* ASA6, no. 166.

Lone Eagles or Sitting Ducks?
...*a human "motor."* (p. 35) ...*a body without fatigue*... (p. 44) Rabinbach 1990.
...*the American system of manufacture.* Smith 1985.
...*psychotechnicism*... to ...*rhythm of the blood.* Rabinbach 1990, pp. 284–287.

Revolt of the Microserfs against the Sociotechs
Quotes are from Coupland's book *Microserfs*, pp. 4 and 15.
...*informate*... Zuboff 1988.

...body/machine system... (p. 73) *...Mom, part woman/part machine...* (p. 369) Coupland 1995.

Human-Machine Learning Systems
...amplification of human intelligence... (p. 22) and *...computer or a human being.* (p. 43) Noble 1989.
...Man-computer Symbiosis. Licklider 1960.
...desiccation of human intellectual potential... Noble 1989, p. 15.
Virtual U. is a real joke... Associated Press 1996.

'Borging the Professional Athlete
...win without drugs. and *...athletes have to be treated...* Quoted in Bamberger and Yaeger 1997, pp. 62 and 63.
It doesn't hurt... Hudak 1992.
...young bodybuilder... Trappen 1992.
...prosthetic leg. Associated Press 1998d.
...team of people behind them. McDonald 1996.
...a shocking 1995 poll... and *...incredibly sloppy, incredibly stupid...* Bamberger and Yaeger 1997, pp. 62, 63.
...doping is defined as... McDonald 1998.
...morals go out the window. Quoted in Kimbrell 1993.
...Tour de France... Evagora 1998.
...lethal concentration... Sports Illustrated 1998a.
...stricken from the list of banned substances... Rosenthal 1998.
...retracted his statements. Associated Press 1998e.
...It's legal. Wilstein 1998, p. C-1.
...a $100 million industry... to *Somewhere in between Sports Illustrated* 1998b.
...Engineered Nutrition... Mihoces 1998.
...filled with drugs and devices... Bamberger and Yaeger 1997, p. 70.
Shortness is being labeled a disease... Dr. Lantos quoted in Kimbrell 1993, pp. 151–152.

CHAPTER 13

...science rather than religion. Reeve 1998, p. 266.

The Gaze of Science
...reproductive politics of genetic investment. Haraway 1989, pp. 355, 358.

The Human Use of Human Beings
Render unto man the things which are man's... Wiener 1964, p. 73.
The cybernetics of men, as you... From Plato's *Clitophon*, in a loose translation by Parsegian 1973, p. 1.
We might regard patterning... Bateson 1972, p. 1.
Identifying information with both pattern and randomness... Hayles 1993, p. 70.
The nine laws of God... Kelly 1994, pp. 468–472.

Small Is Powerful
...*machines ad infinitum.* Quoted in Kimbrell 1993, p. 232.

Science of the Artificial and the Reflexive Turn
Everything said is said by an observer. Maturana and Varela 1980, p. xxii.
Nazism is applied biology. Quoted in Kimbrell 1993, p. 254.
...*take a rat...* Gruber 1994, p. 112.
...*peculiar form of computation.* Quoted in Bass 1995, p. 168.

CHAPTER 14

Man is an invention... Foucault 1973, p. 371.
...*modify ourselves.* Wiener 1989, p. 46.

Cyborg Epistemologies, Ethics, and Epiphanies
...*last victim is himself.* Fiedler 1996, pp. 60–61.
Bodies are beautiful... Douglas 1996, p. 17.

Subjectivities of Posthumanity
...*FUCK THE OLD FLESH!* Quoted in Dery 1996a p. 248.
...*American "Body-Machine" complex.* Seltzer 1990, p. 141.
...*human or, for that matter, unhuman.* Stone 1995, p. 178.
...*oppositional consciousness...* Sandoval 1995.
...*postcolonial cyborgs...* Gabilondo 1995.

Carnival Cyborg
...*raptures and ruptures of our time.* Braidotti 1998, p. 12.
...*the great future problems...* Wiener 1964, p. 71.
...*man free to explore...* Clynes and Kline 1995, p. 27.
...*the cyborg carnival...* Casper 1995.

The Future Is Not Yet Written
...*organizational scheme for bodies...* Martin 1997, pp. 555–556.
...*the brain and central nervous system.* Reeve 1998, p. 135, italics in the original.
Zamir Net Gessen 1995, p. 228.
...*empathetic future vision...* Kimbrell 1993, pp. 298–299.
It is a moment... Stone 1995, p. 183, original italics.
...*democratic technological order.* Sclove 1995, p. 244.
...*your own DNA destiny.* Quoted in Dery 1996b, p. 303.
How crude the governmental... Ward 1992, p. 52.

bibliography

Published in New York unless otherwise noted.

Agigian, Amy Carol
1994 We Are (Cyborg) Family: Lesbian Artificial Insemination. Working Paper No. 8, Waltham, MA: Brandeis University Woman Studies Program.

Alldridge, Peter
1996 "Who Wants to Live Forever?" in *Death Rites*, Robert Lee and Derels Morgan, eds., Routledge, pp. 11–36.

Altman, Larence
1992 "First Human to Get Baboon Heart," *New York Times*, June 20, p. B6.

Alwall, Nils
1986 "Historical Perspective on the Development of the Artificial Kidney," *Artificial Organs*, vol. 10, no. 2, pp. 86–99.

Andrews, Lori B.
1998 "Human Cloning," *Chronicle of Higher Education*, Feb. 13, pp. B4–B5.

Associated Press
1983 "Electronic Leash for Malefactors," *San Francisco Chronicle*, March 10, p. 24.
1993 "Twin Survives Separation," *New York Times*, August 21, p. A7.
1994 "Twin Who Survived Separation Surgery Dies," *New York Times*, June 10, p. A14.
1996 "Western Governors Move Ahead with Cyberspace U.," *Great Falls Tribune*, Sept. 29, p. 6B.
1997a "Cloning Cows," *Great Falls Tribune*, August 8, p. 6S.
1997b "Scientists Reportedly Create Headless Frog Embryo," *Great Falls Tribune*, Oct. 19, p. 7A.
1998a "Maverick Pushes Human Cloning," *Great Falls Tribune*, Jan. 8, p. 3A.
1998b "Advocate of Cloning Willing to Relocate," *Great Falls Tribune*, Jan. 12, p. 3A.
1998c "High-Tech Tracking Awaits Killer's Parole," *Great Falls Tribune*, May 16, p. 2A.
1998d "Amputee Climbs Everest," *Great Falls Tribune*, May 28, p. 5A.
1998e "Olympics," *Great Falls Tribune*, July 29, p. 3S.
1998f "Is Privacy in Public a Thing of the Past?" *Great Falls Tribune*, August 2, pp. 1A, 10A.
1998g "How Much Is That Clone in the Window?" *Great Falls Tribune*, August 26, p. 2A.
1998h "Chicago Physicist Says He'll Clone Himself with Help from His Wife," *Great Falls Tribune*, Sept. 7, p. 2A.

Balsamo, Anne
1996 *Technologies of the Gendered Body*, Durham: Duke University Press.

Bamberger, Michael, and Don Yaeger
1997 "Over the Edge," *Sports Illustrated*, April 1, pp. 60–70.

Barber, Benjamin
1996 *McWorld versus Jihad*, Ballantine.

Basinger, Julienne
1998 "19 European Countries Sign Pact Prohibiting the Cloning of Human Beings," *Chronicle of Higher Education*, Jan. 23, p. A48.

Bass, Thomas
1995 "Gene Genie," *Wired*, August, pp. 114–117, 164–168.

Bateson, Gregory
1972 *Steps to an Ecology of Mind*, Ballantine.

Baudrillard, Jean
1983 *Simulations*, Semiotext(e).
Bell, Daniel
1976 *The Cultural Contradictions of Capitalism*, Basic Books.
Benedikt, Michael, ed.
1991 *Cyberspace, First Steps*, Cambridge, MA: MIT Press.
Bennahum, David
1997 "The Internet Revolution," *Wired*, April, pp. 123–128, 168–173.
Bey, Hakim
1991 *T.A.Z.: The Temporary Autonomous Zone, Ontological Anarchy, Poetic Terrorism*, Automedia.
1996 "The Net and the Web," in *CyberReader*, Victor Vitanza, ed., Boston: Allyn and Bacon, pp. 366–371.
1998 "The Information War," in *Virtual Futures*, Joan Broadhurst Dixon and Eric Cassidy, eds., Routledge, pp. 3–10.
Biddick, Kathleen
1993 "Stranded Histories: Feminist Allegories of Artificial Life," in *Research in Philosophy and Technology*, Joan Rothschild and Frederick Ferre, eds., Greenwich: JAI Press, pp. 165–182.
Bolin, Ann
1992 "Flex Appeal: Fool and Fact: Competitive Body Building, Gender and Diet," *Play and Culture*, no. 5, pp. 378–400.
Bonchek, Mark
1995 "Grassroots in Cyberspace," MIT Artificial Intelligence Laboratory, Working Paper 95–2.2.
Borenstein, Nathaniel
1997 "One Planet, One Net," *CPSR Newsletter*, vol. 15, no. 4, Fall, pp. 1, 3–5.
Braidotti, Rosi
1998 "Cyberfeminism with a Difference," http://www.let.ruu.nl/womens_studies/rosi/ cyber fem.htm.
Brand, Stewart
1994 "Foreword," in *The Millennium Whole Earth Catalog*, Harold Rheingold, ed., San Francisco: Point Foundation, p. 55.
Brin, David
1992 *Earth*, Bantam.
Bunker, Robert J.
1994 "The Transition to Fourth Epoch War," *Marine Corp Gazette*, Sept., pp. 23–32.
Bury, Stephen
1994 *Interface*, Bantam.
Califia, Pat
1997 *Sex Changes: The Politics of Transgenderism*, San Francisco: Clies Press.
Cartwright, Lisa
1997 "The Visible Man," in *Processed Lives*, Jennifer Terry and Melodie Calvert, eds., Routledge, pp. 123–138.
Casper, Monica
1995 "Fetal Cyborgs and Technomoms on the Reproductive Frontier," in *The Cyborg Handbook*, Chris Hables Gray, Steven Mentor, and Heidi Figueroa-Sarriera, eds., Routledge, pp. 183–203.
Channell, David
1991 *The Vital Machine*, Oxford University Press.
Cherry, J.
1980 "The New Epidemiology of Measles and Rubella," *Hospital Practice*, July, pp. 52–54.
Chomsky, Noan, and Edwards S. Herman
1998 *Manufacturing Consent: The Political Economy of the Mass Media*, Parthenon.
Clarke, Adele
1995 "Modernity, Postmodernity and Reproductive Processes," in *The Cyborg Handbook*, Chris Hables Gray, Steven Mentor, and Heidi Figueroa-Sarriera, eds., Routledge, pp. 139–156.
Cliff, Steven
1998 "Democracy Is Online," *OnTheInternet*, vol. 4, no. 2, March/April, pp. 20–28.
Clynes, Manfred
1977 *Sentics*, Anchor/Doubleday.

Clynes, Manfred, and Nathan Kline
    1960 "Cyborgs and Space," *Astronautics*, Sept., pp. 26–27, 74–75.
    1995 "Cyborgs in Space," (*Astronautics*, Sept., 1960); reprinted in *The Cyborg Handbook*, Chris Hables Gray, Steven Mentor, Heidi Figueroa-Sarriera, eds., Routledge, pp. 29–34.
Collier, Jane, Michelle Z. Rosaldo, and Sylvia Yanagisako
    1997 "Is There a Family?" in *The Gender/Sexuality Reader*, Micaela di Leonardo and Roger N. Lancaster, eds., Routledge, pp. 71–81.
Coontz, Stephanie
    1992 *The Way We Never Were*, HarperCollins.
Coulter, Harris, and Barbara Loe Fisher
    1985 *DPT: A Shot in the Dark*, Harcourt, Brace, Jovanovich.
Coupland, Douglas
    1986 *Microserfs*, Regan.
Crewe, N., and I. Zola, eds.
    1983 *Independent Living for Physically Disabled People*, San Francisco: Jossey-Bass.
Davis-Floyd, Robbie
    1998 "From Technobirth to Cyborg Babies," in *Cyborg Babies*, Robbie Davis-Floyd and Joseph Dumit, eds., Routledge, pp. 256–282.
Davis-Floyd, Robbie, and Joseph Dumit, eds.
    1998 *Cyborg Babies*, Routledge.
Delgado, Jose
    1971 *Physical Control of the Mind*, Colophon.
Dery, Mark
    1996a *Escape Velocity*, Grove Press.
    1996b "Slashing the Borg: Resistance Is Fertile," *21*C*, no. 4, pp. 74–76.
Diamond, Jared
    1995 "Father's Milk," *Discover*, Feb., pp. 83–87.
Dibbell, Julian
    1999 *Tinylife*, Owl Books.
Douglas, Billy
    1996 "Jo Ann," *PFIQ: Piercing Fans International Quarterly*, no. 47, pp. 16–17.
Downey, Gary Lee, Joseph Dumit and Sarah Williams
    1995 "Cyborg Anthropology" in *The Cyborg Handbook*, C.H. Gray, Steven Mentor, and Heidi Figreroa-Sarrierer eds., Routledge, pp. 347–362.
Dumit, Joseph, and Robbie Davis-Floyd
    1998 "Cyborg Babies," in *Cyborg Babies: From Techno-Sex to Techno-Tots*, Robbie Davis-Floyd and Joe Dumit, eds., Routledge, pp. 1–20.
Dutton, Diana
    1988 *Worse than the Disease*, Cambridge, UK: Cambridge University Press.
Edwards, Paul
    1996 *The Closed World*, Cambridge, MA: MIT Press.
Ehrenreich, Barbara
    1987 "Iran Scam," *Ms.*, May, p. 26.
Etzioni, Amitai, and Oren Etzioni
    1997 "Communities: Virtual vs. Real," *Science*, vol. 277, July 18, p. 295.
Evagora, Andreas
    1998 "Five Riders Admit Drug Use," *Great Falls Tribune*, July 28, p. 3S.
Everard, Jerry
    1999 *Virtual States: The Internet and the Boundaries of the Nation-State*, Routledge.
Fausto-Sterling, Anne
    1993 "The Five Sexes," *The Sciences*, March/April, pp. 20–25.
    1997 *Myths of Gender*, Basic Books.
Fiedler, Leslie
    1996 "Why Organ Transplant Programs Do Not Succeed," *Organ Transplantation*, Stuart Youngner, Renée Fox, and Laurence O'Connell, eds., Madison: Wisconsin University Press, pp. 56–65.
Fitzgerald, Alison
    1998 "Cloned Calves May Aid Drug Production," *Tacoma News*, Jan. 21, p. A4.

Flax, Jane
    1987 "Postmodernism and Gender Relations in Feminist Theory," *Signs*, vol. 12, no. 4, Summer, pp. 621–643.
Forberg, Friedrich
    1967 *De Figuris Veneris*, Halloway.
Foucault, Michel
    1973 *The Order of Things*, Vintage Books.
Fox, Renée
    1996 "Afterthoughts," in *Organ Transplantation*, Youngner, Fox, and O'Connell, eds., Madison: Wisconsin University Press, pp. 252–267.
Fox, Renée, Laurence O'Connell, and Stuart Youngner.
    1996 "Introduction," in *Organ Transplantation*, Youngner, Fox, and O'Connell, eds., Madison: Wisconsin University Press, pp. 3–18.
Fox, Renée, and Judith Swazey
    1974 *The Courage to Fail*, Chicago: University of Chicago Press.
    1993 *Spare Parts*, Oxford University Press.
Gabilondo, Joseba
    1995 "Postcolonial Cyborgs," in *The Cyborg Handbook*, Chris Hables Gray, Steven Mentor, Heidi Figueroa-Sarriera, eds., Routledge, pp. 423–432.
Gannett News Service
    1998 "Cloning Takes Leap Forward," *Great Falls Tribune*, July 23, pp. A1, A8.
Gee, William F.
    1975 "A History of Surgical Treatments for Impotence," *Urology*, vol. 5. no. 3, pp. 401–405.
Gessen, Masha
    1995 "Balkans Online," *Wired*, Nov., pp. 158–162, 220–228.
Gitlin, Todd
    1989 "Postmodernism Defined, At Last!" *Dissent*, Winter, pp. 52–61.
Gonsalves-Ebrahim, L., and M. Kotz
    1987 "The Psychosociological Impact of Ambulatory Peritoneal Dialysis on Adults and Children," *Psychiatric Medicine*, vol. 5, no. 3, pp. 177–185.
Goodman, Ellen
    1994a "Conception Advances Need Limits," *The Oregonian*, Jan. 11, p. B9.
    1994b "An Easy Choice Was Made Hard," *The Oregonian*, June 19, p. B3.
    1995a "Insemination: Law, Biology in Conflict," *The Oregonian*, Jan. 30, p. B6.
    1995b "Treatments Reproduce Dilemmas," *The Oregonian*, June 13, p. A9.
Gray, Chris Hables
    1979 "The New Libertarians," *Black Rose*, vol. 1, no. 3, pp. 29–39.
    1996 "Medical Cyborgs: Artificial Organs and the Quest for the Posthuman" in *Technohistory*, Gray, ed., Melbourne, Fl.: Krieger, pp. 140–178.
    1997a *Postmodern War*, Guilford.
    1997b "The Ethics and Politics of Cyborg Embodiment: Citizenship as a Hypervalue," *Cultural Values*, vol. 1, no. 2, Oct., pp. 252–258.
Gray, Chris Hables, and Mark Driscoll
    1992 "From Virtual to Real: Anthropology in the Age of Simulation," *Virtual Anthropology*, Fall, pp. 39–49.
Gray, Chris Hables, and Steven Mentor
    1995 "The Cyborg Body Politic," in *The Cyborg Handbook*, Chris Hables Gray, Steven Mentor, and Heidi Figueroa-Sarriera, eds., Routledge, pp. 453–465.
Gray, Chris Hables, Steven Mentor, and Heidi Figueroa-Sarriera
    1995 "Cyborgology," in *The Cyborg Handbook*, Chris Hables Gray, Steven Mentor, and Heidi Figueroa-Sarriera, eds., Routledge, pp. 1–16.
Griffin, David Ray
    1988 "Introduction," in *The Reenchantment of Science*, Griffin, ed., Albany State University of New York Press.
Gross, Paul R., and Norman Levitt
    1994 *Higher Superstition: The Academic Left and Its Quarrels with Science*, John Hopkins Press.
Gruber, Michael
    1994 "Neurobotics," *Wired*, Oct., pp. 111–113.

1997 "Map the Genome, Hack the Genome," *Wired*, Oct., pp. 152–156, 193–198.
Guernsey, Lisa
1996 "The Electronic Soapbox," *The Chronicle of Higher Education*, May 3, pp. A29–A33.
Hall, Diedre
1995 "Interview" on *20/20*, April 21.
Halperin, James L.
1996 *The Truth Machine*, Del Rey.
Handy, Bruce
1998 "The Viagra Craze," *Time*, May 4, pp. 50–57.
Hanson, Victor
1989 *The Western Way of War*, Knopf.
Haraway, Donna
1985 "A Manifesto for Cyborgs," *Socialist Review*, no. 80, pp. 65–107.
1988 "Situated Knowledges," *Feminist Studies* 14, no. 2, Fall, pp. 575–599.
1989 *Primate Visions*, Routledge.
1995 "Cyborgs and Symbionts," in *The Cyborg Handbook*, Chris Hables Gray, Steven Mentor, and Heidi Figueroa-Sarriera, eds., Routledge, pp. xi–xx.
Hartouni, Valerie
1991 "Containing Women," in *Technoculture*, Constance Penley and Andrew Ross, eds., Minneapolis: University of Minnesota Press, pp. 27–56.
Hayles, N. Katherine
1987 "Denaturalizing Experience," paper presented to the meeting of the Society for Literature and Science.
1993 "Virtual Bodies and Flickering Signifiers," *October 66*, Fall, pp. 69–91.
1999 *How We Became Posthuman*, Chicago: University of Chicago Press.
Heinlein, Robert
1959 *Starship Troopers*, Signet.
Hill, Anne
1998 "Children of Metis," in *Cyborg Babies*, Robbie Davis-Floyd and Joseph Dumit, eds., Routledge, pp. 330–344.
Hilton, Bruce
1992 "How to Tell When Someone Is Dead," *Cleveland Plain Dealer*, July 19, p. 3C.
Hitchcock, D. R.
1965 "Introduction," *Medical and Biological Applications of Space Telemetry*, July, Washington, DC: NASA.
Hogle, Linda
1995 "Tales From the Cryptic," in *The Cyborg Handbook*, Chris Hables Gray, Steven Mentor, and Heidi Figueroa-Sarriera, eds., Routledge, pp. 203–218.
Hori, Motokazu
1986 "Artificial Liver," *Artificial Organs*, vol. 10, no. 3, pp. 211–213.
Hudak, Stephan
1992 "Boy Keeps Charging on Artificial Leg," *The Plain Dealer*, June 29, p. 4B.
Hutcheon, Linda
1987 "The Politics of Postmodernism," *Cultural Critique*, no. 4, pp. 179–207.
Huyssen, Andreas
1984 *After the Great Divide*, Bloomington: Indiana University Press.
Isin, Engin
1997 "Who Is the New Citizen?" *Citizenship Studies*, vol. 1, no. 1, pp. 115–132.
James, Walene
1988 *Immunization*, Bergen and Garvey.
Jameson, Fredric
1984 "Postmodernism, or on the Cultural Logic of Late Capitalism," *New Left Review*, no. 146, July/August, pp. 53–92.
Johnsen, Edwin
1968 "Teleoperators," presented to the 1968 FJCC Panel, Human Augmentation Through Computers and Teleoperators, Dec. 10, NASA History Office archives.
Jordon, Tim
1984 "The Pediatric Vaccine Controversy," Editorial, *Journal of the American Medical Association*, Dec. 7, pp. 3013–3014.

1999 *Cyberpower: The Culture and Politics of Cyberspace and the Internet*, Routledge.

Kaplan, David, and Andrew Marshall
1996 *Aum The Cult at the End of the World*, Crown.

Katz, Jon
1997 "The Digital Citizen," *Wired*, Dec., pp. 68–82, 274–275.

Kaufert, Joseph, and David Locker
1990 "Rehabilitation Ideology and Respiratory Support Technology," *Social Sciences and Medicine*, vol. 30, no. 8, pp. 867–877.

Kelly, Kevin
1994 *Out of Control: The New Biology of Machines, Social Systems and the Economic World*, Addison-Wesley.

Kiernan, Vincent
1997 "The Morality of Cloning Humans," *Chronicle of Higher Education*, July 18, pp. A13–A14.
1998 "Senate Rejects Bill to Ban Human Cloning," *Chronicle of Higher Education*, Feb. 20, pp. A40–A41.

Kimbrell, Andrew
1993 *The Human Body Shop*, San Francisco: HarperSanFrancisco.

Knox, Richard
1976 "A Shot in the Arm, A Shot in the Dark," *Boston Sunday Globe*, Dec. 26, p. B1.

Kolff, Willem
1979 "Questions and Predictions," in *Assisted Circulation*, Felix Unger, ed., Berlin: Springer-Verlag, pp. 11–12.
1989 "The Artificial Heart, the Inevitable Development," *Artificial Organs*, vol. 13, no. 3, pp. 183–184.

Kroker, Arthur, and Marilouise Kroker
1987 *Body Invaders*, St. Martin's Press.

Kruger, Jeffrey
1997 "Will We Follow the Sheep?" *Time*, March 10, pp. 69–72.

Laqueur, Thomas
1990 *Making Sex*, Cambridge, MA: Harvard University Press.

Latour, Bruno
1993 *We Have Never Been Modern*, C. Porter, trans., Cambridge, MA: Harvard University Press.

Lee, Robert, and Derek Morgan
1996 "Preface—Law, Ethics and Death," *Death Rites*, Routledge, pp. x–xvi.

Levidow, Les, and Kevin Robins, eds.
1989 "Introduction," in *Cyborg Worlds*, London: Free Association, pp. 7–12.

Lewontin, R. C.
1997 "The Confusion over Cloning," *New York Review of Books*, Oct. 23, pp. 18–23.

Licklider, J. C. R.
1960 "Man-Computer Symbiosis," *IREE Transactions on Human Factors in Electronics*, March, pp. 4–11.

Los Angeles Times
1998 "Procedure Could Advance Cloning—and Controversy," *Great Falls Tribune*, Jan. 19, p. A2.

Lubeck, Deborah, and John Bunker
1982 Case Study No. 9, *The Artificial Heart*, Washington, DC: Congress of the United States Office of Technology Assessment.

Lyotard, Jean-François
1985 *The Postmodern Condition*, Minneapolis: University of Minnesota Press.

Mackenzie, Debra
1984 "Hidden Menace of New Chicken Pox Vaccine," *New Scientist*, June 7, p. 27.

Maines, Rachel
1989 "Socially Camouflaged Technologies," *IEEE Technology and Society Magazine*, vol. 8, no. 2, June, pp. 3–11.

Manning, Dr. Richard
1987 *Impotence—How to Overcome It*, Farmington Hills, MI: HealthProlink.

Martin, Emily
1991 "The Egg and the Sperm," *Signs*, vol. 15, no. 3, pp. 485–501.

1997 "The End of the Body?" in *The Gender/Sexuality Reader*, Leonardo and Lancaster, eds., Routledge, pp. 543–558.

Maturana, Humberto, and Francisco Varela
1980 *Autopoiesis and Cognition*, Dordrecht: D. Reidel.

Mazlish, Bruce
1993 *The Fourth Discontinuity*, New Haven: Yale University Press.

McDonald, Kim
1996 "A Top-Secret Campaign to Build the Ultimate Bike," *Chronicle of Higher Education*, Jan. 12, pp. A11–A13.
1998 "Scientists Debate the Benefits and Hazards of a Seemingly Magical Powder," *Chronicle of Higher Education*, June 26, pp. A15–A16.

McKenzie, D. S.
1965 "Still a Long Way to Go," *Artificial Limbs*, vol. II, No. 2, Autumn, pp. 1–4.

Mendelssohn, Robert S.
1984 *How to Raise a Healthy Child... In Spite of Your Doctor*, Random House.

Mentor, Steven
1996 "Manifest(o) Technologies," in *Technohistory*, Chris Hables Gray, ed., Melbourne, FL: Krieger, pp. 195–214.

Mihoces, Gary
1998 "Debate over 'Andro' Builds," *USA Today*, August 25, p. 3C.

Miller, Steven
1996 "The Building Blocks of Electronic Democracy," *CPSR Newsletter*, vol. 14, no. 2, Summer, pp. 1–2.

Miller, t al.
"Multiple Sclerosis and Vaccinations," *British Medical Journal*, April 22, pp. 210–213.

More, Natasha Vita
1998 "Future of Sexuality," http://www.extropic-art.com/sex.htm.

Mumford, Lewis
1970 *The Myth of the Machine*, Harcourt Brace, Jovanovich.

Neustadt, Richard, and Harvey Fineberg
1978 *The Swine Flu Affair*, Washington, DC: U.S. Department of Health, Education, and Welfare.

Noble, Douglas
1989 "Mental Materiel," in *Cyborg Worlds*, Les Levidow and Kevin Robins, eds., London: Free Association, pp. 13–42.

O'Connell, Laurence
1996 "The Realities of Organ Transplantation," *Organ Transplantation*, Stuart J. Youngner, Renée C. Fox, and Laurence J. O'Connell, eds., Madison: Wisconsin University Press, pp. 19–31.

O'Keefe, Mark
1995 "Family Values Back with a Twist," *The Oregonian*, Feb. 20, p. B1.

O'Neill, Patrick
1995 "The Complex Case of Baby Ryan," *The Oregonian*, Feb. 19, pp. D1, D7.

The Oregonian
1995 "Surrogate Father Murders Son," Jan. 19, p. D1.

Pakulski, Jan
1997 "Cultural Citizenship," *Citizenship Studies*, vol. 1, no. 1, pp. 73–86.

Parsegian, V. L.
1973 *This Cybernetic World of Men, Machines, and Earth Systems*, Doubleday.

Pohl, Frederick
1976 *Man Plus*, Bantam.
1982 *The Cool War*, Del Rey.

Rabinbach, Anson
1990 *The Human Motor*, Basic Books.

Rajchman, John
1985 "The Postmodern Museum," *Art in America*, Oct., pp. 116–129.

Rawson, Hugh, and Margaret Miner, eds.
1986 *The New International Dictionary of Quotations*, Signet.

Reeve, Christopher
1998 *Still Me*, Random House.

Reid, Jeff
    1988 "Just What Is Postmodernism?" *Utne Reader*, Sept./Oct., pp. 32–33.
Renshaw, Domeena
    1979 "Inflatable Penile Prosthesis," *Journal of the American Medical Association*, vol. 241, no. 24, pp. 2637–2638.
Restak, Richard
    1973 *Pre-Meditated Man*, Viking.
Richardson, Ruth
    1996 "Fearful Symmetry," *Organ Transplantation*, Stuart Youngner, Renée Fox, and Laurence O'Connell, eds., Madison: Wisconsin University Press, pp. 66–100.
Rifkin, Jeremy
    1993 "Foreword," in *The Human Body Shop*, Andrew Kimbrell, HarperSanFrancisco, pp. vi–x.
Rosenthal, Bert
    1998 "Drug Scandal Rocks National Track Program," *Great Falls Tribune*, July 28, p. 1S.
Rothbard, Murray
    1978 *For a New Liberty*, Collier.
Roy, Jean-Hughes
    1996 "Way New Leftists," *Wired*, Feb., p. 109.
Sale, Kirkpatrick
    1995 "Setting Limits on Technology," *The Nation*, June 5, pp. 785–788.
Saletan, William
    1998 "Fetal Positions," *Mother Jones*, May/June, pp. 58–59.
Sandoval, Chela
    1995 "New Sciences: Cyborg Feminism and the Methodology of the Oppressed," in *The Cyborg Handbook*, Chris Hables Gray, Steven Mentor, Heidi Figueroa-Sarriera, eds., Routledge, pp. 407–422.
Scarry, Elaine
    1985 *The Body in Pain*, Oxford University Press.
Schmidt, Matthew, and Lisa Jean Moore
    1998 "Constructing a 'Good Catch,'" in *Cyborg Babies*, Robbie Davis-Floyd and Joseph Dumit, Routledge, pp. 22–39.
Sclove, Richard
    1995 *Democracy and Technology*, Guilford.
Seltzer, Mark
    1990 "The Love Master," in *Engendering Men: The Question of Male Feminism*, Joseph A. Boone and Michael Cadden, eds., Routledge, pp. 141–149.
Silber, Jerome, and Sydelle Silverman
    1958 "Studies in the Upper Extremity Amputee," *Artificial Limbs*, vol. 5, no. 2, pp. 88–116.
Silver, Lee
    1998 *Remaking Eden*, Avon Books.
Silverstein, Arthur
    1983 *Pure Politics and Impure Science—The Swine Flu Affair*, Baltimore: John Hopkins Universtiy Press.
Smith, Marc A., and Peter Kollock, eds.
    1999 *Communities in Cyberspace*, Routledge.
Smith, Merritt Row
    1985 "Army Ordnance and the 'American System' of Manufacturing, 1815–1861," in *Military Enterprise and Technological Change*, M.R. Smith, ed., Cambridge, MA: MIT Press, pp. 39–86.
Sokal, Alan
    1996 "A Physicist Experiments with Cultural Studies," *Lingua Franca*, May/June, pp. 62–64.
Sports Illustrated
    1998a "Whiskey Business," *Sports Illustrated*, August 17, p. 25.
    1998b "Hurricane Andro," *Sports Illustrated*, Sept. 7, p. 22.
Stacey, Judith
    1990 *Brave New Families*, Basic Books.
Stelarc
    1997 "From Psycho to Cyber Strategies," *Cultural Values*, vol. 1, no. 2, Oct., pp. 242–249.

Sterling, Bruce
     1990 "Swarm," in *Crystal Express*, Ace, pp. 3–26.
Stewart, G. T.
     1979 "Vaccination against Whooping Cough: Efficiency vs. Risks," Lancet, Jan. 29, pp. 234–237.
Stock, Gregory
     1993 *Metaman*, Simon and Schuster.
Stone, Allucquere Rosanne
     1991 "Will the Real Body Please Stand Up?" in *Cyberspace: The First Steps*, Michel Benedikt, ed., Cambridge, MA: MIT Press, pp. 81–118.
     1995 *The War of Desire and Technology at the Close of the Mechanical Age*, Cambridge, MA: MIT Press.
Strauss, Michael J.
     1984 "The Political History of the Artificial Heart," *New England Journal of Medicine*, Feb. 2, pp. 332–336.
Talmadge, Eric
     1997 "Robo-Roach Will Boldly Go Where No Bug Has Before," *Great Falls Tribune*, Jan. 10, p. A2.
Taylor, Chris
     2000 "Behind the Hack Attack," *Time*, Feb. 21, pp. 45–47.
Teitelbaum, Sheldon
     1996 "Privacy Is History—Get Over It," *Wired*, Feb., p. 125.
Theweleit, Klaus
     1989 *Male Fantasies, Vol. 2, Male Bodies*, Minneapolis: University of Minnesota Press.
Tiefer, Lenore, Beth Pederson, and Arnold Melman
     1988 "Psychological Follow-up of Penile Prosthesis Implant Patients and Partners," *Journal of Sex and Marriage Therapy*, vol. 14, no. 3, Fall, pp. 184–201.
Tiefer, Lenore, Steven Moss, and Arnold Melman
     1991 "Follow-up of Penile Prosthesis Implant Patients and Partners," *Journal of Sex and Marriage Therapy*, vol. 14, no. 3, Fall, pp. 113–127.
Titmuss, Richard
     1971 *The Gift Relationship*, Pantheon.
Toffler, Alvin, and Heidi Toffler
     1993 *War and Anti-War*, Warner Books.
Trappen, Michelle
     1992 "Flexing His Future," *The Oregonian*, Nov. 10, pp. G1, G8.
Turing, Alan
     1950 "Computing Machinery and Intelligence," *Mind*, vol. LIX, no. 236, pp. 47–79.
Turkle, Sherry
     1984 *The Second Self*, Simon and Schuster.
     1995 *Life on the Screen*, Simon and Schuster.
Turner, Bryan
     1997 "Citizenship Studies," *Citizenship Studies*, vol. 1, no. 1, pp. 5–18.
Turner, Stephanie
     1997 "The Politics of Intersexuality," paper presented to the Science, Technology, and the 21st Century conference, Cameron University, Lawton, Oklahoma, March 21.
Tzamaloukas, A. H., P. G. Zager, B. J. Quintara, M. Nevarez, K. Roberts, and G. H. Murata.
     1990 "Mechanical Cardiopulmonary Resuscitation Choice of Patients on Chronic Peritoneal Dialysis," *Peritoneal Dialysis International*, vol. 10, no. 4, pp. 299–302.
Van Gelder, Lindsy
     1996 "The Strange Case of the Electronic Lover," in *Computerization and Controversy*, 2nd ed., Kling, ed., Academic Press, pp. 533–546.
Van Nieuwkerk, C. M., R. T. Krediet, and L. Ariez
     1990 "Voluntary Discontinuation of Dialysis Treatment by Chronic Dialysis Patients," *Netherlands Tijdschrift Voor Geneeskunde*, vol. 134, no. 32, August 11, pp. 1549–1552. (In Dutch, translated on Medline.)
Varley, John
     1986 "Options," in *Blue Champagne*, Berkeley Books, pp. 154–181.
     1993 *Steel Beach*, Ace.

Waisbren, Burton
    1982 "Swine Influenza Vaccine," *Annals of Internal Medicine*, vol. 97 no. 1, July, p. 149.
Ward, Colin
    1992 *Anarchy in Action*, London: Freedom Press.
West, Jessica
    No date "Sybian: Plug Into the Ultimate Joy Ride" from www.sybian.com.
Wheeler, David
    1996 "Creating a Body of Knowledge," *Chronicle of Higher Education*, Feb. 2, pp. A6A7, A14.
Wiener, Norbert
    1948 *Cybernetics*, Cambridge, MA: MIT Press.
    1964 *God and Golem, Inc.* Cambridge, MA: MIT Press.
    1989 *The Human Use of Human Beings*, Boston: Houghton-Mifflin.
Wilson, Rir Graham
    1967 *The Hazards of Immunization*, Oxford University Press.
Wilstein, Steve
    1998 "McGwire Sees No Harm in Bulking Up With Steroids," *Salt Lake City Tribune*, August 23, p. C1.
Winner, Langdon
    1988 *The Whale and the Reactor*, University of Chicago Press.
Wolcott, D., et al.
    1988 "The Quality of Life in Chronic Dialysis Patients," *General Hospital Psychiatry*, vol. 10, no. 4, July, pp. 267–277.
Wolfe, Tom
    1983 *The Right Stuff*, Bantam.
Young, Jeffrey R.
    1998 "Technorealists Hope to Enrich Debate Over Policy Issues in Cyberspace," *Chronicle of Higher Education*, March 23, pp. A11–A12.
Youngner, Stuart
    1996 "Some Must Die," *Organ Transplantation*, Stuart Youngner, Renée Fox, and Laurence O'Connell, eds., Madison: Wisconsin University Press, pp. 32–55.
Zimmermann, E.
    1989 "Quality of Life in Artificial Kidney Therapy," *Wiener-Klinische-Wochenschrift.*, vol. 1010, no. 22, Nov. 24, pp. 780–784. (In German, translated on Medline).
Zuboff, Shoshana
    1988 *In the Age of the Smart Machine*, Basic.

index